# Praise for *The Wonder of Girls*

"Excellent."

*—Library Journal*

"Bound-to-be-controversial."

*—USA Today*

"Michael Gurian shares intriguing insights in THE WONDER OF GIRLS."

*—Seattle Times*

"Gurian is at his best when it comes to the nuts and bolts of rearing a daughter."

*—Los Angeles Times*

Gurian's attention to the physiology of how girls develop is tapping into a growing field among researchers. . . . THE WONDER OF GIRLS has won universal praise for Gurian's focus on the importance of maintaining personal connections with girls.

*—Chicago Sun-Times*

"Expect Gurian's arguments to stir controversy and inspire thought."

*—Publishers Weekly*

# Previous Books by Michael Gurian

### PARENTING

**THE SOUL OF THE CHILD**

**THE WONDER OF BOYS**

**A FINE YOUNG MAN**

**THE GOOD SON**

**WHAT STORIES DOES MY SON NEED?**
(WITH TERRY TRUEMAN)

### EDUCATION

**BOYS AND GIRLS LEARN DIFFERENTLY!**
(WITH PATRICIA HENLEY AND TERRY TRUEMAN)

### PSYCHOLOGY

**LOVE'S JOURNEY**

**MOTHERS, SONS AND LOVERS**

**THE PRINCE AND THE KING**

### FOR YOUNG ADULTS

**UNDERSTANDING GUYS**

**FROM BOYS TO MEN**

### FICTION AND POETRY

**AN AMERICAN MYSTIC**

**THE ODYSSEY OF TELEMACHUS**

**EMPTYING**

# *the* WONDER *of* GIRLS

UNDERSTANDING
THE HIDDEN NATURE
OF OUR DAUGHTERS

MICHAEL GURIAN

**ATRIA** BOOKS
New York   London   Toronto   Sydney

ATRIA BOOKS
1230 Avenue of the Americas
New York, NY 10020

Copyright © 2002 by Michael Gurian

Originally published in hardcover in 2002 by Pocket Books

Library of Congress Cataloging-in-Publication Data

ISBN-13: 978-0-7434-1702-0
ISBN-10:    0-7434-1702-X
ISBN-13: 978-0-7434-1703-7 (Pbk)
ISBN-10:    0-7434-1703-8 (Pbk)

First Atria Books trade paperback printing February 2003

20  19  18  17  16  15  14  13  12

ATRIA BOOKS is a trademark of Simon & Schuster, Inc.

For information regarding special discounts for bulk purchases,
please contact Simon & Schuster Special Sales at 1-800-456-6798
or business@simonandschuster.com

Printed in the U.S.A

*For Gail, Gabrielle, and Davita*

# ACKNOWLEDGMENTS

Many people deserve thanks for this project—most especially my wife and partner, Gail, who advised me so thoroughly, and my daughters, Gabrielle and Davita, who allowed me to pick their brains and even to write about them.

I owe much gratitude as well to Alan Rinzler, my longtime mentor and friend, and Candice Fuhrman, my agent, both of whom guided this project to Pocket Books and the Simon & Schuster group.

At Pocket, my thanks are due first and foremost to Tracy Behar, my editor, whose vision has enhanced this book greatly, and to Judith Curr, who oversaw our work with grace. Many thanks also to the Pocket publicity staff, the copy editing staff, and the rest of the Pocket family, people who labor behind the scenes and deserve such great credit.

To the trainers, teachers, students, and staff at the Gurian Institute, I give my profound thanks. They, along with my clients in Spokane, have allowed me to explore issues faced by girls through the eyes of diverse families and communities. Special thanks to Gurian Institute colleagues Terry Trueman and Stacie Wachholz for their extensive research on female and male neurobiology.

Finally, my profoundest thanks are due the many girls and young women who have let me be a helpful part of their lives. They are courageous in their search for life skills and for meaning. I am sure I have learned more from them than I have been able to teach.

# CONTENTS

PART II

# What Girls Need

# INTRODUCTION

*"Truth tends to shake us to our very bones."*

—Marilyn Sewell

Soon after my first daughter was born, I wrote of my hope for our lives together:

*in early spring*
*the world cool*
*green leaves open first*

*Gabrielle, two weeks old,*
*shivers*
*in my green intentions.*

I was thirty-two years old, and knew little about what it means to have a daughter. I knew next to nothing about girls, though I thought I knew a lot about women. I had not yet acquired the wisdom to know that knowledge is never certain, and children are the best teachers.

I had specialized thus far in two kinds of work: writing itself—mainly novels and poetry—and the teaching of writing and literature; and psychological and neurobiological research, preparatory to becoming a therapist and educator in child development. Now here I was, father of a baby daughter; it was time to learn what that *really* meant.

My wife, Gail, also thirty-two, knew a great deal more than I did about girls, and yet, she too felt inadequate. What parent, upon having their first child, does not feel lost?

Now, many years later, I know from experience and research somewhat more of what it means to have a daughter. Yet so often, still, I feel that what I know is even too subtle for poetry. It exists in a wordless quiet when one of my daughters is reading silently beside me on the couch. It weaves through words while Gabrielle tells me about the latest discomfort she's had with her friends, or Davita, three years younger, details her day of exuberant events. My intentions with my daughters are less green than they were at Gabrielle's birth, but they are no less passionate.

Recently I asked Gabrielle what it should mean to me to have a daughter. She answered, affecting an actress's pose, "To love me beyond measure." I asked Davita the same thing. She giggled, "I don't know," and gave me a bear hug. Not poetry, not science, not even flawed memory can do justice to the emotions that surround the love of parent and child.

It is a love that is lived as one soul embraces another throughout the life journey.

*The Wonder of Girls* hopes to become a comprehensive part of your own answer to the question, What does it mean to have a daughter? While ever respectful that no *book* can be a *complete* answer, I will cover everything I can think of that a daughter needs—yet still there will be more.

*The Wonder of Girls* has grown not only from my own research and my own care for my daughters, but it has grown from my interactions with other parents and caregivers. If one is going to try to write a book that hopes to aid the life journey in a comprehensive way, it must be one that grows in that place where an expert's ability to serve and an audience's need come together. Even though there are numerous books about girls on the shelves these days, I think you'll quickly discover that this one is needed, because it reveals the *nature* of your daughter.

Because I am fortunate to meet thousands of people every year, and receive numerous e-mails and letters, I am constantly learning parents' needs from them. As both a parent of daughters and a professional, I came to fully realize that the book you are about to read both grew in me and was needed in the world when I read this beautiful letter from a mother of four, Cheryl McKenzie.

Dear Michael Gurian:

I have three daughters, 16, 13, and 9, and a son, 12. I've read a lot of books on parenting. I'm writing you because your book, *The Wonder of Boys*, changed our family. I'm hoping you'll write a book like it for raising girls.

I've read *Reviving Ophelia*, which scared me to death. I've read *Schoolgirls* and know how to advocate for girls. I've read *Ophelia Speaks*, *In a Different Voice*, and *Don't Stop Loving Me*. These were all good books. I understand how girls need to watch out for dangers, and need to have a voice. I'm an avid reader of magazines, like *Parenting* and *American Girl*. They teach me a lot about how our culture influences girls.

But I still don't understand my girls like I need to. I don't mean I'm ignorant or naive—I'm a smart woman and a smart parent. I mean that I want to know more about what makes my daughters *tick*. I felt this way about my son too, and then I read *The Wonder of Boys*. You told me what was actually going on in my son's hormones and brain. Some big truths in my son's life were right there, in his nature. Now I have the insight to help him find these truths.

You've helped me raise my son, now will you help me raise my daughters? Will you write about girls' hormones and their brains and the hidden world girls live in? I've lived it, I know it's there. Maybe it's strange asking a man to do this, but you seem to know a lot about biology and psychology—most professionals in your field don't deal much in the biological aspects. And I met a friend of your wife's. From talking to her, I think Gail could help you and keep you honest.

To start you along, here are some things our family cares a lot about.

My husband and I have noticed that girls care more about character and morality than anyone really talks about. Everyone talks about self-esteem, and it's sure important, but my girls and their friends are very moral young people. I wish someone would go into this part of girls' lives more deeply.

Amelia, our eldest, is very curious about how different her nature is from boys. She can't find the deep answers she wants. Because she's spinning, I'm spinning too! Amelia is athletic and smart. She desperately wants to know how to love a boy, and how to understand herself when she's with a boy. The other day she came home from school and said, "Mom, we women are stronger than men, aren't we?" She's beginning to see that life is very complex. I want her to receive the kind of wisdom that understands that complexity.

Mary Ellen is my "relational girl," always paying attention to how everyone's interactions are going. She's not very competitive at all. She wants a lot of kids when she grows up. I want her to be accepted for this and not feel what I felt when I cut back to part-time to raise my children—that I hadn't lived up to cultural expectations. I have a feeling that if people really understood why so many girls are like Mary Ellen, people would also understand that it's important to really nurture that quality of relationship girls have. In my mind, it's more important than being able to compete with boys and men. Does saying this make me old-fashioned?

Mia is very emotional. I'm always afraid I'll destroy her self-esteem by trying to get her to focus on other things besides tears and dramatic outpourings. I know she needs to manage herself better. I would like to understand why she and I are so gushy with our feelings. This is very "female," as I've been reading, and I'm not ashamed to say it. I like how emotional I am. But Mia needs help learning to see through emotions to the truth behind them.

Amelia and I talk about feminism and gender roles a lot. She is very smart about feminism, and sees its uses. But she's a new generation. Recently she said, "Mom, we girls are not Gloria Steinem." I know she's not satisfied with what feminism has become. I'm not either. A lot of this new generation of girls is looking for a new logic for girls' lives. These girls don't want to throw out the advantages feminism has given us, but they don't want to take on the narrowness of the feminist view anymore. I wish you could help form a new vision. In *The Wonder of Boys* you called on the carpet some of the feminist notions about boys. I think this was helpful. As a parent, I am searching for a new logic of girls' lives, and as kids, my girls are looking for a new logic of women's lives. We need help!

Please put your mind and research to girls' lives. I know you are the father of two daughters. Besides Gail, they can help you. I hope this letter finds you, Gail, and your daughters well, and I hope you'll teach others what you've learned about the wonder of girls. Maybe you could call the book that.

In my career I can say that this is one of the most challenging and mind-expanding letters I've received, and I thank Cheryl McKenzie, its author.

I am, indeed, the father of two daughters. This has become quite ironic to many of my readers, because I've written six books on raising *boys!*

"Where are your sons?" people ask me.

Or: "Without raising your own boys, how do you test out your theories?"

Or: "How has this happened to you?"

Before Gail and I had children, I had begun my interdisciplinary research in applied neurobiology, anthropology, and psychology. There was very little published in our culture on male development, and I felt called to apply my research to that field. Thus, I had written two books on male development by the time Gabrielle, our first child, came to us. By the time Davita came to us, I had written the manuscript for *The Wonder of Boys*. Now Gail and I had our second girl—no boys—and I was about to publish my fourth book on male development!

"Hmmm," Gail smiled mischievously, "I guess we'll just have to have a third child."

But we had decided on two, and two we have, and I cannot see life any other way. Gabrielle and Davita complete me. I'm fated to be known by some of the media as "the Dr. Spock for boys," yet to have no sons!

As I look back now, especially in the context of letters like Cheryl's, I realize that it has actually been of immense value that a male parenting expert and social philosopher, like myself, producing books on raising boys, has done so while living with a woman and two girls—it has created a balance in me, an ability to see more than "only the boys' side of things," a constant measurement of whether what I say makes sense in the real world (as my wife and daughters always remind me, the real world is "the world of girls"!). And it has always provided me with the best motive to help boys: I want to help parents, teachers, mentors, and policymakers raise a loving, wise, and responsible generation of men who will, one day, adore my daughters.

Meanwhile, I have been raising daughters and, as a family therapist, providing counseling to not only boys but girls, not only men but women; I have also been a researcher in female development. I've been preparing to write *The Wonder of Girls* for over a decade. Boys' and girls' lives are intertwined in all facets of our culture; their biological heritage is also intertwined. Their needs are intertwined. To study one sex responsibly is to study the other thoroughly.

This has been the premise not only of my family therapy practice, which I share with Gail, but also of my research and educational training programs at the Michael Gurian Institute, which began as a two-year pilot at six school districts in Kansas City, Missouri. Our goal has been to find the essential currents of human understanding by which to help girls and boys in family, school, and community life. We began publicizing our studies in our coauthored book, *Boys and Girls Learn Differently!*

While I am the sole author of *The Wonder of Girls*, it is also a kind of collaboration. It could not be written without the help, insight, direction, and critique of Gail and many others, as well as the stories and insights of the many girls and families we've worked with. Many of its stories and anecdotes come from my own and Gail's family practice, the research of teachers and professionals who have specialized in girls, and also the work in school districts we've been doing in Missouri and elsewhere. I've asked (begged!) Gail to give me editorial advice and professional input so that she, as a woman, mother, professional, and former girl, can check everything I write for veracity and accuracy. Because she is my partner in parenting our girls, she appears often in this book, as do the lives of Gabrielle and Davita—with their permission, of course.

My goal is to make groundbreaking scientific research accessible here—research that leads with nature and what is natural to a girl's development, while simultaneously providing you with a practical, inspiring guide to raising girls. While I find that most girls, with enough love and attention, can grow up healthy and safe, their natural wonder a delight to observe, many girls today are not doing well. Many are confused, many are hurting. I will speak to the needs of the wide spectrum of girls, those doing well and those in trouble.

Since they could speak, my daughters have asked, "Dad, when are you going to write just about *girls?*"

"Soon," I've promised, "very soon."

Finally, the time has come.

## Toward a New Logic of Girls' Lives

At the outset, it is fair to say that the perspective of my work and studies, and thus of this book, shares qualities with the many very fine books on girls that have come out in the last two decades—some of which Cheryl referred to in her own library—but only to a point. The basic perspective of *The Wonder of Girls* is quite different from the books you may have read. As one mother told me, "Don't write just another book on girls. There are lots of those. Give us a new way of understanding girls, give us a book we can't live without."

That is my aim. Fortunately for any parent raising daughters, there are many resources on bookshelves. I'll refer to some of them in this work, but I won't repeat what they've done. For your special needs or concerns—those that merit more information than this book provides—specific resources are listed in the appendix.

My approach to parenting, and coaching and training parents, is a *nature-based* approach. Its theoretical base lies in human nature, not in ideological theory. "Human nature" is revealed, as you'll notice throughout the book, by an acute emphasis on human sciences—neurobiology, biochemistry—checked by experience, human history, multicultural application, and just plain common sense. *The Wonder of Girls* finds wisdom in many disciplines, and thus has the temerity to call itself a comprehensive guide for parents.

By the final chapter of this book, I hope you will experience four things specifically:

- a fundamental challenge to many of the ideologies and conventions by which our culture has, since 1960, conceived of girls' lives and development;
- an in-depth understanding of girls' actual biological and personal development;
- comprehensive, practical help in applying your new understanding, whether you are raising a girl of two or twelve or twenty;
- a passion to move beyond many of our present, dominant ideologies into a new stage of social thought regarding the lives of girls and women.

Any one of these in itself is a tall order, and all four together may seem especially daunting, but I hope you'll join me in high expectations of all of us. Even while the bulk of this book is written to help parents and other caregivers with the daily raising of girls, for those interested in social theory, I will very clearly be calling for fundamental changes—not only in patriarchy, but also in feminism.

In *The Wonder of Boys* I ask the reader to engage in revolutionary thinking in regard to boys' lives and male development. In *The Wonder of Girls*, I ask you to do the same for girls: Engage in a revolutionary perspective—like the feminist call of Gloria Steinem, Betty Friedan, and others was four decades ago—but this time, a grassroots effort to move beyond feminism into *womanism*, a term fully defined in Chapter 8. The call to find a new logic, a *womanist* logic, will lead, I hope, to a quiet revolution; one that transpires first and foremost in our care for our individual daughters—from there, who knows how loud it will become.

## QUESTIONS AND ANSWERS

"How do I talk to my fifteen-year-old?" a mother asks.

"Why are girls getting so much nastier these days?" a grandmother asks.

"How do I, as a father, handle my daughter's sexual yearnings?" a father asks.

Over the last decade and a half, Gail and I have been asked questions like these, and hundreds of others, which we will answer with practical strategies.

"Are the issues of American girls the same issues girls face around the world?"
"How do I help my daughter get through my divorce?"
"How can I help my daughter handle her own feelings and emotions on a daily basis?"

As you read this book, I hope you'll find that we've covered most of your questions. The answers I provide may startle you, and you may disagree with some. I hope that even as you disagree, you'll still receive enough hard information to deal with dilemmas you are experiencing in your daughter's life. Even disagreements are part of the process of creating a quiet revolution in our girls' lives.

"How can I provide the best discipline for my daughter without crushing her independence or her self-esteem?"
"How much backtalk should I allow with my daughter?"
"My daughter is really searching for herself. How do I help?"

As we explore girls' lives, don't be surprised to notice that you are learning a lot about the lives of grown women, especially women from puberty until menopause. The fields of neuro- and sociobiology teach us that the life of the pubescent girl and the thirty-something adult woman have more in common, biologically and therefore relationally, than people have understood. The same holds true, in many ways, for boys; thus I have often heard, "*The Wonder of Boys* helped me understand not only my son, but my husband." I hope *The Wonder of Girls* will help you understand not just the girl, but the woman, and I've written it to accomplish that goal.

In the end, I offer *The Wonder of Girls* as a heartfelt vision, hoping you'll be inspired and touched by it. I've worked to bring together the best of the new wisdom on girls without losing the best of the old. I want to thank Gail and my daughters, Gabrielle and Davita, for helping me understand many of the secrets of girls' lives. And I want to thank all of the girls, mothers, grandmothers, fathers, grandfathers, caregivers, mentors, and counselors who have shared their lives and stories with me over the years. Without their efforts and wisdom, this book would be incomplete.

I have learned the wonder of girls from all of them.

# PART I

# Why Girls Are the Way They Are

*"'Who in the world am I?' Ah, that's the great puzzle."*
—LEWIS CARROLL,
*Alice's Adventures in Wonderland*

# 1

## BEGINNING OUR SEARCH

### A NEW LOGIC OF GIRLS' LIVES

*"We have to look beyond patriarchy, that's for sure. But, you know, it's starting to be that we also have to look beyond feminism too. Our daughters' lives are limited by both theories."*

—Gail Reid-Gurian, mother of two girls
and family therapist

On a sunny day in June, I took my daughters to Manito Park, our neighborhood play area. Gabrielle was seven and Davita four. Beyond the normal swings and slides, the girls always enjoyed a sculpture there, built from logs and shaped like a Viking ship. On this particular day, we arrived early, and the girls, who had brought some of their stuffed animals, began to play a game involving two mothers caring for children on an ocean voyage. I offered to be part of the game if they wanted me, but then, as they enjoyed their "girl world" without me, I settled into a book on a bench at the periphery.

Their play went comfortably, filled with creative ideas and adjustments, in that way girls have with each other. They could have gone on happily, alone together, until they got hungry for lunch. But a car pulled up, and out stepped a mom and two boys, around five and eight years old. The mom and I waved as strangers do in parks when the sweet energy of children is about. Her two sons dashed onto the ship loudly. I watched, fascinated at first, then disquieted.

The complex game Gabrielle and Davita had created was interrupted by the louder and more aggressive energy of the boys. Within seconds, my girls abandoned their game and took to observing the boys' action and cries. "I'm captain now!"

"Shoot the shark!"

Watching this usurpation of my girls' play-world, I felt a growing irritation. I thought sadly of how often this happened between boys and girls.

There it is, I thought. What we are so often warned about: that when the boys come around, the girls step aside. The girls' self-esteem drops and the boys take over.

My protective instincts for my girls rose even while I harbored no ill will toward the boys, who were, after all, just enjoying the world through their own way of being. I felt almost like a crime was being committed to my daughters. I felt like I should *do* something.

A professional student of human nature, I spend a lot of time observing children's behavior. When I'm not sure what to do, I fall back on watching. On this morning I did just that. And I learned a valuable lesson.

For about five minutes, my daughters tried to return to their game. This became impossible, given the noise and interruptions. Then Gabrielle said something to the older of the boys, made some suggestions, began a negotiation I couldn't hear from my bench. The boys slowed down a little, listened, talked in the midst of their bouncing and playing. Gabrielle, as the alpha female on the ship, seemed to talk mostly to the older boy, the alpha male. She pointed; he pointed. She told Davita to move one of the dolls over to where he was, and he instructed his little brother to take hold of it and prop it up on the aft rim of the ship.

Within ten minutes from the boys' arrival, the "set" was rearranged. Now the four children were in a group near the helm of the ship, each of them with a different job, and all of them engaged in some new game, even more rich and complex than had been my daughters' or the boys' original intentions for play, this one featuring princesses, giants, pirates, treasures, and, I found out later from Davita, Cinderella's lost shoe.

My disquiet, my irritation, even my hidden anger were replaced now by admiration. As so often happens in the world of children, something small was really something large. The kids were living out their nature wholeheartedly, and it was worth a lot to observe it at work.

## A Moment of Awakening

This moment at the park was the first of many incidents that cried out for me to think beyond our culture's present ideas about girls, about girls and boys, and about women and men. If you think about it, how many times have similar things happened on playgrounds, in workplaces, in homes, among children, teenagers, adults? Initially, there is overwhelming energy from males, but soon, gradual assessment, then guidance, from females. As a married man, I am no stranger to this circumstance!

And in the five minutes of negotiation that went on between Gabrielle, Davita, and the two boys, I realized I needed to revise the timeline by which I watched for drops in girls' self-esteem. Among these four children there was no drop in self-esteem, though initial observation seemed to show there was a sad drop for my girls. Instead, there were the natural interpersonal relationships that emerge when we are patient enough to observe them.

This incident occurred many years ago. It was one of the times in my life that I've felt dissatisfied, as a parent, by what our present, conventional conversation about girls has taught me about "gender stereotypes," "girls' self-esteem drops," "girls in crisis." A number of catchphrases dominate our dialogue about girls, but our girls actually live far beyond the words. That morning, I went home and began a list of these phrases, as well as some of the theories that indoctrinate me nearly every day—in some form in our media and pop culture—to see girls in a way that allows very little for the subtleties in which girls really live their lives.

I told Gail about my observation. As she does so often, she smiled at me, a little bemused. Quite often she sees things more clearly and much earlier than I do, but just doesn't tell me about it. "Mike, hardly anyone anymore really looks under the surface of girls' lives," she said. "Feminism used to do it twenty, thirty years ago. It was deep. But now it's skidding on the surface." It was during the rest of that day that Gail and I talked about this, talked about my writing this book, and acknowledged something we, brought up in the feminist tradition, had avoided dealing with.

The great ocean of girls' lives actually lies beneath the surface of the simple formulas we are now taught about "girl power" and girls' self-esteem. Feminism is, we realized, no longer the best theory to care for many of our girls.

In this book, my primary objective is to help parents and caregivers raise daughters. I am a teacher and counselor who greatly enjoys working intimately with people and their families. I am not seeking to be a political figure on one "side" of a political debate.

And yet to write about girls in any way different from current convention is to immediately become a person of the fight. My experiences from around the world, my research, and my own parenting lead me to somewhat different conclusions from my peers. Thus, in offering this parenting guide, I feel compelled to speak not only as a helpful professional but as a figure in a social debate. I don't think *The Wonder of Girls* would be comprehensive if it did not briefly explore some of the ideologies and theories our girls are now being raised in.

This chapter, then, is about the social debate we raise our girls within. If you are uninterested in politics of this kind, you might want to move to Chapter 2. If, however, you want to revise some of the political logic by which girls have been raised for the last few decades, then this chapter will be enjoyable. It is an analysis of feminist theory, specifically of feminist theories about factors predominant in making girls the way they are. It is also a call to move beyond feminism, to a new logic of girls' lives.

The central core of the new logic is this: Feminism as we know it today is "power feminism"—based in acquiring more and more social and workplace power for females. While this acquisition is important, it is being pursued at the expense of what I will argue that my daughters, and yours, need and want as much or more. Feminism has, in its worthwhile and useful search for power, neglected this other world of girls' needs. In the last chapter of this book, we will define a set of principles by which to provide our girls with an even wider scope of happiness and success than present-day feminism offers.

## Looking Beyond Feminism: Old Myths and New Theories

Almost four decades ago, Gloria Steinem, Betty Friedan, and others based their feminist revolution on showing us the Victorian and patriarchal myths that impeded the progress of girls and women. The myths they fought against—and many of us along with them—went something like this:

- *Since a girl's ultimate social goal should be to catch the right husband, girls don't need equal opportunity for education, especially higher education.*

- *Girls don't need to become leaders in society and business; their job as women will be to serve men and raise a man's children.*

- *Women's rights, including reproductive rights, voting rights, right to work outside the home, and right to physical safety, should be controlled by men.*

- *If women do work outside the home, they don't need equal pay for equal work, and girls should not expect it.*

Because of the inspiration and direction provided by the feminist movement, we have each, over the last decades, seen amazing changes in the home, the workplace, the school classroom, and the media. There are still many battles to fight in pursuit of women's equality, but many have also been won. Because of the inspiration of feminists, we've worked to change our culture, and we've succeeded.

Yet if you are like Gail and myself, while ready to congratulate feminists for the powerful work the movement has done for our girls and women, you have begun to suspect, over the last few years, during moments of your own awakening, that feminist theory is often static and overreactive, sometimes unfair, and generally incomplete in its assessment of human nature. But you may also feel like the villagers in the story "The Emperor's New Clothes," hesitant to to cry out, "But look! There's something wrong with this picture!"

Let's feel this hesitancy no longer. Let's explore some of the most predominant feminist theories in our culture, and make decisions about whether they really do apply to our homes, our classrooms, and our culture.

Let's look at the four most prevalent feminist theories, and the imperatives they impose on our thinking as parents, regarding why girls are the way they are. To fully care for girls in this millennium, these four theories will have to be broken through.

### THEORY 1
### HUMAN NATURE IS NOT VERY IMPORTANT TO GIRLS' LIVES.

*Girls are who they are predominantly because of the way they are socialized in our society. Nature plays a smaller part in why girls are the way they are.*

What we need to know about girls, we are told, can be learned by studying "socialization." In our society, a girl's socialization is patriarchal and male dominated, and females are second-class citizens. When a girl experiences a self-esteem drop, a problem, an unrequited desire, or a fear of life itself, interpretation of "socialization" provides the reason. To spend time looking at hormones, the female brain, and the natural evolution of the female is to risk limiting girls' potential, so we must avoid it. Human nature (as girls live it) is a subject too risky for contemporary parents and teachers, for spending a lot of time on the nature of a girl will lead, ultimately, to her oppression.

This first feminist theory found its genesis just under forty years ago. It was a logical response to the misuse of biology and nature-based observations by nineteenth- and early-twentieth-century neu-robiologists and psychologists. When, over a hundred years ago, we discovered that the male brain was ten percent larger than the female, some male scientists cried, "You see, men are smarter than women!" Sigmund Freud, a genius in many ways, based his own the-ories on just a few people—his patients—and found in them penis envy; he claimed this to be natural to females, and overburdened this "nature-based" theory with male chauvinism.

Early feminists reacted strongly and effectively to the limitations and just plain bad theory of many of the men in the early century. In the 1960s and '70s, academic feminists buried neurobiological and sociobiological research. They've continued this trend unflinchingly. In a 1995 television interview on male/female brain differences, Gloria Steinem told 20/20 reporter John Stossel that to talk about biology was to continue the patriarchy.

Hormonal and biochemical research—so useful in helping adult women understand pregnancy, menopause, and daily life—has been largely absent from the books and resources on raising girls. In 1998, I asked Mary Pipher, author of *Reviving Ophelia,* whether she thought biology played a part in the lives of girls, especially the girls who were suffering so deeply in her book. Biology, she told me, plays a much smaller part in what's going on for girls than socialization does.

Christina Sommers, author of *Who Stole Feminism?* told me she saw the feminist hyper-emphasis on "nurture" and nearly complete lack of emphasis on human nature to be a "feminist fear of what is natural, because feminists see what is natural as being defined through a male lens." Early feminism had to disconnect itself from many of the scaffolds of human life in order to develop as a domi-nant theory. Nature was owned by men. Biology was owned by male theorists who got their guidance not just from science (dominated by men for hundreds of years) but also religion (dominated by male imagery). The imperative behind Gloria Steinem's sense that to talk of biology is to be patriarchal was crucial to early feminism's time and place.

And yet, even given the immense liberation for women that femi-nism has accomplished, the basic questions of human nature remain.

They especially remain for parents who are trying to raise children of nature without understanding the original nature from which the children have come.

*The Wonder of Girls* hopes no longer to skirt questions involving human nature, for the very soul of the human is lost when human nature is taken out of the human dialogue. At the Gurian Institute, where we train teachers and parents, classrooms and homes become very different places when communities learn the hidden secrets of human nature. We have found that parents, teachers, and community members who are not equipped with the wisdom of nature in understanding their children make painful mistakes both in action and in thought—they think themselves to blame for things in which they play little part; and they neglect to provide ways of love and nurturance that they did not know they should provide. They become embattled in causes, but discover they do not understand the girl herself, or the boy beside her. And they often try to direct their daughter toward certain social and political goals that may not be right for the personality and nature of that particular girl. They become cut off from the child, especially during adolescence, when their child wants desperately to be understood. A great deal of our society's woes grow from the isolation adolescents feel from their caregivers.

When parents don't fully understand their children, much of the wonder of parenting is lost. In the minds of both parents and children, parenting becomes like a business, always on the verge of failure or bankruptcy.

There is another way, available to us once we push beyond the simplistic idea that girls are who they are "because they are socialized that way," and notice that "girls are who they are as much or more because of their hidden nature" in which socialization plays an important, but, surprisingly, *not a life-defining role.* New sciences (especially neurobiology and biochemistry) that will not be submerged in politics any longer have made it very possible, as Chapters 2 and 3 will reveal, to *know our daughters from the inside out.* Distinctions like nature vs. nurture become relatively trivial: What comes to matter is the knowledge of how a girl's brain, hor-

mones, and physiological development, within her everyday enviro-
ment, are affecting her life.

As a mother of two girls put it to me after learning about the biology and biochemistry of girlhood: "This is incredible. Now my girls
make sense."

### THEORY 2
### WOMEN DO BEST WHEN THEY ARE INDEPENDENT OF MEN.

*To be safe and successful as human beings, women must become, for the*
*most part, independent of men. Boys and men are not inherently trust-*
*worthy; girls and women must compete with them as needed, become*
*more like them as it is strategic to do so, and seek a social position in*
*which they don't need the other sex.*

When I was a boy my mother told me what her life was like in the
1950s. "A woman got married and had children, and her husband
got a job and supported her and the children. I was alone in my own
house, and I relied on your father so much that for years I just didn't
know who I was, or what I could be. I felt so second-class, I came to
resent him, myself, and the world."

My mother's sense of loneliness, of utter dependency on a man,
and of social inequality was shared by many women of that time.
When Betty Friedan cried out, "We want equality! Now!" to a huge
crowd gathered at the Washington Monument, a nation listened. The
dependency of a wife on a husband's social status had become destructive to women's psychological health, and thus to human society.

Our culture took up the cause of women like my mother, and continues to do so to this day, through one of the best outlets available:
the workplace. In order to extract themselves from the loneliness of
the wife at home, and the low status they were given (and for other
economic reasons), women entered the workforce en masse, and discovered a mainly male-dominant environment. Women saw that they
needed to compete with men. And the most efficient female strategy
appeared to be for women to become more like men. If they became
like men, they would compete and succeed in the male world. And
many women have.

Because of feminist theory and strategies, the financial worth and social independence of most women in Western economic cultures is now not primarily controlled by a man's money. "Women need men like a fish needs a bicycle," said Gloria Steinem in the 1970s. Her thinking inspired young women seeking to make it on their own. Feminist theory, and our cultural adjustment to it, has helped create an economic culture in which most women can, should they choose to, create a life separate from intimate dependency on men. In a recent poll, however, reported by the Associated Press, the majority of women who were asked if they were happier than their mothers said no. The number-one item on the list of what they felt they missed? Stable relationships. This was especially true for women raising kids.

While the compelling need for a woman to be independent was a dominant necessity of my mother's generation, what was not clear thirty to forty years ago, but is clarifying for many of us now—especially when the sciences of neurobiology and sociobiology are applied to the lives of girls and women—is this natural fact: In most cases, human females and males need to form intimate, long-lasting, and symbiotic relationships in order to feel safe and personally fulfilled and in order to raise the next generation safely. Furthermore, the safety of civilization as a whole depends on the social guidance, protection, and valuing of bonds between males and females who are in the nature-based process of raising children. Couples who are not raising children can often experiment with serial mating, divorce, and social independence without structurally harming a society; but couples, families, and extended families that raise children without valuing the bonds among the caregivers have a higher probability of raising troubled children. The weight of this greater probability falls on not only individual families, but the civilization as a whole.

In the old patriarchal logic of raising girls, females were overly dependent on males and got in return a family arrangement that would give most women the relational stability in which to raise children.

In the feminist logic of raising girls, there is a high emphasis on female independence and social status, but the reward of relational stability is downgraded. Females are constantly embattled by having to make it on their own.

All this might not seem like a crucial issue to you or me were we not raising the next generation of daughters. But because we are, we must firmly establish where we stand, as parents, on how female independence from males will be encouraged in our house. Even if we don't spend time thinking about it, we are either pushing our girls toward competition with males or holding them back; we are either teaching them to trust males, or not. As parents in our era, we are in the thick of matters of female independence.

As we search for new logic for girls' lives, every parent and caregiver may find themselves challenged to develop a *womanist* vision— one that is neither predominantly patriarchal nor feminist: one that provides for the equal status of girls and women without robbing them of *the natural need for dependency on men*. Meeting this challenge will be a major, and very practical, subject of this book. For if we succeed in meeting it, our girls will fully achieve personal identity, relational stability, and social success.

### THEORY 3
### GIRLS ARE VICTIMS.
*Today's girls are, first and foremost, victims of a male-dominant society.*

For about a year, between 2000 and 2001, I watched the popular nighttime crime drama *Law and Order: Special Victims Unit*. This program deals very realistically with some of the sickest perpetrators of sexual crime in our culture. In one episode, a fifteen-year-old girl from Romania is manipulated by a pedophile to not only become the au pair of his daughter, but a victim of his violent sexual fantasies. Her developing self is erased by his dominance; he withholds food from her, convinces her to become utterly dependent on him, locks her up, ties her up, constantly rapes her. When she is rescued by the detectives, she is nearly dead, locked in a coffinlike box in which she cannot move and can barely breathe.

This is only one episode of *Special Victims Unit*, and not even the most frightening.

I stopped watching the show because it was so effectively written, acted, and directed. As a father of daughters, it was constantly like watching my own girls being hurt, and I simply could not stand it anymore.

Like so many television shows, movies, and newspaper stories, *Special Victims Unit* displays the dangers that girls face, and the sickness, violence, and harassment that males are capable of perpetrating upon them. One in four females will experience rape or sexual abuse at the hands of males during their lifetimes, according to the FBI. Just under one in ten will experience domestic violence at the hands of men. Many will experience sexual harassment at school or in the workplace.

Some girls and women experience victimization, and many live in a kind of fear males do not understand. This undeniable fact was— like the fact that some women felt second-class in marriage and society—a foundation of early feminist thinking.

As feminism developed in scope and power, this fact-for-some women became a truth-for-all. Feminist theorists, such as Anne Wilson-Schaef, argued that not only are *some* girls and women victims of males, but *all* girls and women are inherently victims of the male-dominant system. Very quickly the "victim theory" developed, teaching that male identity is linked to victimizing females, and that men, masculinity, male social systems, and "male-dominant society" are inherently hostile to girls and women. It also taught that female identity itself is largely based on girls' victimization by male systems; girls and women are victims or sisters of victims or former victims or potential victims of males or male systems.

As a young feminist, I recall being moved by the victim theory years ago. It filled me with sympathy for the women I cared about, and cautioned me to be the best man I could in their presence. Years later, watching *Special Victims Unit*, anyone would be prone to agree with the females-are-victims theory.

But mustn't we ask ourselves if victimization by male-dominant society is a *predominant* factor in the lives of *all* girls and women? And mustn't we further ask if victim identity is ultimately useful, as a self-image, to *our daughters' developing identity*? Might there be

long-term effects of the girls-are-victims theory on human relationships as a whole, and thus on our civilization?

In the mid-1990s, Christina Crawford, the author of *Mommie
Dearest*, told me during a dinner party: "Males destroy, females create. That's just the way it is."

Years ago we might not have noticed that in order for comments
like hers to make us more conscious of the abuses of males and the
trials faced by girls and women, social thinkers like Crawford made a
choice—to promulgate a universal enemy: destructive masculinity.
Thus, the majority of girls and women—who are not victims of violence, rape, date rape, or harassment—are nonetheless, in theory, still
very much victims, because the enemy does not need to be an individual man; it is "masculinity." As recently as 1998, the feminist Carol
Gilligan told me that we could not protect either our girls or our
boys until we completely deconstructed masculinity. It is inherently
dangerous, in her opinion, and has to go.

In *Reviving Ophelia*, one of the most effective books to map girls'
distresses at the end of the twentieth century, psychologist and
author Mary Pipher utilized the female victim/male villain theory.
She argued that among the causes of a girl's loss of self during adolescence is that "most fathers received a big dose of misogyny training
[training in women-hatred]." In her very powerful and important
book, she shows us the many ways that our daughters are potentially
victimized by their socialization in this culture: their spirits crushed,
their bodies emaciated, their minds manipulated. When I spoke with
Mary before a seminar we gave together, she admitted that she
thought part of the success of *Ophelia* was due to its ride on an ideological wave of victim thinking.

She didn't consciously try to exploit this feminist idea, she told
me, but it had ended up being very effective.

Mary's book is effective, because, like no other, it tells the story
of girls in distress with beauty and grace; it has had a profoundly
important impact and is very useful to those people raising daughters who have been hurt and are hurting. At the same time, it participates, like so many other girls' books, in propagating the myth
that girls' lives are dominated by distresses predominantly caused

by female socialization in a misogynistic male-dominant society.

For my daughters' sake I must ask: What happens to a culture that promotes the idea that males are inherently defective, violent, or women-hating, and females are inherently victims? How will my daughters make the compassionate alliances they need when they are adults if they are trained to believe boys and men are predominantly destructive to them?

Since most boys and men are good people—according to the FBI, 1 percent of men commit our crimes—and most girls and women are not born victims of bad men, isn't it my responsibility to help my daughters live, as much as possible, in *trust* of males? How am I to do this if the voices of female culture condemn men so constantly?

Gail and I, and many like us, strive to protect our daughters' abilities to love, trust, and be compassionate. We hope they trust not only men, but also the highest moral standards of masculinity as well, without acceding to the bad boys and men out there. *The Wonder of Girls* is written in that spirit of trust. I hope it challenges you to explore where you stand, as a parent of daughters, on issues of victimization and masculinity. I hope it challenges you to ask and answer these questions: Do I choose to like boys and men, or not? Do I choose to fear masculinity, or do I take the time to guide my daughters through it? Our daughters are making these choices all the time. How will we guide them in our own thinking and living?

Throughout this book, and especially in Chapter 8, I note how vigilant a girl must be about boys, men, and the masculine; but also, how equally vigilantly those of us who care about girls must focus on seeing human love for what it is: an adaptable, but also an established, dance between a flawed but essential feminine way of being and a flawed but essential masculine way of being.

When we explore girls' lives from a broader perspective than a set of feminist theories, when we listen to girls and boys—and women and men—with tender ears and eyes, we discover that *most* girls' lives are *not* dominated by their victimization and by misogyny; *most* males are *not* trained to hate women; and *all* girls experience normal developmental crises which, by understanding female nature, we can best help *without* attacking and distancing males, but instead by noticing how they are ready to be our allies.

## THEORY 4
### GIRLS' LIVES ARE DOMINATED BY GENDER STEREOTYPES THAT LEAVE GIRLS ONE-DOWN AND POWERLESS.

*Most of our girls' social problems, especially as adolescents, grow from the gender stereotypes females are forced into by our culture. These gender types—Barbies, images of thin women, and female gender roles in the workplace and home—are the primary causes of the low self-esteem we see in young women.*

Kristen, fourteen, came into Gail's office with her mother, who confessed to being unable to help her daughter. "Kristen suffers from low self-esteem," she explained. "I think she's being stereotyped by everyone, not just boys but the girls too. She's pretty. It can be a problem." Kristen agreed that kids picked on her for her large breasts, and even her model-like looks.

Kristen was tall for her age, and very developed physically. She had long brownish-blond hair that was cut high above her right eye but hung below her left. She wore a lot of makeup, in that way adolescent girls do, that makes us think they are trying to look adult. Within a half hour of talking with her, Gail ascertained that she felt anything but grown-up. She felt overwhelmed by life. Two years before, her parents had divorced. Her grandmother, with whom she'd been close, had died a year before. In school, she'd discovered she had to study harder now than before, but no longer had motivation.

"And my mother's on me all the time," she complained. "She wants me to be more like this or like that. It's always something." At some level she knew her mother was "on her" because she worried for her daughter; nonetheless, Kristen felt more inadequate in the face of her mother's love, rather than more safe and more accomplished.

Margeaux, twelve, a straight-A student, was just beginning puberty, talkative, self-aware—yet seemed to be moving toward anorexia.

"I just hate food," she told me. "I hate everything about it. I'm sorry I make trouble for my parents. But I just don't want to eat." This had been going on for about four months, since just after her menses began. Her mother told me, "The problem is, she reads all the magazines about thin girls and wants to be like them." Many adolescent girls who struggle with eating disorders will not admit their compulsion. Margeaux admitted it, but couldn't change it, so she would eat for a few days, even a week, then starve herself for a few days.

In the cases of Kristen and Margeaux, Gail and I were both faced with adolescent girls about whom the conventional idea that gender stereotyping in school, in magazines, and in the culture was destroying self-esteem could have been easily applied. In this fourth feminist theory—promulgated mainly during the 1990s through studies put out by the American Association of University Women, Carol Gilligan's research at the Harvard School of Education, David and Myra Sadker, and then spreading throughout the news media—those who care for girls, whether parents or professionals, are warned of the destructive power of gender stereotypes on adolescent girls' self-esteem. In some cases, the work behind these theories is called "the self-esteem research."

Gail and I, as therapists, have enjoyed the fruits of that research—learning more about how images of thin women can affect girls' self-image, how boys are sometimes called on in class more than girls, how girls are judged on their looks and boys on their achievement. However, for us, the cases of Kristen and Margeaux helped us to notice something we had suspected, as professionals and as parents of girls, for some time: While the feminist idea that girls experience stereotypes and lose self-esteem is irrefutable, *in most cases, gender stereotypes are not the primary cause of a girl's developmental issues.* To focus on them, while worthwhile, is often destructive, because it distracts parents, schools, and the culture from the deeper issues facing our girls.

In working with Kristen, Gail was aware immediately of having to help her family push through their ideas about "low self-esteem" and "gender stereotypes" in order to get to the real cause of a girl's problems. While Kristen was ostracized at school by girls because she was beautiful and hit on by boys for the same reasons, and while these did affect her growth, her developing self was at risk from a different root cause: She was terrified by the consequences of her parents' divorce, and the broken family bonds. The gender stereotypes issue was, in large part, a smokescreen. The whole family had bought into the smokescreen with the best of intentions; however, Kristen's healing, and the family's, began when the smokescreen was pulled away.

As I worked intensely with Margeaux's family, I discovered that her eating issues mimicked complexities (to be dealt with further in Chapters 3 and 6) in her hormonal cycle—her hormones and neurology were out of balance. When I referred her to an appropriate physician, treatment for biological, hormone-cycle issues were the most instrumental in dealing with her anorexia. Stereotypes regarding thin women—while a factor—were not the causal factor that the family initially perceived.

Like all therapists working with girls, Gail and I have counseled girls in trouble: girls with low self-esteem, girls who are depressed, girls who have been abused, girls whose core selves are being trampled, girls who are anorexic, and girls on anabolic steroids. Many girls have become anorexic after looking at magazine pictures of very thin women. Many girls have experienced drops of self-esteem in sport or classroom situations where they were not treated with as much respect as boys were. Girls do feel immense pressures to fit in, to be popular, to become a Barbie, a sex object, a voiceless object of a young man's quick, then flagging desires.

However, we have come to understand a deeper reason than "stereotypes" for the disintegration of these girls' lives. While Gail and I respect the research on the impact of cultural imagery on girls, in *The Wonder of Girls*, you'll find me downplaying its importance on female adolescence. Gail and I protect our daughters as much as possible from destructive gender stereotyping, and help empower them to be who they are in the face of cultural typing; we also teach methods of doing this to clients, and many will appear in this book. But after years of noticing the Kristens, the Margeauxs, and the smokescreens, we have come to understand that Theory 4 is just that, one theory. So often other things weigh heavier on our girls and yours: issues of attachment, of family bonds, of grief, of lack of self-knowledge during traumatic adolescence, of physiological change, of brain development, of hormone cycles. These are far larger causes of self-esteem drops than we have realized in our late–twentieth century focus on gender stereotypes.

Furthermore, Gail and I have also come to understand—and the biological research in the next two chapters will reveal this in depth—that a large cultural issue hides behind the gender stereotypes theory, an issue all parents of daughters must, in some inspiring way, come to terms with in our fast-paced society, so often unfriendly to family stability: *Our early-adolescent girls do not get enough attachment, bonding, and information from the family and extended family into which they've been born.*

Kristen, Margeaux, and millions of other adolescent girls are moving through three to five years of internal transformation to womanhood while feeling abandoned, in differing ways, by family members and community. For hormonal, neurological, and psychological reasons, a girl of this age group is now desperate for love. Adolescence is, after infancy, the most vulnerable time in a child's developing life. As we will explore in Chapters 2 and 3, our culture as a whole has forgotten how normal it is for children to experience a series of self-esteem drops in early to middle adolescence: The changing brain and hormones require these. The mistake our culture has primarily made in nurturing its daughters is the pull-away that occurs among the generations when a girl enters puberty.

How often have you yourself seen it in your community? By the time a girl discovers puberty, the family has moved on to the business of parents back in the workforce, of kids left alone, of parental divorce, all of which may in some way be necessary for the adults in the family system, but all of which also affect the attachments and bonds the girl feels during this most tumultuous time in her development.

Gail and I have found ourselves using two primary strategies to help parents look behind the smokescreen of "gender stereotypes" and into the attachment needs of girls. The first is to educate parents fully in female adolescent development. Usually, when parents fully "get" their daughters, they know how to make life better. The second is to help families make choices that keep and build *three or more very close family attachments* for the growing girl. Often these three are mother, father, and grandparent, but there can be many different sets of this adolescent triad, as we will explore in later chapters.

Guiding Kristen's and Margeaux's parents, as well as the girls themselves, through deepened knowledge of themselves and their broken attachments was life-changing for them. Anorexia began to make etiological and biological sense to a girl and a family that had earlier defined itself by the idea that "girl diseases" were not biological or chemical but caused by cultural imagery and stereotypes a mother and father had not protected a daughter from. Margeaux's "I can't get my mother to understand me" hid a deeper pain. Her mother, who had worked part-time during Margeaux's early childhood, had gone back to work full-time when Margeaux was in fourth grade, and her father was not around every other week because of his work schedule—a high-tech sales rep, he traveled a great deal. With both mother and father working, Margeaux, the eldest of three, entered adolescence among fading attachments. Her family was pulling away from her (and she from them), but it hurt, and she suffered unnecessarily.

During counseling the trauma of divorce was dealt with honestly in Kristen's family. Kristen explored with her parents how the broken attachments had altered her ability to live. The family learned to heal its daughter by becoming closer—not in remarriage, but in postdivorce restructuring of family time, rituals, and bonds.

## A THEORY FOR SOME, NOT FOR ALL

In providing what I hope is useful insight into four of the defining theories of our last half century of feminist thought, I have tried to stay focused on what is most important to parents, teachers, and other intimate caregivers of girls. When offering an analysis such as I have in these last few pages, there is the risk of overstating one's case—of saying, "Well, there, you see, that feminist theory is all bunk, and we should throw it out." That kind of overstating regarding our patriarchal history has led to excesses of feminism. I am not offering an extremist response to feminist theory. Feminist theory is crucial for the lives of many girls.

What might interest us most now, in the new millennium, is *which* girls.

Based on a review of statistics from the National Institute of Mental Health, as well as the Department of Justice, the Department of Education, and a number of independent data collectors, it appears that around 10 to 20 percent of our girls are in some form of crisis—an ongoing physical, emotional, or mental circumstance that increases their cortisol (stress hormone) levels to a degree which interferes with normal, healthy female development.

These are many of the girls Gail and I might see in our family practice. These are the girls who are most written about in the media. No one knows for sure, but between girls in personal crisis and girls and women in dangerous, demeaning relationships, the figure is probably just under one quarter of our population.

For abused, disturbed, or systemically disrespected girls, feminist theory is very helpful. In some ways, feminist theory is most useful to these girls because it is a crisis-response theory. It has forced our culture to make remarkable gains for girls suffering domestic violence, exploitation, sexual abuse, and eating disorders. Were my daughter beaten by her boyfriend, the services that feminist agendas now provide to her would be a miracle in her life. Feminist theory and services have acted as miracles in the lives of many.

Herein lies the hardest truth for me and for Gail, as parents of daughters—the truth that shakes us to the bones. Feminist theory is the right model for that minority of girls who are in crisis. Yet, for us, given the myths it labors under, it is not the right model for the majority of girls, who are not at this time in crisis, including our daughters.

## FROM SELECTIVE FEMINISM TO WOMANISM

Gail and I and many others in our personal and family community have practiced what our daughters' godmother, the counselor Pam

Brown, once called "selective feminism." This selective feminism is supportive of some aspects of "girl power" but disheartened by others; supportive of "female risk-taking" but disheartened by the pressure on girls to judge themselves inadequate if they can't best boys; supportive of girl-assistance programs in schools but disheartened by lawsuits against schools that attempt to help boys; supportive of sports programs for our daughters, but disheartened by erasure of sports programs for boys who also, desperately, need them; supportive of providing help to women and girls who have been abused, but disheartened by constant attacks on males in agencies charged with helping females in crisis.

Over the last decade, our selective feminism has been whittled down in our minds, mainly because we have discovered that feminist theory is able to take into account neither the hard sciences, like neurobiology, nor the sheer variety of emotional, moral, and spiritual needs girls have. Girls' lives are far more about the four-million-year human history than they are about the few decades, or even centuries, of social life that feminism helps us understand.

## A NEW THEORY: THE JOURNEY AHEAD

The foundation for the language and ideas of womanism, which I hope will be useful to you in the rest of this book, does not mainly lie in the four theoretical imperatives we've explored in this chapter but, rather, in an *intimacy imperative*, to be fully introduced at the end of Chapter 2: *the hidden yearning in every girl's and woman's life to live in a safe web of intimate relationships*. In following this imperative in girls' lives, *The Wonder of Girls* seeks to protect what is most beautiful and inspiring in our daughters even while protecting their social rights to equality and physical right to safety. By noticing, first, how female biology seeks the magnetism of intimacy and attachment, we will then provide a clear vision of how to rethink our society toward greater attachment and stability for girls and for women, not just with boys and with men, but with their families, communities, and other girls.

The next two chapters, and the practical application of their material throughout the rest of this book, utilize *nature-based* theory and *nature-based* parenting. This is an interdisciplinary approach to neurobiology, biochemistry, psychology, anthropology, moral theory, and sociology. In preparing to provide you with this new approach, I have studied thirty cultures' (listed in the Notes and References section at the end of this book) approaches to parenting girls, and included studies conducted in six school districts in Missouri; I have also relied on my own family practice, and on the daily journey of raising daughters. In all walks of life, I focus on the base, in human nature, for a child's actions. As you read Chapters 2 and 3 especially, you'll find new sciences of female biology on display which are groundbreaking and provide one of our best, natural allies in raising our girls.

You'll discover that many of your daughters' interests, moods, attitudes, self-esteem drops, desires, and ways of relating, once thought to be caused by culture, are products of their neurobiology, and as you find their minds and hearts clarified, you'll be able to alter the way you relate to them, especially during their adolescence, between ten and twenty years old. You'll discover how large a part biology plays in girls' distresses—from depression and anorexia to self-esteem crises—and what you can do, from the inside out, to help girls in trouble.

You'll discover the ways in which girls' biology differs significantly from boys' biology. Because of structural and functional differences in the female and male brains, girls sense, remember, enjoy, and experience personal needs and desires differently than boys. They use their bodies differently, and their words. They even experience God, religion, and spirituality in neurologically differing ways.

As you explore this book, I hope you'll experience the degree to which *femininity* (being female) is an immensely complex neurobiological process that takes place, even more than masculinity, *in separate stages, which each have discernible needs.* This staged female development process is not suitable for the kinds of theoretical simplifications we've based social policy on over the last decades. It can only stand for so long the attempt to limit itself to one stereotype of what a woman is or should be: financially independent and able to compete successfully in the workplace with males. This "different stages/different needs" femininity is a process, a way of being, which we have neglected for decades—but one on which human civilization has always been grounded.

As you gain support in these pages for your daughters' journey through life, I hope most of all that you will enjoy a deep sense of peace for yourself and your girls, the kind of peace that comes, almost like a whisper, late at night, when we know we are living out to the best of our ability our fragile parent–daughter relationship.

# 2

## HOW HER MIND WORKS

### SECRETS OF THE FEMALE BRAIN

*"There's a lot more going on inside my head than people think."*
—Erin, seventeen

*"I'm a girl! Don't you get it? Not a boy—a girl!"*
—Gabrielle, at eleven, to her friend Josh, ten

Erin came to see Gail when she was sixteen. She had been having trouble concentrating in school, she had been losing enough weight to frighten her family, and she had lost friends because of angry episodes. Her grades had started to drop, even in easy classes. She spent a lot of time on the Internet, telling her mother, "You don't understand me. On the Internet I find people who do." Erin's sleeping, eating, and daily cycles had changed enough to indicate to Gail that her brain was going through a series of small traumas, often daily. She was an unhappy, sometimes desperate young woman, and she suffered from mild depression.

Along with providing her and her family a number of family therapy options, including referring her to a psychiatrist for medication, Gail took seriously Erin's feeling that no one understood her. Gail knew that adolescents of any age and gender can be prone to dramatic utterances and narcissistic claims of uniqueness. Yet Gail had been hearing more and more lately from girls who did not feel understood, and who had trouble communicating who they were and what they needed to parents, extended family, and school communities. She was noticing an increased number of girls relying on the Internet for communication of self, and she noticed that Internet communications fulfilled a need for intimacy; yet she noticed that while it let girls feel heard, it did not in the end satisfy a girl's deep need to know *herself,* and know herself in the presence and safety of *a nurturing group*—her close family—who inherently loved her.

Parents, grandparents, teachers, and neighbors who once taught girls how to look within and gave them enough basic knowledge of themselves to lead them to the doorway of self, were busy, or did not live nearby or had little knowledge of the workings of the adolescent girl's mind. Gail realized that Erin, at sixteen, knew very little about herself, could say very little about how her own brain, mind, and soul worked in the world. Gail came to call this "the self-knowledge gap" in girls, for she noticed it in so many (and I had been noticing it as well in boys). Children were growing up understanding a great deal about social and mechanical technologies—peer groups and Internets—but lacked deep self-knowledge.

Given her realizations, Gail asked Erin, "What don't you feel people understand?"

"I don't know, I mean, it's like this . . ." Out came a series of stories of moments when Erin had tried to relate to people.

"I know Colin understood what I was saying, he must have—but he didn't. He thought I was dissing Brittany."

"I read a lot and I know a lot about girls, but no one explains *me* to *me.*"

"My dad and my brothers treat me like I'm an alien, or someone to just tease. They think I like being teased all the time."

"Do you explain to them what you don't like?" Gail asked.

"Usually I just tease them back."

"Why not tell them you don't like being teased? Why not just stop the cycle?"

"Because I like it too. Don't you get it? I'm a hundred things at once. I can't get a grip. You want me to get a grip on myself but I can't!"

Gail came to realize that while Erin benefitted from Prozac, to give her medication without also giving her education was to betray her. Erin needed help with neurochemical stabilization, but she also needed people—parents, grandparents, teachers, and, in Gail's case, a counselor—to help her fill in the self-knowledge gap.

Gail taught Erin a great deal about how her own mind worked, her brain, her hormones, her female culture, giving her books to read, sites to check about girls' development; Gail helped her create a questionnaire to ask her own parents and grandparents about what they were like as adolescents, what they thought and felt and knew, and about their ancestry and family history. Erin's nature—who she was—resided to a great extent in her genes and family past.

For Erin, this kind of therapy—something Gail and I have come to call "self-knowledge therapy"—was life-changing. Erin began to see who she was, what her values were, what she stood for; over a period of a year, she filled in a great deal of the self-knowledge gap. Her mother told Gail, when Erin was eighteen and graduating from high school, "It's like she didn't know who she was at all, but now she does. She's not lost anymore." She had gained some of this new self simply by living two more years—and she had gained it in two years (instead of needing ten years of extended adolescence) because she learned who she was at sixteen and seventeen.

There are a lot of Erins in our lives, a lot of girls who are trying to become adults without knowing even the basics about how their own minds work. And there are a lot of parents, grandparents, teachers, and others—in fact, let's be honest, it's most of us—who couldn't begin to explain how a girl's mind, and therefore her heart and soul, work.

Let's end a huge part of that knowledge gap now. Let's go deep into the female mind, and let this be a doorway into wonderful mysteries. By the end of this chapter, I hope you'll understand the female mind as you have not understood it before.

## Girls and Boys Are Different

When discussing the female brain, hormones, and environment/culture in this book, I will generalize for efficiency, but not in ways that negate common sense, good science, personal observation, or basic human intuition. In working with neurobiological information, I check what I learn cross-culturally and anthropologically, in order to make sure that the conclusions, for instance, of a study on hormonal systems, are similar around the world, and in many different cultural systems. I have checked results of biochemical and neurobiological research in thirty cultures, having lived in seven of these cultures myself. Through the Gurian Institute, which has studied students in six Missouri school districts extensively over two years, I have been able to check these results even further.

As we explore these wonders together, it is crucial to agree that each girl and woman is an individual. Hormonal and brain systems develop on a wide spectrum. Both females and males are affected by some of the same hormones, but to different degrees. All of us are also affected by similar neural stimulations to differing degrees, and each of us is exposed to those stimulants differently. Hormones, brain, and environment work together in vast and constant fluctuations.

Even given our daughters' inherent individualities, it is amazing to notice how different girls and boys can be.

Brenda Goff, a middle-school teacher in Kansas City, described her family in a way most of us can recognize.

"Before I became a parent, I firmly believed that behavior of boys and girls was mostly molded by society and parents. Girls learned to be feminine, boys learned to be masculine. I had a girl first. At fifteen months, this little girl cried about her socks not having flowers on them. She was even born with feminine qualities that I do not have, so how could she have learned them? I was stunned!

"Then I had a son. I was still convinced that I could have a boy who wasn't aggressive—no guns, war toys, etc. No violent TV shows—actually very little exposure to TV at all. Then my son 'shot' me with his banana around the time he turned two! And my hair dryer became a space gun at around three. It was extremely obvious that he was different from her and yet we felt, as parents, that they'd been treated in much the same manner."

Brenda's story has been the story of many parents. And why shouldn't it be? It is human nature.

In our grandparents' time, the obvious natural differences between boys and girls were accepted as not only natural but also inherently, even mysteriously, essential to human life. Science wasn't needed to confirm or deny them.

During about a quarter century, from about 1965 to about 1990, our society engaged in what is surely one of the most interesting social illusions in human history: that sex differences in neurology, temperament, psychology, biochemistry, and physiology didn't matter much.

As a retired psychologist, Marty Morris, seventy-three, recalled to me recently: "When I was coming up the academic ranks in the '70s, we were told that males and females were the same. We didn't have neurological evidence to turn to—we didn't actually study the brains of boys and girls or women and men. You have to remember, we weren't trained in neurobiology. We were trained to help people with their minds but didn't acquire hard data on the mind itself."

I asked Marty if, while he was practicing psychology and raising his family, he would have benefitted from "the hard sciences."

"Are you kidding!" he responded. "It would have been great. Now the hard sciences are everywhere, and I'm glad. We all thought we had the inside dope on men and women and that inside dope was 'sameness,' but now we're *really* seeing through the looking glass."

As a practicing psychologist, Marty didn't have access to what we have now because Marty had to practice his craft during a time in which nature-based thinking was suspect. Ironically, as ordinary parents, we now have better access to biosciences than he did as a professional. These hard sciences, like neurobiology, endocrinology, and microbiology, have actually been collecting data about "maleness" and "femaleness" since the 1960s, but the major change in the public's perception of these sciences has been occurring just in the last few years as MRI and PET scan technology has advanced so significantly that we can now look "through a looking glass" into the brains of boys and girls themselves. The vision we now have of the brain leads us to some secrets of the female brain that may startle you.

## A Quick Look at Your Daughter's Brain

The human brain is the seat of all daily human activity; it is both the hidden cause and effect of much of your daughter's existence. Modern philosophers and scientists are even beginning to wonder, now, if the brain is not the seat of the soul.

Let's get to know it.

Your daughter's brain is basically divided into three parts: the cerebral cortex, the limbic system, and the brain stem. The cerebral cortex—four lobes at the top of the brain—evolved latest in human development; the limbic system, in the middle of the brain, evolved just before; and the brain stem, at the base of the brain and top of the neck, evolved first.

In the brain stem is the seat of our fight-or-flight responses ("Should I run away from that attacker or fight back?") as well as basic functions like breathing and digestion.

In the limbic system is the lion's share of our emotive processing, as well as directional management—like an air traffic controller—of sensory, memory, stress, and other stimuli. The limbic system—mainly through the offices of the hypothalamus gland within it—controls things like body temperature, sleep cycles, and the menstrual cycle.

In the cerebral cortex, at the top of the brain, is most of our thinking and decision-making, imagination and creation of language.

Millions of years ago, all we had was a brain stem, then the limbic system grew to wrap around it, then the cerebral cortex grew around and above those. What we like to call "gray matter" is this cortex, divided into the occipital, parietal, temporal, and frontal lobes—each lobe composed of billions of cells wrapped together. These four lobes exist, physiologically, as right and left hemispheres, connected by a bundle of nerves between the two hemispheres. There are smaller "lobes" within these four lobes, existing as "sections" of the four lobes: for instance, the "prefrontal lobe," also known as the "prefrontal cortex," just behind the forehead, which partially controls moral and executive decision-making.

One of the miracles of nature is the fact that all human beings grow all their brain cells by the time the fetus is eighteen weeks old!

When people say of a three- or six- or twelve-year-old, "She's maturing so much!" or "Her brain seems to be growing in leaps and bounds," they are referring not to the actual growth of *new* cells in the brain, but to maturation due to constant alterations in the way the already set cells *communicate* with one another.

As your daughter's brain develops alongside the brains of boys, it is developing in similar areas—the frontal lobe, the temporal lobe, the prefrontal cortex, the limbic system, and so on—but is doing so very differently. As we explore your daughter's brain further, let's focus both on how it develops as a *girl's* mind, and also how that girl's mind differs in its development from a boy's mind.

## The Stages of a Girl's Brain Development

Of the many distinct stages in a girl's development, four stand out. These four stages of a girl's brain development comprise a human journey in four episodes.

STAGE 1: *The Child: Birth to Five Years Old.* In this stage, we find that girls and boys are relatively alike, at least in comparison to all the later stages of life. Bodies look the same, and you often have to look closely to see physical, emotional, and mental differences.

STAGE 2: *The Girl: Six to Ten Years Old.* By now, the girl has "gender identified." A girl knows she's a girl, and knows she's not a boy. Male/female differences are also becoming clearer to her and to everyone around her.

STAGE 3: *The Adolescent Girl: Eleven to Fifteen Years Old.* Adolescence often does begin before eleven years old (if menses or pubertal growth begins earlier), so this age-beginning is not set in stone. Now the girl is not just a "child" and "girl" but she is an adolescent too.

STAGE 4: *The Young Woman: Sixteen to Twenty Years Old.* In this final stage of childhood, the girl makes the passage to womanhood. Many girls, in fact most in our culture, do not complete that passage by twenty, but we work hard to help them do so, and they generally yearn to.

Each of these stages is distinct as a stage because of brain development milestones. For instance, by five, the brain is, in general mass, nearly completely formed; at around ten, the epic use-then-prune of brain cells begins, as does the cognitive development that makes an adult brain think like an adult; at fifteen, these cognitives are nearly fully formed, and puberty, for the most part, concluded; by twenty, myelination of brain cells (the protective, oozy white coating over the brain) is mainly completed, thus the brain is technically adult.

## Stage 1: The Child

Your daughter's brain has been developing before birth, layering the limbic system onto the brain stem, and the neocortex onto the limbic system. By the time she's born, your daughter's brain will be a mass of millions of cells communicating with one another via neurotransmitters. Its structural growth will be encoded genetically, i.e., it will grow a right and left hemisphere and so many other parts of the brain already coded in. Further encoded are some of the ways—the "how"—of that growth in *your* particular child.

For instance, all brains are coded to grow from the right hemisphere over to the left. The female brain, however, is coded to grow more quickly from right to left than the male. This is one of the reasons that female children, at very young ages, already use a higher quantity of words and more coherent language than boys. They speak, in general, earlier than boys. The left hemisphere, where most language takes place, develops earlier in girls.

Both female and male brains are coded to develop neurotransmitter tracks in the brain, so that the brain can learn, live, and accomplish. But *quantity* of neurotransmitters can differ. The female brain, for instance, is coded to secrete more serotonin than the male. Higher serotonin secretion is directly related to greater impulse control. This is one reason one- or two- or three-year-old girls will tend to be physically calmer than same-age boys. The female brain also secretes more oxytocin than a male's. Oxytocin secretion directly relates to play with "care objects" or babies. Girls of any age play with dolls and other "care objects" more than boys do. New studies indicate that oxytocin in the brain rises when not just human females but other female primates as well are near a baby, small animal, or other object needing care.

All brains will develop neurotransmission and tissue in the four lobes of the brain, but again the toddler girl and boy differ. She will probably have accelerated development of the occipital lobe, which is one reason her brain takes in more sensory data than the male brain, making her more able to distinguish a parent's voice from background noise, making her more sensitive to loud noises than boys, causing her to seek "tactile longevity," to handle an object—such as a doll—for longer periods than boys do.

She's feeling, hearing, smelling more than he is, and enjoying those senses; and she's creating an interior world that is much more sense- and contact-laden than is a boy's.

While he too seeks contact, of course, his brain works with this yearning differently: His brain is more dominant in the right hemisphere, giving him a less sensory and more spatial perspective. He fidgets, moves around, tries to throw things, tries to jump, and walks earlier than girls, explores farther out into the backyard than the average same-age girl. He has less brain development in verbal areas to utilize (by age 4½, 99 percent of his speech is comprehensible, in contrast to age 3 for girls), so he relies more on his own body and on motion for enjoyment of the world, learning, and communication.

You might be thinking, "Couldn't this all be a matter of socialization?" It's worth noting: Even in infancy, from as young as four months old, girls can better distinguish family members' faces from photographs they look at. Boys have more trouble. As the cerebral cortex develops, Stage 1 girls and boys already show profound differences. As early as one week old, girls are better able to distinguish another baby's cry than boys. There is hardly an area of the brain where from very young ages we don't see girls emerging somewhat different from boys, and these differences appear in studies on all continents, in all cultures.

## Stage 2: The Girl

By five years old, the brain is greatly formed. Often we have heard people say, "If you don't do right by the kid in the first five years, you may have blown it." Or, "Better teach her everything she needs to know by five, or she'll be behind." These comments have a doom-saying quality to them that isn't necessarily accurate, but then again, the first five years are more crucial than we realize. The brain stem, limbic system, four lobes, two hemispheres, as well as corpus callosum, hippocampus (where memory goes on), amygdala (which handles emotions inside the limbic system), as well as countless other brain structures and patterns are well set by five.

If ever there is a time to protect brain development, give the girl constant physical and emotional bonding, and protection from harmful media messages, dangerous people, bad influences—this is the time. By five, her rate of brain growth decelerates, and she has a somewhat stronger, more resilient brain. All children at five are still very fragile, but five is a milestone in brain growth. It is the time we start our children in kindergarten, and it is the time we begin to treat them with more independence, for good reason.

Having said that, while fetal life to five years old is perhaps the most crucial time of brain development, we should think of it as the laying of the foundation. Foundation is not enough to live in. We need the house of self too. Beginning at around five, your daughter starts constructing the house (and you are her architect, skill provider, and materials technician).

Her limbic system is becoming more developed. For instance, it is moving more and more emotional data up to the four lobes of the brain now. Whereas, at two, she might have just thrown a tantrum when something went wrong for her (this tantrum transpiring mainly in the brain stem and limbic system and from there, into her voice, arms, and kicking legs), now, at five or six, she might hold back, think, even talk when she's hurt or angry. This ability, of course, will grow and grow over the next five years. Hormonal flow will probably confuse it as early as nine or ten, then by middle to late teens, she'll hardly tantrum at all in the ways she did at two; she'll express herself somewhat more like a young woman.

By eight or nine, another fascinating part of the brain is coming into its own: the hippocampus. The hippocampus is one of many areas of the brain that develops differently in girls and boys. It lies on a ridge along the lower section of each lateral ventricle of the brain. One of its biggest jobs is memory storage. The hippocampus is larger in a girl than in a boy, and just as important, the number and speed of neuron transmissions in it is higher in females. *There's a lot more going on in the hidden world of female memory than in the male.* This comes as no surprise to us, at an intuitive level. Women often complain about husbands' and sons' memories. A seven- or eight-year-old girl will tend to be better than the average boy at complex memory function. For instance, if you tell an eight-year-old boy to do three things—clean up his room, take out the garbage, and wipe the table—and tell the same to an eight-year-old girl, you are more likely to see the girl complete the three tasks with less reminding. There are a number of reasons for this: more limbic/neocortical connection, better hearing, less impulsivity and distractability—but also better hippocampal memory.

As we notice differences between girls and boys by nine or ten years old, we often wonder why male and female brains are coded for differences—differences that show up as early as four weeks old and continue throughout child development. Why should girls' hippocampus be structured for better memory, especially of concrete details related to concrete places and things? Why does the female mind move more-emotional material more quickly to thinking centers of the brain than boys' minds do? Why does the girls' brain system start out, from the beginning, ready to use more words? Why are girls' brains set up for less physical impulsivity?

From a scientific standpoint, the answer lies in evolution. For millions of our ancestral years, females needed to do infant and child care, as well as gather tubers and roots. They needed to gain superiority in left hemisphere development (word production and vocalizations), and in structures like the hippocampus, which helped them remember intricacies of intimate needs. They needed to be more sensory than males—hear a baby's cries better, enjoy long-term tactile contact more. They needed to calm themselves down more quickly than males did and think first, act second; fragile children were at stake.

Males needed to hunt—up until about ten thousand years ago, when agriculture emerged as dominant. Hunting is a spatial task, one that requires less use of words and more of action. Males needed to be more impulsive, aggressive, and more "act first, ask questions later." Male survival—whether by attack of beast or other warrior—required this.

We are not completely determined by our historical past, but it is worth paying homage to it, since it is the foundation of our minds. Physicists have recently understood that in our DNA are microscopic particles of the Big Bang itself. Each of us is both "present" and "past." So too is the brain both present and past. Your daughter is as much her ancestors' as she is your daughter. My Davita and Gabrielle are modern girls of the new millennium—but also, when I look deep into their eyes, I see the past smiling at me.

By ten years old, your daughter's brain will probably be hungry for input, information, new designs (like algebra), and new emotive stimulants (more friends, more alone time with one or the other parent). She will probably be wondering about whether she'll be popular, whether she'll be liked, whether she is pretty. Her drive to "connect," to "make contact," both intellectually and emotionally, is entering high gear.

She will definitely feel by now that she's a *girl*. The gender differentiation that has led her through life so far, the same differentiation that accelerated around first grade, now accelerates further as hormones just begin to enter the brain system. My daughters, when they were in Stage 2, loved to quip, "Girls are always right, boys are always wrong." (Another, more incisively humorous one: "Girls go to Mars to get more candy bars; boys go to Jupiter to get more stupider.") This kind of male/female "we are different from one another" comment is a gender-identity comment, a normal indication that a girl clearly knows that her neural system, personality, and body are somehow different from a boy's, and will be different from a man's.

She is ready, now, for Stage 3.

## Stage 3: The Adolescent Girl

The age of about ten to fifteen is like a second birth for your daughter. In infancy, she was born into and became a child of your family and the world. During Stage 2, she continued to grow. Now, puberty and early adolescence are her next major life passage; in these, she is born into and becomes an "adolescent," half-girl, half-woman, and adolescence, like her first birth, is a neurologically traumatic crisis, in the most positive sense.

But because of the physical, mental, and social changes involved during this time period (and exacerbated by how little information and self-knowledge we provide our girls), puberty is also perhaps the most frightening episode of life a girl experiences. Your daughter may not experience another neuroendocrinological crisis like this until menopause, and during menopause she'll have the advantage of being a wiser, experienced adult. During puberty, everything is changing within and around a girl and she's still, basically, an inexperienced, needy child.

The Stage 3 crisis of growth and experience requires the same sort of vigilance we practiced during Stage 1. Our daughter is—though more independent and self-sufficient than an infant—also very vulnerable, emotionally and physically.

In Chapter 3, we will explore the hormonal reasons for this crisis. Throughout this book we will explore the cultural reasons. For now, let's look at the neurological reason—the brain itself—and the pressure it puts on the growing girl, pressure she will often pass on to us as she grows in our family and community. Many of these neurological pressures are faced by boys too. But yet again, we notice differences in the ways the female and male brain pressure, and guide, our children.

## THE ADOLESCENT GIRL'S BRAIN GROWTH

By about ten, and continuing till around twelve, connections in the frontal lobes of the brain are growing almost as fast as they grew during your daughter's infancy. In other parts of the limbic system and the cerebral cortex, gray matter doubles during this short period of time. This again mimics infancy. This kind of brain growth was probably obvious when your daughter was six or twelve months old because you were always there to observe changes in her abilities.

"Oh my gosh, did you see that!" you cried to your spouse, a grandparent, or a friend. Your daughter's abilities were growing in leaps and bounds.

This same kind of brain growth is less obvious now because you are not around her as much, or she may not reveal as much. Nonetheless, it's present. This brain growth makes her able to take on new skills, new insights, new abstract concepts, new abilities to think and argue with you. But it also causes numerous crashes, "self-esteem drops," and social miscues as she tries to develop and manage adult character and adult emotional structure.

At around twelve, after two years of accelerated neural activity, her brain will begin to focus neurotransmission on areas of the brain most often utilized and not on areas underutilized. Especially where an area of the brain is underutilized, the brain automatically "prunes" itself—gets rid of excess gray matter. A girl's relationships, intimacies, sports activities, art and musical activities, as well as academic learning during the ten-to-twelve period have a great likelihood of "sticking" or at least "reappearing" later in her life because of their interconnection with the massive brain growth. There is also a greater likelihood that she will not be as good at things she didn't practice during these two years.

This is why, generally, we can say that if she enjoys piano at eleven, she'll probably remain somewhat musical during her life. If she reads a lot at twelve, she'll probably enjoy reading throughout life. If she's in stable relationships at ten, she'll probably feel safer in stable relationships throughout life. (In the age-ten-to-twelve pruning process, girls and boys are similar, except for yet again another interesting difference: Because during these ages girls are generally pubertal more often than boys, the pruning occurs for girls in greater connection with the hormonal systems we'll detail in Chapter 3.)

We wouldn't want to say that everything a girl does from ten to twelve will stick, or that she can't learn something at sixteen, twenty, or thirty that she didn't do at eleven. Yet it is amazing to see how often it does work out that what we care about in early adolescence resurfaces in later adolescence, and throughout life. In my own experience as a soccer coach, I have noticed how much more difficult it is for any child to learn subtle soccer footwork in her middle teens if she hasn't earlier in life, certainly by mid-puberty.

Fifth and sixth grade are amazing learning years for children because of brain growth. High school teachers in the Gurian Institute in Missouri noticed a correlation between math, science, and verbal training in those grades and abilities in high school years. "I know a lot of the teachers in the elementary schools," one high school science teacher told me. "I know the ones who are really good at teaching math, or science, or English. And I can sometimes tell which students had which teachers by what they're really good at when I get them as juniors. If a girl was in Mrs. Jackson's class in fifth grade, I know she'll be better at math. If she went to Mr. Zervas for science, I know she'll be better at science. It just works out that way a lot of the time."

What this teacher noticed was, in large part, the upper elementary teacher's academic immersion of the student during a very "vulnerable" brain growth period. By twelve or so, the brain pruned what didn't get used. If the student was immersed in very effective math teaching at ten, the brain pruned less of these neural cells than those that were unused (for instance, cells in the left hemisphere that might have been used for immersion in reading).

## SOCIAL AND EMOTIONAL CHANGES

Between ten and fifteen, becoming even clearer during puberty and just beyond, are a number of social and emotional changes that match growth in frontal lobes, prefrontal lobes, the limbic system, and the hormonal system:

- Your daughter will start a major push toward independence and self-sufficiency.

- She'll want more privacy.

- She'll notice and ponder differences between people, parents, boys and girls, ethnic groups.

- She'll ask a lot of questions about what she's interested in.

- She may increase athletic performance in one or more sports.

- She'll compare and contrast environments, like home vs. school, or "my home" and "my friend's home."

- She may become like a lawyer, arguing with you a lot. You may also notice that she always liked to argue, but now she just has more to say, a quicker wit, and more motivation to disagree with parents and others.

- She'll start thinking more abstractly—about larger social principles, justice, and how she as an individual might fit in larger social ideas.

- Her memory will get better in many ways, but worse in a few. For instance, she'll remember concepts, equations, and language items more prolifically. But she might not remember where she put something just an hour ago. The hippocampus grows in different sections at different times.

- Things feel very personal to her—she takes comments personally and makes decisions based on how she'll personally be affected. Life becomes more of a social game, to be thought out ahead.

- She'll begin intense experimentation (that will continue, as many of these things do, into Stage 4)—social, emotional, moral, and physical life are all up for experimentation.

- She will probably become judgmental of others in ways she regrets later. She may become nasty in ways you don't like (ways she will feel bad about when she's lying in bed at night reviewing her day internally).

- She may feel like an outsider and struggle to find a crowd in which to feel like an insider. At some point in Stage 3 everyone has this feeling. Some children have it more than others, and much of the cause of the insider/outsider feelings is based in genetic personality. The shyer the girl, by personalilty, the more an outsider she will tend to feel.

Overall, what an adolescent girl experiences is a brain growing in different areas at different speeds. This brain, growing quixotically, has the added pressure of interacting with the most socially complex environment the human brain has had to deal with since it began its present structural growth (about two million years ago). Make no mistake: The social technologies (such as media, peer groups, school institutions) of early adolescents today are overwhelming to brain growth in ways they were not a hundred years ago.

## CARING FOR YOUR DAUGHTER'S BRAIN GROWTH

Given the immense brain growth, pruning, and emotional changes during this time, parents and communities need to be more involved than they often realize. When the brain is going through crisis, it needs *increased*, not *decreased*, attachment from its guides and allies (parents, extended family, teachers, coaches, faith communities). Though our daughter is twelve or thirteen she needs us to lie down and cuddle with her at bedtime and hear about what she's been thinking. She needs structure, a well-disciplined life, sounding boards, limits. The people to whom she is most attached are the scaffolding within which she builds her house of self.

Brain science shows us the wisdom of attachment research at every turn: Those to whom the girl is bonded need to increase the conviction and passion with which they guide girls *toward* things and *away* from things, now utilizing the subtle management skills of a high-level executive (how to do this is the subject of later chapters). This sense of I-must-grow-as-a-parent-the-more-my-child-becomes-an-adolescent can be difficult because as your daughter's brain grows, she seeks more independence and privacy. Your daughter, by twelve or thirteen, may appear not to want you as involved in her life, especially in "telling her what to do."

But she needs you profoundly.

## THE ADOLESCENT GIRL'S SELF-ESTEEM DROPS

As Gail and I raise our daughters, we utilize *natural parenting*—we learn about our daughters' minds and follow their movements, life journeys, successes, and failures with knowledge of the brain in tow. This has especially helped us not to worry as much about "adolescent girls' self-esteem drops" as other contemporary social philosophers and parents do. While we are vigilant about our adolescent girls' happiness and success, and especially watchful of female clients in distress, we notice that *most of girls' self-esteem drops in Stage 3 are normal in self-development of brain and body.* The brain is right on target here. If adolescent self-esteem did not drop, on and off, throughout adolescence, we would have reason to worry for our daughters (and sons). The human brain is growing fast—it has no choice but to learn by failures and by fears of rejection; it must experience loss, confusion, the stress of new ideas and principles. It must go through times of feeling that it does not fit in with others.

We are also cognizant that while both girls and boys experience equal self-esteem drops, girls begin their consistent series of drops before most boys—their brains develop into Stage 3 brains, on average, earlier than boys. As we'll see when we discuss hormones and biochemistry, these differences can cause substantial confusion in relationships between adolescent boys and girls.

Helping our girls navigate not only their own journey but also the difference from the male journey is a primary job for all of us as Stage 3 parents, one we will explore practically in Part II. Meanwhile, protecting a girl's innocence and her family attachments for as long as possible in Stage 3 brings us the best results for brain growth and psychological safety.

"My daughter," a mom told me, "wants to be so grown-up.

But she's only fourteen! She still loves being a kid. I figure she'll grow up soon enough. What I try to do is help her be a kid as long as possible." This simple statement speaks volumes; it's good wisdom for Stage 3. It is also wisdom that runs counter to some people's ideas of "making a girl grow up so she can compete and succeed." In my two decades of brain, attachment, and adolescent development research I have only seen increased evidence of the fact that if a child is guided to navigate Stage 3 in relative innocence, protected safety, and constant primary attachments, *she ends up developing an even stronger, more competent, and less neurotic self* by twenty-five or thirty than had she been "hypermatured" (forced to mature early) in Stage 3. When we speak here of "innocence" or "protection" we aren't talking about hiding a girl away; we are speaking, for instance, of the difference between a home in which a girl is surfing the Internet unsupervised at thirteen and one in which she does not begin this adult occupation until sixteen. Odds are that while the girl who surfs the Net at thirteen will become more mature in some ways (as well as more attached to a computer) than her peer who does not, she is also probably living in a home where primary attachment relationships are not as secure, thus her brain growth may well limit itself to certain areas of comfort (chat rooms) but neglect more primal ways of being soothed and guided (her parents). Every family must make its own call on social technologies of our age; when deciding on policies for the brain growth—and therefore emotional and social growth—of Stage 3 girls we can hardly err if we make sure to put primary family attachments first.

It is also crucial to remember that at this point in our cultural history the social technologies we notice everywhere—in schools, on TV, in peer conversation, in music, in our homes—play the role of pushing the child to maturity no matter what we do, yet most often without emphasizing moral and spiritual development. This is a profound difference between our present-day social technologies and the social technologies of our recent and distant relatives. Moral and spiritual growth was primary to the social technologies of the past—churches, extended-family storytelling, farm work, nature time. The lack of moral and spiritual growth in our own social technologies would not be a problem if Stage 3 girls did not crave, for full frontal-lobe development, moral and spiritual growth. But, in fact, the Stage 3 brain is hungry for moral and spiritual connection and development.

## MORAL AND SPIRITUAL GROWTH IN THE ADOLESCENT BRAIN

As you may have noticed, your Stage 3 girl is becoming a deep moral thinker. Her frontal lobes, prefrontal lobes, and temporal lobes are growing—these are areas of moral and spiritual thought processes. She vacillates between being a "black and white" thinker about morality, and seeing complexities of intentions. She understands high moral principles—sometimes! She is developing her own sense of what or who God is (please substitute your family's words for divine spirit).

She craves help with moral boundaries and rules. Her brain development, especially toward cognitive and abstract skills in the cerebral cortex, actually *forces* her to see the moral layer to things, and to wonder about the unknown.

In school the adolescent brain is getting a lot of stimulation toward abstraction in academic study—language arts, literature, calculus—and so does not often present itself to parents with "What is God?" "How am I divine?" "What are the hidden mysteries of life?" Adolescent girls talk about a reading assignment, or a TV show, because that's what's on the brain's surface agenda right now. Yet when an adolescent girl is guided through a Rite of Passage experience (see Chapter 4), or sees a film that emphasizes spiritual mystery, or goes to her church group, she becomes immensely moved and excited. Her half-girl, half-woman brain is hungry for spiritual mystery (which is, in cognitive terms, "high abstraction").

Especially in Chapters 7 and 8 we will emphasize moral and spiritual growth for our daughters. They are a beautiful hidden agenda for Stage 3 girls especially.

## WHY STAGE 3 GIRLS AGONIZE OVER DECISIONS

By the time a girl is pubescent, PET scans and MRIs of her brain already show increased brain activity in more parts of the brain at once than in boys. There is, on average, more going on at a given moment in her brain than in a boy's at this age, and, in fact, all ages. Boys' brains tend to be more single-task oriented. They tend to be more deductive in their reasoning, and they don't tend to take in five or ten elements of a small situation before making a decision. Girls often seem just the opposite—they think everything out and take lots of things very personally.

The disadvantage for girls of thinking a lot about a lot of things almost all the time is that girls, especially during all the changes of early adolescence, can develop *a malleable self*: a self that relies on others to make decisions for her. This is especially the self that gets talked into early sexual activity by adolescent boys. Girls often find it easier to just let someone else think for them; or they agonize and make no decision at all.

This is an area of special vigilance for parents of girls, and one we'll develop further as this book continues.

## GIRLS' STRESS RESPONSES

Over the last few years, neurobiological researchers have discovered specific ways the female brain handles stress. These show up very well by Stage 3, and involve some of the same neurological elements we've already discussed, but even more powerfully.

When a child or adolescent is being abused, feels perennially attacked by peers, is unable to comprehend social technologies, or finds herself in any other ongoing stressful situation, her cortisol levels in the brain rise. When the levels of this protective stress hormone rise, other brain and hormonal activity decreases or shuts down. When a child is under inordinate stress for a prolonged period at any time in life, *her brain development will definitely be affected*. She will be "rewired" neurologically. For instance, a girl who experiences perennial psychological abuse may discover, years later, that her brain has been rewired for depression. When a boy, for his part, has experienced ongoing and highly invasive sexual abuse over a pro-longed period, his brain may be rewired for pedophilia. The stress hormone, cortisol, (as well as adrenal and other "lower" brain functions) have dominated brain growth during the time of stress, and this affects normal brain growth patterns of both girls and boys in many similar, but also many different ways.

Those of us raising girls—especially pubescent Stage 3 girls, who are already under great internal stress—should pay particular attention to our culture's general social overstimulation and hyper-stress today. More and more early-adolescent girls are overstimulated by social technologies than they were a hundred years ago. Simultaneously, they experience this increased stress without compensatory family and extended family safety. This is a "double whammy" on our Stage 3 girls. They experience their family's pulling away from them (just as they pull away from their families); they experience a general breakdown of families and protective communities (i.e., increased divorce, decrease in extended family life); they may already have experienced other trauma, like abuse. Stage 3 girls today are set up for increased cortisol levels and thus for developmental difficulties.

Often people ask: Why are we noticing more and more early-adolescent girls with depression today than a hundred years ago? While we can always say, "Because we record the cases now, whereas a hundred years ago depression went unrecognized," this would be tantamount to keeping our heads in the sand. As extended and nuclear families break down, as our social technologies—large schools, media, Internet, peer groups—increase their pressure on the brain, more Stage 3 girls are susceptible to less emotional safety, thus higher cortisol levels, thus higher chances of depression and disorders, raising our heads out of the sand requires a nature-based response: We are messing with girls' brains and have to stop.

The brains of highly stressed girls show higher-than-normal cortisol levels previous to or during the depression, and abnormalities in other brain activities (as well as hormonal activity). Their brains possess more-than-normal corticotrophin-releasing factor, a brain chemical that increases a brain's stress response. These girls often become quiet, withdrawn, unable to eat, and unwilling to communicate.

It is useful to note that adolescent boys, on the other hand, who have similarly suffered abuse or overstimulation and undernurturance tend toward less-overt depression and more physical outlays of violence. The male brain (combined with male hormones), when under stress, tends to emphasize fight responses more than the female. The male brain responds to higher cortisol levels by moving more brain activity to the lower limbic system, the amygdala, and the brain stem than does the female brain. Thus it tends to act out its stress in violence, as well as increased drug and alcohol use, and other "high-risk" behavior.

Male/female brain differences in stress responses show up well before Stage 2, of course, but by twelve years old they become so obvious that they can be almost overwhelming. I have often wondered if social theories that ask us to raise adolescent children without biological wisdom have done so in some part because trying to fully understand the brain life and the male/female differences in this brain life just adds another layer of confusion to our already overwhelming task of raising adolescents in a fast-paced society that is so unfriendly to stable family life.

## Stage 4: The Young Woman

Stage 3 is the period of time most discussed in our contemporary literature on girls, and rightfully so. For both boys and girls, Pulitzer Prize–winning author and journalist Laura Sessions Stepp calls it *Our Last Best Shot*, in her study of early adolescents around the U.S.

Stage 4 continues and refines the changes begun in Stage 3. Fifteen is the age we are using as a milestone of transformation, but for your daughter the age might be fourteen or sixteen.

Because your daughter has had a few years now to start getting used to her new self, she may well manage herself more effectively than at twelve. By the same token, if she was involved in a great deal of emotional stress and crisis behavior, that behavior or disorder may become even more serious by fifteen or sixteen.

In the brain itself there is continued generation of cells toward greater intellect, giving her more tools to deal with stresses. Life is supposed to get easier for her by the middle of Stage 4 as she now focuses on love relationships and activities she enjoys, her education, and her future.

Much of her new ease with life is based in her brain's abstraction abilities, which are now nearly adult in their development.

## THE FOUR ABSTRACT SEARCHES

By the middle teens, your daughter will be involved in four major developmental searches that you can use to guide her brain growth as you parent her into adulthood. These are four areas of abstraction that the brain searches through in late adolescence. Adulthood becomes a journey based on the adolescent brain's ability to complete its search through these four areas of individual humanity:

- the search for identity
- the search for autonomy
- the search for morality
- the search for intimacy

No one can pinpoint for sure how the complexity of brain development creates the web of synapses that lead adolescents worldwide toward these universal searches, but we know it goes on mainly in the interaction of the limbic system (stimulated by hormones we'll look at in the next chapter) with the four lobes at the top of the brain. Whether the culture is a tribal one with fifty people in the village, or one of high population density and complexity of social technology like our own, young women want to know who they are, how to exist not as children but adults, what moral values to guide their adulthood by, and how to love effectively and passionately.

The search a young woman is on will take her through peer groups and back out the other side. Sometimes, as she has throughout life, she'll want desperately to belong to a certain group or garner widespread respect. Other times, she'll want to "go her own way," and she'll be critical of "the group." As her brain grows, it gets better at seeing where she herself fits and does not fit in society (school is the adolescent's crucible for society, then she graduates into the larger culture). Most of her thoughts and decisions in this regard take place in an interaction of her emotion-laden limbic system and idea-laden four lobes in the upper brain.

## COMPLETING BRAIN GROWTH: YOUNG WOMEN AND MEN ARE DIFFERENT

While your daughter's frontal, parietal, occipital, and temporal lobes learn to manage interactions with her limbic system, her whole cerebral cortex goes through a process called myelination of the brain. The white gooey stuff on the brain is myelin, a coating which helps neurotransmission and synapses work more quickly. By about twenty, this myelination completes and your daughter's brain is nearly fully formed. Your role as parent, caregiver, support system, guide, mentor may shift now toward "adult friend." Her brain, now grown, compels this.

Yet she will still have moments of "being childlike," of neediness, of dependency.

In all this she will have many moments of similarity to her male peers, but quite interestingly, even in the myelination process, the female and male brains differ. The *female brain completes the myelination of the brain earlier than the male,* mirroring so many other brain maturation elements in which the female outpaces the male.

All in all, a number of differences between the male and female brain become about as crystal clear as they can be by sixteen or seventeen.

- The female corpus callosum is by now about 25 percent larger than the male. This bundle of fibers connects the right and left hemispheres, giving young women (indeed, women in general) more cross talk between hemispheres of the brain, and making the verbalization of emotions more possible for young women than men.

• The female frontal lobes are generally more active (on average) than the male; young women tend to think consequences out more fully, and tend to use more words in general. Areas in the left hemisphere, called Broca's and Wernicke's areas, are also more active in young women; these areas handle a great deal of speech and written verbals. Young women are, on average, more careful and effective writers and use more words than young men.

• A young woman's occipital lobe (which, among other things, manages interpretation of visual stimuli) creates certain advantages for young women (for instance, they see better in dim light, and experience a wider variety of light sensitivities). Young women, more than young men, can read emotions on faces accurately, and even more accurately in lower light.

• More data moves through a young woman's parietal lobes than a young man's. The parietal lobe handles such perception of bodily sensations as touch and pain. Young women tend to feel pain more fully than males and enjoy long-term tactile contact (longer physical touch) more than males. If you've watched teen girls doing each other's hair or, at slumber parties, giving each other massages and leaning against each other in tactile enjoyment, you're seeing a more active parietal lobe at work.

• There are stronger neural connections in the young woman's temporal lobe than in the male's that lead to greater memory storage and better listening, especially for tones of voice. Your sixteen-year-old daughter will tend to remember sensual memories better than most men because of this temporal lobe difference, and differences in the hippocampus we discussed earlier. She will tend to hear more of what is said to her and catch inflections more completely.

• The female thalamus, which regulates emotional life and the sense of physical safety, processes data more quickly in the mature female brain than in the male. This probably explains some of why males put themselves in harm's way more than females (another biological reason is testosterone, the dominant male hormone); it certainly explains one reason young women process emotional information so much faster than their boyfriends.

- Perhaps most indicative of the difference between the Stage 4 brains of males and females is the greater mass, variety, and speed of neurotransmission in the female cerebral cortex. There is more going on more quickly with more variety in more parts of the female brain than in the male.

- To add to all this, the prefrontal cortex in young women finishes its basic development before it does in young men, so that a sixteen-year-old female is often more mature, in moral terms, or in terms of understanding consequences and being able to put herself in another's place empathically, than is a twenty-one-year-old male.

In all this there are, of course, numerous exceptions: for instance, young men who are far more mature, empathic, and effective speakers than young women. And yet, if you conduct a one-month study of your own, comparing in your observation five young men (or earlier-stage boys) and five young women (or earlier-stage girls), then keeping a journal of your comparisons, you'll see that most of these differences hold true for all stages of female development.

## The Goal of the Journey

In this brief developmental view of your daughter's hidden mind, I hope you've noticed that much of why girls are the way they are in your home, neighborhood, or school lies in *the brain* they are developing. The feminist imperatives we explored in Chapter 1 certainly identify factors that play a part in each stage. If you've read other books on raising girls, or if you've read magazines and watched television shows on the subject, you've probably noticed that their imperative, mainly bolstered by feminist theory, and neglectful of the whole spectrum of female biology, mainly talks about "empowering" girls.

As one applies nature-based research on the female brain to girls' very complex journey through life, "empowerment" is only a part of the puzzle. A girl's mind certainly benefits from more social power and protection against gender stereotypes; but it is also developing along a course set by an *intimacy imperative*. This need for intimacy is certainly as important to it as social power

## The Intimacy Imperative

One of the most humorous ways Gail and I have noticed what I am calling the intimacy imperative occurred when both our daughters started playing soccer. In both cases, the first few years of soccer were as much about socializing as playing the game itself. When we watched the games of our friends who had sons, the game itself—moving the ball aggressively from one end of the little field to the other—was already more important to the boys than it was for six-year-old girls. Boys would knock boys over and would not stop to help the other boys up. A girl would knock a girl over and be much more likely to stop, wonder over the welfare of the other girl, and let a goal be scored despite the parents on the sidelines calling out, "Watch out, watch the goal!"

In your own life, you have certainly noticed your own version of this. We watch our girls and intuit an intimacy imperative in them. But is it that big a deal? we might ask. Should we really delineate it as something as important as or more important than our other intuitions: that our girls are victims of gender stereotypes, and culturally precluded from competing effectively with men?

Ironically, a wonderful response comes from early feminism itself: The Harvard feminist Carol Gilligan in the early 1980s based her theories on the fact that females and males were psychologically different—females by nature more relational, males more independence-oriented—and that modern psychology neglected that difference to its peril.

In *In a Different Voice,* her landmark critique of modern psychology, she writes, "Choosing like Virgil [the Roman poet] to 'sing of arms and the man,' psychologists describing adulthood have focused on the development of self and work. Recent depictions of adult development, in their seamless emergence from studies of men, provide scanty illumination of a life spent in intimate and generative relationships."

Modern psychology, she rightfully noted two decades ago, was very much an imposition of male point of view onto women's lives. Women and men were very different, she believed, and needed to be seen differently.

To prove her point, Gilligan and other feminist researchers asked women to describe themselves and compared their self-descriptions with men's. Women spoke of their sense of identity, of purpose, of passion. They spoke differently than men. Men tended to speak more of their search for independence, women of their search for intimacy. Men tended to speak with more focus on a singular goal, women with more confusion of goals. Gilligan noted that this confusion of goals was only a negative or a distress if we viewed it through the male lens.

Summarizing the viewpoints of a number of women, Gilligan wrote: "In all of the women's descriptions [of themselves], identity is defined in a context of relationship and judged by a standard of responsibility and care. Similarly, morality is seen by these women as arising from the experience of connection . . . the underlying assumption that morality stems from attachment is explicitly stated . . ."

Gilligan did not use brain research as I am doing in this book, but she came to a similar conclusion through another route. Perhaps Gilligan could not have known that feminist theory would end up guiding women further toward independence imperatives and competition with men for male separateness than toward the protection of intimacy and attachment. But now, as we add brain science to her ideas, the brain itself echoes her early intuitions about differences between women and men.

When you look into your daughters' eyes, do you notice your daughters defining themselves, to a great extent, by how they connect with others? Sometimes as I watch my daughters—watching especially from the viewpoint of one so different from them—I see girls who like to be alone sometimes, but also girls *who are searchers into the webbed mysteries of intimate connections in nearly all their interactions.* I watch girls who, even when alone, are often mentally focused on how relationships went or are going.

When I watch the way they handle boys on the playground, or on the telephone, or in my home; when I talk to them about what they think most about; when I ask Gail for her understanding of how our daughters are developing, I witness and experience a constant journey of intimacies. I know myself, as a man, to be capable of both beautiful and cruel intimacies, and yet I know I am different from my wife and daughters. There is something about the female experience of intimacy that I will never fully know because I don't live it.

This experience, this treasure, is what I have come to call *the intimacy imperative.*

Boys certainly possess an imperative to intimacy. And yet, the male's need for intimacy is not quite the same thing as the intimacy imperative that so completely awakens a girl's heart—and her brain.

Let's go deeper than we have into the female brain to see the natural foundation of female intimacy.

## BASIC BLOOD FLOW DIFFERENCES

There is 15 percent greater blood flow in the female brain than in the male. Within that difference, there is a difference in where blood flows in the brain: For instance, in the female brain, blood is more likely to flow to both hemispheres than in the male. When a girl is listening to you, she is listening with more of her brain, and in both hemispheres. When a boy is listening to you, he is more likely to be listening with predominantly one side of his brain.

Basic blood flow differences are one reason that females seem to "think so many things out" more than males do; they "process" more. One of the foremost neuroscientists in the field, Ruben Gur of the University of Pennsylvania's neural imaging unit, has chuckled when pointing to PET (Positron-Emission Tomography) scans of male and female brains.

He notices: "There's more going on in the female brain than the male. The female brain is more revved up."

Not only is there 15 percent more blood flow in the female brain, and energy flowing to *more areas* than in the male, keeping the female brain more broadly active than the male, but the female brain experiences this greater flow even in states of rest.

Have you noticed how hard it is for a girl or woman to "turn her brain off," and how much easier for a male? Girls tend to be more attentive to more people more of the time than boys. Boys tend to focus their energy on narrower stimuli—think, perhaps, of a videogame—and they are more successful at shutting off relationship stimuli.

Female/male "channel-surfing" patterns show us this. Males often "zone out" in front of the TV, channel-surfing and not stopping for any long-term engagement, especially with any material that will require a lot of mental or emotional processing. They are channel surfing as a form of brain-rest. Females, on the other hand, more often stop surfing at a drama that involves scenes in which people are talking or otherwise in interaction and relationship. There's more natural blood flow in her brain, and she seeks stimulation for it. There's less in his, which he seeks to mirror with less complex stimulation.

Among children we notice that girls, more often than boys, get bored with videogames. Girls seek talk and other relational stimulations that excite more parts of the brain at once. Videogames excite only limited parts of the brain, mainly in the right hemisphere. More blood flow in the female brain is occurring in more parts of the brain; that brain seeks the kinds of relational and intimate stimulants that will satisfy the neurology she is living out. If a typical thirteen-year-old girl has to choose between a videogame and giving her friend a call, she'll generally choose to pick up the phone.

In our research at the Gurian Institute, we found another example of differences in male/female blood flow among children. Our research revealed that boys are more likely to "zone out" in class-rooms—stare out the window, become glassy-eyed (this is certainly not a new discovery we should take much credit for—it's intuitive to many people—but it was good to be able to substantiate the intuition with research). Teachers reported this difference at a rate of about two boys "blanking-out" to every one girl, and their findings have been corroborated elsewhere in the United States and overseas.

Neurologically, a key reason for the greater and more diverse attention of the females to stimuli is the higher level of blood flow in the female brain. In the female brain, more blood flow means a higher ability to maintain attention on others. Given this blood flow difference, it is no wonder males are about seven times more likely than females to develop an Attention Deficit Disorder. The female brain is, by genetic structure, less prone to an attention problem because it is internally, inherently, and more constantly attending to others and to the flow of connections, lessons, learning, and relationships.

At the Gurian Institute, teachers have been using their findings in order to explore innovative ways to stimulate both boys' and girls' brains to more effective academic and social performance. In all their work is the implicit finding that the female brain feels like it almost never turns off and thus craves increased bonding, attachment, and intimate stimulation because intimacy stimulation is the most challenging, and in many ways the most fruitful, for a busy brain.

Ruben Gur and his research partner and wife, Raquel Gur, have discovered another interesting thing about blood flow in the female brain: It flows upward to a greater degree than in the male brain. When Ruben and Raquel performed a study in which males and females were asked to make their minds blank, they found that 1) the limbic system in females remained more lit up on the PET scans—which means there was more flow in the limbic areas than in males; 2) more female flow moved upward toward the four lobes of the brain, where constant "cognitive and relational searching" is going on; and 3) less female flow went downward toward the brain stem, where thought and search and intimacy play small parts, but defensive distancing instincts play larger parts. Males differed from females—they experienced greater blood flow toward the fight-or-flight center, less to the more complex areas of thought, emotive, and relational processing, like the four lobes at the top of the brain and the cingulate gyrus, in the limbic system.

The Gurs found out, also, that the male/female difference in blood flow extends even to specific emotional or relationship "tasks." For instance, the female brain more easily identifies emotions on people's faces. On PET scans the Gurs found that there was less change in the positronic imagery in the female brain than in the male when subjects were shown pictures of faces in differing emotional states—sad, grief-stricken, etc. The male brain had to work harder than the female to accurately identify emotions, and still underperformed in relation to the female brain.

All these brain differences add up to something pretty significant. The female brain is set up for greater facility at creating intricate, intimate webs of relationship. Whether it's the identification of the emotion on a face, the desire to stick with intricate relational stimuli, the simple act of giving attention or listening, or even the level of relational understanding itself, the female mind creates and participates in intimate connection in ways the male mind does not.

## LANGUAGE AND CONNECTION

The use of language—a primary form of relationship building—is another different mental and emotional experience for girls and boys.

Language centers in the brain are one-third larger in the female than in the male brain. Many boys talk a lot—that's a given. But average boys and girls together, and you'll generally find more words produced by girls. This crosses into personality types as well. Shy girls and boys both use fewer words, but shy girls use more words than shy boys.

Adding to this language difference are the differences between your son's and your daughter's corpus callosum—in your daughter, it's about one-fourth larger. This bundle of nerves connects the right hemisphere, where emotive processing moves upward from the limbic system into the top of the brain, over to the left, where most language occurs. This is another structural reason for the greater reliance among girls and women on talking in order to express emotions. Males rely on more "spatial" strategies—punching, hitting, walking it off—which don't rely as much on language. Talking is, of course, a relationship strategy that leads to longer-term, more intricate connectivity. Hitting tends to distance another, walking it off is a separation strategy. The corpus callosum helps females process and cross-talk within the brain so that they can keep relational connectivity longer.

The corpus callosum also means more ability to multitask in the female brain. Girls and women tend to be able to do more different tasks at once than boys and men—thus relating and connecting to more people at once. Here, again, we are averaging male/female difference. Some girls can't stay on task at all, much less do more than one thing at a time! But, still, you'll find that boys tend to single-task, doing one thing very well at a given time, whereas girls may begin more things at once and pursue more than one task at once: holding the hamster while doing homework while talking to someone while keeping a diary open for writing in.

In large part because of brain differences between males and females, language researchers have been able to discover the intimacy imperative in female language use quite specifically—by watching what females use language for.

Deborah Tannen, linguist and author of the bestselling book about women, men, and language *You Just Don't Understand,* has identified female talk as "rapport talk" and male talk as "report talk." Females tend to spend more time talking in order to bond; for them, language is a way of establishing connections and relationships; men spend more time talking in order to report events, and position themselves within the events. Another linguistic researcher, Barbara Johnstone, studied stories women and men tell. She discovered that women's stories tend to be about community building, and men's stories about contests, even subtle ones. She also discovered that the majority of men she studied were happy working alone; the majority of women felt they suffered by working alone.

## MORE HIDDEN SEATS OF THE INTIMACY URGE

Structural brain differences add to our picture of girls and boys. The blood in the female brain flows more quickly to more parts of the brain, and moves through structures of the brain better set up for connectivity and complex, interwoven relational strategies.

Here are some more components of "relationship centers" in the female brain.

*The Cingulate Gyrus.* In your daughter's brain, within the limbic system, is this very important set of cells. This gyrus is directly linked to maternal bonding, upon which all species rely for survival, and to female bonding behavior in general. Females have more activity in the "bonding gyrus" than males. This is true not only for humans, but other primates as well.

The neuroscientist Paul MacLean has been studying the gyrus for decades. He discovered in 1981 that when female hamsters lack a certain part of the gyrus, they give birth to pups without bonding or caring for their own offspring. He further discovered that it is in this part of the brain that females specifically locate the "separation cry" of the infant (the cry a child gives off when separated from Mom). If the part of the gyrus that hears the cry is gone, the mom doesn't hear the cry and thus does not respond to the child, even though the child is her own.

MacLean, among many others, has come to understand that a great deal of what we think of as "empathy responses" exist because of this gyrus. The female brain has more blood flow in this gyrus, even at rest.

*Oxytocin.* The cingulate gyrus is one of the areas of the limbic system that carries receptors for an important brain chemical: oxytocin. Oxytocin activity, like the gyrus, gives us a wonderful illustration of how complex your daughter's brain is: When your daughter hears a baby cry in a crowded theater, her oxytocin level rises just slightly. When she hears the baby cry next to her, it increases even more. When she sees a baby near her (or sometimes, even when she sees a baby on a television commercial), her oxytocin rises further, compelling her to want to hold the baby. When she holds the baby, oxytocin surges again.

The imperative to intimacy in your daughter's brain is unmistakable. When people refer to the "maternal instinct," they are speaking, in part, of oxytocin. Among males, oxytocin changes are minimal in comparison.

*The Hippocampus.* The hippocampus, which looks like a seahorse, is, like the gyrus, located in the limbic system. We've looked earlier at its responsibility for storing memory and retrieving it; but the hippocampus has other functions. For instance, it modulates emotions, and ties emotions to memories.

With a larger hippocampus, and more blood flow and neural pathways to it in the female brain, girls attach more feelings to memories than boys do. With more memory storage and retrieval present among females, more emotive material is linked to memory in females than in males. Quite often a girl (or a woman) will remember a detail from the past *and feel the memory* in a way the boy or man will not. She might say, "Don't you remember that day? You said, ————, and it really hurt me." He might remember saying something, but he might very well not remember her being hurt.

When memory and emotion are so well linked in a mind, intimacy is most often the subject of the memory. In the hippocampus itself, the female brain is generating constant connection with memories of intimate detail and intimate alliance. Your daughter is running over memories of relationships gained and relationships lost, how it felt in both cases, and feeling some of it all over again.

## BUILDING A HOUSE OF PROOF

These, then, are further details of the female mind provided to you in hopes that we are, together, beginning to build a house of proof that girls want something specific from life which it is our duty, as parents and as a society, to give them.

When I observe my daughters and think back to being a boy, I do not see as clearly as I saw in my own life the simplistic "good guy" and "bad guy" psychology that dominated my boyhood. Instead, I see more interaction in girls' lives of the prefrontal cortex with the limbic system and frontal lobes. My daughters are more interested in subtleties of relationship than in black and white.

I do not see as much physical fighting as I and my brother did—as much wrestling. I do see more the swords of words constantly at play.

Though my daughters enjoy soccer and other competitions, I see less will to compete and more will to connect.

I see very different ways of establishing hierarchies, different ways of testing each other, different ways of viewing moral and spiritual life.

I see different kinds of fragility in my boyhood and in my daughters' girlhood: Gabrielle's and Davita's selves seem more malleable than mine was.

Gail once said, "The worst thing for a girl is to feel left out and alone." I remember yearning to be alone as much as possible. When I was left out, it was often my first instinct to say, "That's all right. I'll show them one day."

In Gabrielle's and Davita's lives I see a few stereotypes; more so, I see the cerebral cortex, the neurotransmitters, and blood flow working inside the brain to give me daughters, not sons. And I am challenged, as are each of you, to ask: What does it mean to have a daughter?

As much as I help protect my daughters from taking direct hits to their self-esteem, as much as I encourage them to compete and to be independent, I find myself worrying about one thing especially: Will I help forge a world in which my daughters can find *the intimate relationships* they need? Will I help forge a world of stable, loving, and long-term relationships for my daughters? Not only does the brain science show me a female mind electrified by the constancy of contact and attachment, but I observe it among my wife and daughters, among my female clients, and among the happy and the struggling marriages of friends.

As we move, in the next chapter, to deeply explore female biochemistry and hormones, our intuitions about the intimacy imperative will be even further awakened, and our house of proof further built. We will discover the myriad ways the female brain *and female hormones* come together in a beautiful natural design to encourage the intimacy imperative in female life.

In discovering these connections we will be moving closer to fla-grantly using the word "femininity." It is with that word that I would like to end this chapter.

## The Future of Femininity

All of us raising daughters experience various moments when we must take stands to protect girls' development. As we do this, mustn't we take a stand on what we mean by "femininity"?

For many people, the word "femininity" implies only delicacy, for others it implies weakness. From a nature-based point of view, I find the word "femininity" to be infinitely useful, rather than limiting. It is, after all, the word on which "feminism" is based. Whether a social theorist admits it or not, he or she, in promoting women's rights, is making inherent statements (even if concealed) about how she or he judges the character and worth of *the feminine*.

It is my profound belief that neurobiology and biochemistry are scientific fields that can help us reveal and define femininity in its broadest and most freeing sense. I offer my understanding of those sciences to parents and to professionals with this object in mind. Part of that understanding, as I've emphasized, is the idea that *there is an imperative to intimacy* at *the heart of femininity*.

And yet, even armed with the latest information about how the female brain, hormones, and socialization work, I know what it feels like to want to stop short of saying "Girls are hard-wired for something." It's hard, especially in the present age, to buck the trend and say "Femininity is a very natural thing, and it includes a predominance of intimacy activity." This is difficult not only because it goes against some of the present politically correct con-ventions—that women and men are the same, or that women don't have "maternal instincts" per se, or that, if women do have them, they shouldn't listen to those instincts when they get in the way of social success—but it is even more difficult, I think, for a deeper reason. To accept that femininity is definable is to define it, and once defined, it may make us a little bit ashamed of how we've been. The future of femininity, I think, lies in our changing some of the things we do as parents and a society. This won't be easy.

To say that femininity is somehow "hard-wired," then to see the intimacy imperative inherent in the hard-wiring becomes a great challenge. The early feminists, without using brain research, saw it. Carol Gilligan saw it. She saw that intimacy was a lion's share of the feminine imperative. But she, like her feminist colleagues over the next few decades, turned away from it, and occupied themselves with empowering women and girls toward greater male-held social status.

Had Gilligan and others, thirty years ago, stuck to their early findings about the inherent qualities of femininity, it would not seem so alien to say that the future of femininity, no matter our age or era, has always lain in a culture's commitment to providing girls and women with secure webs of interrelationship, bonding, and attachment. Providing girls and women with the ability to compete with men, while very useful, may not lie at the heart of how a society must nurture its girls.

Saying this kind of thing, even thinking about it, then using science to explore it—is difficult, indeed. The difficulty is not just political; it is practical. If it is correct, it will mean that our girls need even more parents, teachers, grandparents, friends, mentors than we give them. All of us will have to spend *more* time guiding them through life than we do in our neighborhoods, schools, and homes; *more* time nurturing them through adolescent stages of life; *more* time learning who they are and helping them gain self-knowledge. Espousing a philosophy that we must take *more* time bonding with our daughters than we do—especially in adolescence—in more intricate ways than we do, means thinking and acting against the currents of postmodern, very busy life.

Yet isn't this where we have to stand as we build our house of proof? In generations past, our ancestors' daughters had tribes, extended family, communities, and large nuclear families in which girls could exercise their beautiful minds, talk their talk, be stimulated by survival and love and the adventure of relationships, stimulate the intimate world around them with their own particular way of being, of grace, of connection. And in any generation, if girls do not get the relationship stimulation, attachment, bonding, and guidance they need, do they not discover unhappiness, loneliness, and difficulties we do not wish upon them?

Mary Pipher, in her powerful book, *The Shelter of Each Other*, speaks of how our children today are "thirsty in the rain." When I think of her phrase, I think of Erin, Kristen, Margeaux, and other girls like them, girls who spend more time in chat rooms than in families, girls who not only do not see grandparents, but have little opportunity to develop relationships with mentors or godmothers; girls who rely fully on peers and the media for identity and companionship, though both peers and the media are fickle.

Nature-based research, both in female life and male, both in seeking to define the masculine and the feminine, corroborates from within the brain and hormones what Mary Pipher finds in the world. Who our children truly are—their inherent needs—often lies at odds with many of the values of our society. Who our girls are—their inherent needs—is often not seen, even by political advocates who strive so hard to care for girls' futures. Who Erin is—her identity, her soul, her nature—was not befriended even, to some extent, by her own busy family.

As you explore nature-based thinking, as you see through the looking glass into your daughter's brain and hormones, I hope you'll come to agree with me, at least to some extent, that the future of femininity lies in embracing our daughters again, embracing them fully as *girls*.

Let's now move to exploring how our *biochemistry and hormones* help define a girl, femininity, and the intimacy imperative. Let's bring an even broader measure of truth to the house of proof we are building about who our daughters are. Then, in Parts II and III, we will look at specific ways to alter families and the culture to ensure the future of femininity. In doing these things, we will be returning, in a graceful way, to not only a nature-based approach to girls, but one that even early feminism, and certainly the early women's rights movement, espoused.

# 3

## THE HIDDEN WORLD

### THE BIOCHEMISTRY OF GIRLS' LIVES

*"How can one learn to live through the ebb-tides of one's exis-*
*tence? Perhaps this is the most important thing for me to take:*
*the memory that each cycle of the tide is valid; each cycle of*
*the wave is valid . . . for the sea recedes and returns eternally."*

—Anne Morrow Lindbergh

There is an ancient Hindu story of a girl with the moon on her forehead, a magical child who lives with her people in a seaside town. She must be kept alive so that the moon will be happy. In this story, if the moon is unhappy, human beings suffer. The moon is as important as the sun, for while the sun's light gives life to plants and people during the day, the moon's light illumes the night, and it is the night that most frightens, and most intrigues.

One day this girl disappears, and everyone in the town stops work, banding together to find her. They search throughout the bordering forest, the mountains, the sea. They search every home, every dark well, every cave, every dream. They ask the animals and the fish where the magical girl could be hiding, or if harm has come to her. An elephant tells them she can be found not in the sea, but inland.

One day, a young fisherman of the village, who has given up fishing to search for her, happens upon a cave hidden far away in the forest. At its mouth is a huge tree. After peering into the cave and seeing nothing except dirt and moist walls, he rests under the tree. He sleeps for an hour or so as night comes, cloudy and thus empty of a moon. When he awakens, he lights his torch and knows he must choose between going onward along the path into the forest, or going into the cave. A little frightened, he nonetheless enters the cave, and upon moving inward he sees both an underground stream and a light far within. He moves along the stream to the light and there sees an old crone at a fire beside the stream, and with her the magical girl.

"You're alive!" he exclaims. "We have all been worried sick about you! We thought you drowned, or got lost!"

The old crone invites him into the circle of the fire.

"You must come back to your people," he admonishes the girl.

"I will return, but not for a while," she responds. "I have things to learn here."

"What things?" he asks.

"I am free here. I will learn what a woman truly is."

As this is a very intriguing subject for him as well, and seeing that he cannot force her back to the village, he says, "Perhaps I will stay and learn this too. Perhaps I will carry water for you here, or do some other work."

Kindly, the old crone shakes her head. "If you will wait outside at the tree of life, she will bring the water to you."

And the girl says, "I won't be long. Please wait for me."

The young man leaves the cave, finds the tree, and sits under it patiently. A day goes by, then another moonless night, then another day. Days and nights pass until he is ready to go to the village and bring all the villagers here, or ready to go back into the cave after the girl. Just at the moment of his supreme impatience, the girl emerges from the cave, carrying a pail of water. She looks like a woman now. And in the heavens, the moon has returned.

"We can return to the people now." She smiles, taking the young man's arm and offering him a drink.

Startled by her beauty, he asks, "Does your beauty come from your increased age, or does it come from knowledge?"

"From knowledge." She smiles. "Now I know who I am."

He drinks the water and finds that he loves her as a man loves a woman. Returning to the village, the woman with the moon on her forehead marries the young fisherman, and the people, who have suf-fered in her absence, are reunited with happiness and their secure life.

When I was a young boy, our family lived in India and I heard from our Aiya (a "mother's helper" who became like an aunt) many stories like these. In telling this one now, I've modified it a little, mainly for lack of perfect memory, but it is not changed much. I could not have known as a boy—nor perhaps did Aiya think about these things—that this story, a typical Indian tale about children growing up and falling in love, could also be seen from a neurobio-logical perspective. A girl, connected to the moon (both literally and figuratively an emblem of female hormonal cycles), lives in her con-nection, even dutifully, but lacks real knowledge of that connection; she must go find that knowledge in order to find freedom, find the heart of duty, and find the whole self. The culmination of that jour-ney lies in bringing the waters of life out of the cave to her people.

Not surprisingly, she marries the searching young man. In ancient fairy tales, marrying a man at the end of the tale is symbolic of the return of equilibrium, stability, and security to the world. Marriage is seen here not as an imposition on a woman but as symbolic of divine union. The waters of life flow most securely, ancient wisdom often tells us, when there is security in a kingdom. And often the moon appears in stories about the waters of life: a common feminine symbol of all of our ancestors. Not surprisingly, there is a great tree, or Tree of Life, in this story. This is a common symbol of life's origins in both ancient mythology and, interestingly, in contemporary neurobiology.

Some may think it strange that I begin this chapter with an ancient fairy tale, yet I could not resist (and I will use myths and fairy tales throughout this book), for there is a bare simplicity to these tales that beckons, especially to we who care for children. They point to the basics in life. In this Hindu tale, the girl cannot become a woman of importance without self-knowledge, and her family and culture has not finished the work of her childhood unless it com-pletes her knowledge (in this story by her time with a wise elder) of who she is and the imperatives by which a woman of character, pur-pose, and self-fulfillment lives her life.

As Gail and I explored and culled the material presented to you in this chapter on female biochemistry, Gail told me, "You wouldn't believe how few girls or even *women* know this stuff about themselves. I never learned this stuff as a girl. How could I really know who I was?"

"How could you not learn about this?" I asked naively. "This is basic!"

Yet I should not have been surprised; as a boy, I learned almost nothing about my own male nature and biology from my parents or others.

Just as Chapter 2 hoped to end our cultural silence about girls' brains, this chapter hopes to end the silence about a girl's hidden world: her hormones, and their interaction with the brain. The "stuff" Gail had not learned as a girl, the "knowledge" the girl in the Hindu story sought are the tip of an iceberg of knowledge available now, with present science, on how sensitive the female hormonal cycle is, and even more than that, how fundamental it is to the personal, emotional, moral, spiritual, and physical development of a girl, wherever she may be in her cycle, and wherever she lives in the world.

By the end of this chapter, I hope you'll find yourself amazed by the workings of your daughter's internal foundations for daily life. Much of her wonder rests in her biochemistry and the place to begin understanding that biochemistry is with the tree of life itself.

## THE TREE OF LIFE: FROM MIND TO HORMONES

When speaking with microbiologist JoAnna Ellington recently, I heard her use a beautiful phrase for the foundational hormonal, biochemical network in the human body. "What most intrigues me about the development of children is the tree of life hidden inside them," she said. "Pretty much everything else depends on this tree because it controls our human energy flow."

When biologists refer to "the tree of life" in human males, they are discussing the hypothalamic-pituitary-*gonadal* (testicular) axis: the signal connections between the hypothalamus in the brain (hormonal mission control), the pituitary, which carries the mission news to the testicles, and the testicles, which create the testosterone. That axis looks like a vertical tree trunk, top to bottom, whose signals flow throughout the body, like branches and leaves of energy.

In females, the tree of life refers to the hypothalamic-pituitary-*ovarian* axis. The hypothalamus tells the pituitary and the pituitary tells the ovaries, which secrete the many female hormones into the female bloodstream, branching them out everywhere. Signals regarding female energy flow occur along this axis, and fluctuations in the workings of that flow will create tremors felt by the branches, the leaves, and whole energy structure of the organism.

The tree of life is different in girls and boys because the female and male hypothalamus are a little different, the pituitary a little more different, and the reproductive organs completely different. Thus, the hormones that comprise the photosynthesis occurring in the tree of male and female life are different.

The tree of life is also different because in the male, hormonal needs are mainly created in the hypothalamus by external stimulants (e.g., if we play or watch hockey our testosterone rises) and by a diurnal (daily) cycle (males from puberty onward to andropause—male menopause—have between five and seven testosterone spikes per day).

The female tree of life, on the other hand, is affected not only by external stimulants (when a female touches a baby her level of oxytocin rises) but also by internal directives males don't have—a monthly reproductive cycle, which controls estrogen, progesterone, prolactin, and many other hormone flows. Furthermore, because the female cycle is not diurnal (reflective of the sun) but menstrual (monthly, reflective of the moon's cycle), the female tree of life is actually far more complex than the male. We've all probably intuited this, but haven't quite known how and why females go through so much daily complexity.

The gender-different tree of life relates to everything from when girls and boys perform best (or worst) on tests and in schools in general, something I have covered in depth in *Boys and Girls Learn Differently!* to why girls more than boys are victims of eating disorders, to why girls are less physically aggressive than boys, to the biological reason girls tend to cry and produce tears more than boys, to why girls so easily give in to pressure from certain media imagery and peer pressures, to differing styles of conversation and hierarchical activity, to different approaches to family and romantic relationships. The list is, of course, endless. Your own list of the wonder of girls is perhaps also endless.

## HAVE YOU WONDERED WHY . . .

Have you ever wondered why your early-adolescent daughter (eight years old and beyond) does the things she does? Let's list some of those things.

Beginning at around eight years old or certainly by around twelve, does your daughter experience:

- Slight (or severe) mood disruptions—does her mood seem to change almost instantaneously at times?
- Slight (or severe) anxiousness—does she get anxious in ways she didn't seem to before, "take things personally," "be less able to shake things off"?
- Times in which concentrating or making decisions is difficult?
- Noticeable drops in self-esteem—does she seem to like herself less, feel she can't do something?
- Anxiety about making or keeping friends?
- Weight gain that seems abnormal—or weight loss that seems abnormal?
- A feeling of being overwhelmed by things?
- Angry outbursts—do these come more frequently now?
- Hypersensitivity to what people say, and to subtle signals people send, especially other girls, then soon, boys?
- A great deal of worry about herself, her appearance, and how others perceive her?
- Too much sleep, too little, lack of REM sleep, or trouble falling asleep?

- Intermittent, recurring sad times, whether minor or severe, and sometimes not attached to any obvious source at school or at home?
- Unhealthy and unremitting self-criticism—does she just not let herself off the hook?
- Energy depletion or loss that lasts for at least a day and sometimes more than three days?

If you've noticed three or more of these states, you've just diagnosed your daughter with a possible mood disorder, or with dysthymia (minor depression) according to the *DSM V*, the working manual for therapists.

Or, you've noticed a normal early-adolescent girl.

Are there other times in your daughter's early-to-mid-adolescence when you notice that she experiences:

- Tangential thinking and speaking?
- A sense of doom or foreboding, often exaggerated?
- A sense of always being rushed (like she's been drinking a lot of coffee)—"Get out of my way, I can't get everything done in time!"?
- An unusual fearlessness?
- A grandiose sense of who she is in the world, even inaccurate beliefs about her popularity or potential—"I'm the best, I'm the most cool, I know it all"?
- Increased irritability?
- Immoral behavior, bad judgment, lack of empathy?
- A sudden love of fun and heightened excitement—"Let's just do it, it'll be fun, who cares what happens!"?
- Less than normal need for sleep?
- A heightened desire for quick stimulations and quick release of tension, including faster talk and more physical activity?
- Lots of energy to spare?

If you have noticed three or more of these states, you've just diagnosed your daughter with the manic portion of bipolar disorder, according to the *DSM V.*

Or, you've noticed a normal adolescent girl.

"I don't like myself," Gabrielle cried one day when it felt to her like life was just too hard. "I hate myself." Gail and I felt the terrible pangs of parents who fear for their child. But we also knew she was a normal girl who vocalized her pleasure and her pain successfully.

Given the complexity of the female monthly cycle, it would be difficult for a girl *not* to experience many of the characteristics of a bipolar or other mood disorder. While environmental stimulants can certainly influence every child, these aspects of girls' lives are rooted far within, underground and in the caves of female hormones, and branching up along the female tree of life.

## The Hidden World: A Girl's Hormonal Biology

Deborah Sichel, M.D., primary author of *Women's Moods*, an immensely valuable book for any woman interested in adult female biology, has noted that clinicians "don't evaluate women as whole beings, taking into account all the elements that contribute to their mental health. Consequently, they misunderstand the interplay of the psyche, brain chemistry, and reproductive state." Quite often, they use sociological and psychological models for adult women's distresses rather than looking to nature-based, biochemical nature.

Dr. Sichel sums up her research, which is based on her work with thousands of women, this way: "A woman's biology is the cornerstone of her *mental* health."

How can she make this bold statement? And is it true for *girls* too?

Answers to the first question will become clear soon. The answer to the second is: Yes.

The lives of girls younger than eight to ten are affected much more by their brain system's genetic development patterns and its experience of the child's environment; hormones don't yet play a large part. This is intuitive for most of us who have said "My girls weren't too difficult, certainly not before they hit adolescence." In our younger girls, we notice relative innocence, ease of care, and adequate social performance, especially if these girls get enough love, attention, and direction. The effects of hormonal biology, and the entrance of hormonal biology into emotional life, begin around eight to ten, when girls' ovaries begin to produce adultlike doses of hormones.

Here's how it all works.

## THE HORMONES

A girl's hormones are miraculous and wonderful parts of her, whose composition and effects we now understand relatively well, though every day some new mystery about them is revealed. Every year now, as biochemical research grows, hormones will get increased credit for female existence, success, happiness, self-esteem, and quality of life. That's how powerful they are.

Hormones have many names in popular understanding: They've been called "brain chemicals," "brain molecules," "maestros of human energy," "the power source," "the body's energy director." They are all of these. In simplest scientific terms, they are molecules that travel through the body and brain telling cells what to do.

One way to think of this is to see the hormones as the codirector (along with the brain system) of a film, telling the scriptwriter (the genes) and the actors (the brain's nerve cells or "neurotransmitters") what to do, and relying on the producer (the tree of life) to make the movie possible in the first place. The young person's physical actions are the movie-in-progress, projected into the world by a projection system called "the girl's body." The family and society in which this movie plays are both its editors (trying to help the film make consistent sense) and "film critics" (mentoring, cajoling, pointing out flaws, praising). The executive producer of the movie—the force that sets it all up—is nature.

This human film is an ensemble effort: Each person and system in it is essential. Some in the film are more consistently crucial than others: for instance, the codirectors. Without the hormones and brain patterns, the film would not happen; it would drift unmanaged, self-destruct, end prematurely. At puberty especially, we can see how the hormones codirect the film. Much of the child's transformation into an adult, both in body and brain, depends on the direction of four primary sets of molecules: growth hormones, estrogen, progesterone, and testosterone.

- Growth hormones in both girls and boys direct physical growth.
- Estrogen and progesterone are the dominant female sex hormones, directing growth of reproductive systems in girls.
- Testosterone is the dominant male sex hormone.

These molecules can't be seen, and so we often miss that they are directing our film. It has been politically incorrect to talk much about them. Since we all agree a girl is far more than just body size and sex organs, and because hormones have been barely understood, we would have to be ready for recrimination if we said in public that these brain chemicals direct her film.

In fact, a few decades ago, this admonition made sense. We couldn't be sure what was really going on. But now we do know a great deal. Thirty years of human biochemical research has taught us that *in order to accomplish the completed adolescent-to-adult transformation of the female body and sex organs, estrogen, progesterone, testosterone, and other lesser hormones must also direct emotional, psychological, and mental transformation; they take primary control of these human functions for a period of a few years of a girl's life, while she (especially her brain system) gets accustomed to their effect on her, and learns to manage the self.* We know also that, even as she grows accustomed to these hormones and learns to work with them, they still play a large part in her adult story, in a monthly cycle, until menopause (and even, in some ways, beyond). In other words, hormones change *everything*, not just a few things, and they don't just change a girl into a woman, they *are*, to a great extent, *the woman herself.*

To many girls and women, knowing this about themselves is liberating. But in the eyes of many people, saying this is a kind of criminal offense. "A girl is not limited to her hormones!" comes the angry cry. "Her environment, her mind, her heart, her soul are what she really is!"

And of course she is all these things. But now we are arguing over words, not the biological character of a human being. No response to environment, no "mind," "heart," or "soul" exists in the human being separate from hormones, which are stimulated by environment, woven through thought, create the baseline for romance and love, and speak directly to the hidden mysteries of the universe. In the minds of some, talking about a girl's hormones is "very limiting." In my mind, understanding a girl's hormones is a way of understanding all that is unlimited about her. Her freedom, like the Indian girl's, comes not in avoiding looking within, but in fully looking within. In my years of presenting this material to girls and women, the vast majority have found a deeper doorway into the self rather than a limitation. Trudy and her daughter are examples.

## TRUDY'S STORY

Trudy is a mother of three children, two sons and a daughter. I met her in Missouri, where she is an elementary-school teacher, her husband a contractor. When I met her, her daughter was fifteen and her sons twelve and eleven.

I met her in training at her school in February; but it turned out she had seen me speak in August of the previous year. During that summer month, I was in Kansas City training teachers in how boys and girls learn differently, and I taught a section on female hormones. Trudy had been in the audience. Her own daughter, Candice, then fourteen, had been angry, distant, rebellious. The girl's eating habits had changed, she was having trouble sleeping. She had been diagnosed with depression. She had gone from being "a very sweet girl," in Trudy's words, to "a troubled teen." Trudy had taken her out of her public school, after three disciplinary incidents, and put her in private school. Her daughter was set up to try a second public school in the upcoming fall, because the private school, while still support-ive, was at wit's end. Candice had also attempted suicide.

"When you presented the hormonal information last year," Trudy told me in February, "a lightbulb went on in my mind. I rushed home after that day, talked to my husband, talked to the psychologist. We checked out the hormonal component and got treatment. You would not believe how Candice is now." Trudy now told the story of a girl no longer depressed, indeed a young woman who had returned to stability and success. School was working out well, grades were where they should have been, the bouts of anger (one of which had been violent and required the police) were gone.

"I had to change psychologists," Trudy reported, "because our psychologist wasn't trained in hormonal diagnoses. But I found one who knew about it, and we changed Candice's diet, especially increasing the proteins and vitamins. We stabilized her progesterone; the progesterone receptors in her brain were not receiving the proges-terone itself. Once we discovered that, everything made sense. We have her on a progesterone patch, but she's not on antidepressants and antianxiety meds anymore. She's living a normal life! Sometimes I wake up in the morning and can't believe how lucky we've been. We almost lost Candice. Your information about hormones changed our lives!"

As Trudy told me about her experience, both her eyes and my own had teared up, and we embraced each other. This person I barely knew had nearly lost her daughter but had recovered her because she gained fundamental nature-based information from a lecture. How many other Trudys and Candices are there in our families, neighbor-hoods, and schools? There are countless girls suffering middle to acute PMS like Candice was, and there are even more who develop "symptoms" of psychological diseases—symptoms parents blame themselves for—because of their hormonal cycles.

I have heard other stories like Trudy's from other women all over the country. One of the keys to success for these parents and daugh-ters has been the sharing of hormonal information with the daughter.

If you are raising an early- or midadolescent girl who enjoys read-ing, please share the following material directly with her. My own daughters have read it and it has led to amazing discussions in our family.

If you are raising a middle-to-late-adolescent boy (or a younger boy who is very mature and a good reader), you might also let him read these sections. It is crucial that males, as they are ready, understand the hidden dance of female hormones. Guys often like science, "The facts, please!" and thus find "the science of femininity" an interesting way of understanding the other sex. Because knowledge into another person leads to empathy, patience, and deeper love, Gail and I have made biological information a crucial part of our relationship. We credit the strength of our marriage, in large part, to our constant investigation of each other's hidden, inner worlds.

## HOW HORMONES DO THEIR DANCE

Let's look at a few of the important partners a girl's hormones need in order to do a dance of life inside her.

Hormones tell a girl's millions of cells what to do by attaching to *receptor sites* in brain cells set up specifically for them. In brain cells there are estrogen receptors, progesterone receptors, testosterone receptors, and so on for every hormone. The hormones attach to these sites, affecting neurotransmission in the brain, which then affects activity in the body.

It is through this system of hormone/receptor cell/neurotransmission that so many things in the girl are affected:

- her mood
- words she uses, speed of conversation, need for conversation
- how she'll do on tests at a given time of the month
- how much she'll eat
- how she'll relate to people nonverbally
- how she'll feel about the people she loves
- how she'll see herself fitting in
- her self-esteem
- her level of competitiveness

- her social ambition
- her aggression
- her primary emotions—like anger, joy, grief

These are "large" effects. Meanwhile, small things you wouldn't think of are affected not only by the primary hormones but also by *lesser hormones* (those that don't do as many jobs as estrogen, progesterone, testosterone, and growth hormones). For instance, a lesser hormone, like prolactin, which directs growth of breasts, breast milk, and tear ducts, directs the natural part of how and how much your daughter cries. If your daughter cries a lot, and especially if her tears drop from her eyes in torrents, she most probably has high prolactin levels, or did during a crucial developmental time, resulting in large tear ducts.

And then there are growth hormones. These affect your daughter's growth spurts, height, weight, and other aspects of body shape. They are most active during puberty.

We will look in greatest detail at the dominant *sex hormones,* for they have the most profound effect on a girl's emotional life.

## ESTROGEN

Estrogen is generally thought of as a single hormone. In fact, it is really a family that includes estriol, estradiol, and estrone and at least five other discrete estrogen-type molecules. Each of these is structured slightly differently and performs slightly different functions under the "estrogen umbrella." Together they comprise estrogen, which is perhaps one of the most dominant forces on earth.

Estrogen is certainly the most influential hormone, on a daily basis, in a girl's physical, mental, and emotional experiences. Progesterone comes close, but estrogen (and its hormonal family) is the primary female hormone.

It is estrogen that controls the firing rates of four essential neurotransmitters (or nerve cells): norepinephrine, serotonin, dopamine, and acetylcholine. These neurotransmitters are mainly in charge of mood stability, thought process, perception, memory, personal motivation, intimacy motivation, appetite, anxiety, how a girl handles stress, and sex drive. Estrogen also enhances the activity of glutamate, a neurotransmitter that accelerates the communication of nerves in the brain. What's crucial here is the fact that this acceleration (or deceleration when estrogen is low) directly affects *a lot;* the stability of a girl's mood, her yearning for intimacy, and her performance on intelligence tests are only the beginning.

## PROGESTERONE

Progesterone and estrogen are often thought of as "opposing" hormones. This initially makes sense just because when you look at their physio-structure, you see opposing constructions. Also, when progesterone rises during a monthly reproductive cycle, it specifically directs cells to make fewer estrogen receptors. It is trying to shut estrogen down. It does this so that reproduction can take place. Unchecked estrogen means no human reproduction.

Progesterone is also called the "bonding" hormone. It literally bonds the fertilized egg to the walls of the uterus. Some scientists believe one reason girls and women emphasize complex, interwoven networks of social bonds is the presence of this hormone, especially as it adds to the mix of other chemicals like oxytocin. Oxytocin is, as we've already noted, identified with holding babies, cooing at small children, and caring for small animals.

Progesterone plays a large part just before menses. Estrogen drops and progesterone takes over. Girls' lives change, often "for the worse," in that they feel withdrawn, irritable, depressed. Progesterone and estrogen both need to be in balance for a girl to feel in balance. Generally, they are in a delicate balance together, and of course this delicate balance becomes even more delicate depending on the time in the monthly cycle.

In all this it is important to keep reminding ourselves that every girl is an individual. Some girls are very affected by progesterone levels, others barely feel the tremors of pre-menses and menses. If, however, your daughter seems to feel the tremors, progesterone is one big reason.

## TESTOSTERONE

Females have up to twenty times less testosterone than males. In girls, this hormone is called an "androgenic hormone," but we often just say testosterone, even when discussing girls, because the word has so completely entered our popular culture.

- In both males and females, higher testosterone levels mean less depression.
- In both males and females, higher testosterone levels mean more aggression.
- In both males and females, higher testosterone levels mean more libido.

Testosterone is not the only factor in these by any means, but it is an important one. Girls tend to be less aggressive than boys, they tend to suffer overt depression more than boys, and they tend to have lower libidos than boys (speaking statistically, of course). Lower testosterone in girls is an important reason.

Testosterone affects female social ambition just as it affects male. Girls and women who climb higher in social hierarchies generally have higher testosterone. In a recent study, for instance, professional women tested as having higher testosterone levels than women who stayed at home or women who held clerical jobs.

Girls are presently experimenting with testosterone through steroid use. This can be dangerous and often illegal. Long-term health risks to girls in this situation are frightening.

Interestingly, as a woman becomes menopausal, the health risks of testosterone experimentation diminish and the benefits increase. For instance, I was recently talking with a menopausal colleague in New York who had been involved in carefully managed testosterone therapy for a year. She had been taking testosterone because she had become forgetful, easily tired, and often felt unable to think. As a corporate executive, she simply could not exist in this situation. For months she tried different doses, but none worked until a third doctor found the right dosage.

"I'm a new person," she told me. "It's as simple as that. The right dosage of testosterone has saved me."

Testosterone injection is rarely, if ever, suggested for prepubescent or pubescent girls.

## HORMONES DO AFFECT GIRLS EVEN BEFORE ADOLESCENCE

Though we've said that hormones don't affect a girl very much before about eight to ten years old, we don't want to say they have no effect. Their main effect is in the wiring of the brain to accept and organize them later: in the womb hormones wire most girls' brains to be "female brains" and most boys' brains to be "male brains."

The female brain is set up from before birth to be an estrogen/progesterone-receptive system. It sets up in the fetus the "female" tree of life. In all humans, even before hormones come in at early adolescence, the brain is already operating in anticipation of them. While the male brain is loaded with innumerable receptor sites for its dominant hormone, testosterone, the female brain is loaded with innumerable receptor sites for female hormones, mainly estrogen and progesterone. These receptor sites exist throughout the female brain, with a heavy concentration in the limbic system of the brain, which houses the lion's share of emotional processing.

So, while a girl of three or four is not experiencing life yet through the wash of a hormonal cycle, she is experiencing the world in a way similar to how she will—more dramatically—once the hormones flow.

When a parent says, "My girl isn't in puberty yet, but she is so much a 'girl.' Why is that?" the answer lies mainly in a brain system set up for an adult hormonal system.

Just as the developing male brain is set up to be a testosterone-receptive system—making three-year-old boys, who have no surging testosterone yet, generally more physically aggressive than three-year-old girls—the developing female brain is set up to receive estrogen and progesterone, making girls generally more sedentary than boys, and, as we'll explore in a moment, more focused on the intricacies of intimate relationships.

Remember, if the female brain were not, by female genetics, set up along female lines already, the adolescent girl would become a completely disordered being. She would possess a brain system not prepared to receive the primary source of adult female energy—her hormones.

## THE FOUR STAGES OF A MONTHLY CYCLE

Hormones and chemicals work in your daughter's life (and in your own if you are a woman) in four stages during the month:

STAGE 1: *The First Half.* Weeks one and two of her monthly cycle. Estrogen and endorphin levels are gradually rising. Her mood is relatively stable, even upbeat, as they rise. Serotonin, dopamine, norepinephrine, and other nerve cells that regulate mood are high in response to high estrogen and endorphin levels. She might be doing pretty well with her math tests, her reading, and other academic skills. She might be living with a certain amount of ease.

STAGE 2: *Midcycle.* Around two weeks before her period begins. Estrogen levels shoot up, then drop suddenly. This is a trauma to the brain, which goes into a kind of withdrawal. Your daughter may experience a lot of the things we listed on pages 71 and 72. This withdrawal—a "down" mood, "she's quieter than usual," "she's moody"—can be even more pronounced in certain girls because of two factors: genetic predisposition and/or external stress.

Many girls are predisposed to "a more difficult cycle" than others, and all girls are predisposed to more or less difficulty at certain times in the cycle.

If your daughter is predisposed to more difficulty in mood regulation during Stage 2, she may confuse you during this time especially. She "may not be herself." Her self-esteem may plummet.

At some point in life most if not all girls and women go through some kind of difficulty in Stage 2 mood regulation. And most go through some measure of it every month. It is part of a female's journey through life.

If she is under a lot of stress (or has been experiencing accumulated trauma, from abuse of some kind or from a divorce or broken relationship), she may also experience severe mood swings during this time. She may do less well in school, lose her focus, and experience a number of the things we listed on pages 71 and 72 with a vengeance.

STAGE 3: *Ovulation and Post-Ovulation.* Ovulation is such a "positive trauma" to the nerve cells that the fog often lifts as quickly as it came. Now estrogen levels begin to rise again. Progesterone levels also rise, reaching their peak about seven to eight days after ovulation, then declining over the next few days. Rising progesterone is a mood-stabilizing influence on the brain: Progesterone attaches to GABA receptors (which quiet the brain) and interacts with serotonin to create feelings of wellness. This is a great time to be a girl!

Testosterone levels gradually rise during the female cycle, becoming highest toward the end of midcycle/beginning of ovulation. Many woman have a higher sex drive at this time. As Stage 2 transitions to Stage 3, the testosterone drops, and generally sex drive will too, bringing the woman closer to Stage 4.

STAGE 4: *The Final Days.* Estrogen drops, followed by progesterone and the endorphins. What may have been experienced in Stage 2 can be even more amplified in your daughter in Stage 4. The sweet, even wonderful feelings of high self-esteem and readiness to face the world experienced by your daughter in Stage 3 can disappear in Stage 4. The brain deals with the traumas of falling estrogen, progesterone, and endorphins by exhibiting anger, hypersensitivity, irritability, sadness, feelings of despair, and lowered self-esteem. It can seem like your daughter is forgetting things a lot; her food intake may change, as she craves carbohydrates. She may hide in her room. You may really come to worry about her. She may well appear very depressed. Her brain is short-circuiting.

Does any of this seem familiar to you? Do you experience the rollercoaster ride of hormones with your daughters?

In an informal study, I asked a set of ten mothers and ten fathers to notice how different their feelings about their adolescent daughters were over a one-month period.

"My girls are so up, then so down," a mother told me. "It's the hardest thing for me. I feel like I'm walking through a minefield."

"I'm always treading on eggs with my daughter," another told me. "No matter what, I say or do the wrong thing, and she gets angry."

"My baby girl has become a b——," a father said in confidence, near tears. "She's turned on me."

These same parents, a week later, reported differently.

"Christina can be so calm and loving."

"Aubrey jumped on my lap and hugged me yesterday. She's fourteen years old! I was so excited."

"That girl is really going to go far in life. She's strong, that's what she is. She's not a b——: She's strong."

The girls were the same girls, the parents the same parents, but the days were different days, and the daughters seemed like they had a twin, or second self—an "emotional" self. This is the adventure of having girls.

## YOUR DAUGHTER'S EMOTIONAL BIOLOGY

Generally, in contemporary language, we talk about a child's "emotions"—grief, love, pain, hate, fear, joy. We don't talk about the biological aspects of emotions; rather, we treat them as feeling states. "I felt sad." "She must have felt happy." This is an important way of dealing with emotions—it is the language of poetry, at its best. From the Hallmark card to the poem "How Do I Love Thee?" to the Shakespearean sonnet, "feelings" are the subject of generous human dialogue.

Yet it is crucial also to find the biological base of emotions—to realize how they work in the brain and hormones. It is crucial because they can then become real, not just poetics or the subject of helpful magazine articles ("How to Feel Good") and self-help books (*Expressing Feelings Passionately*). If we think not just of "emotions" or "feelings" or "feeling states" but also of *emotional biology*, we are focusing in on the hidden, inner world of your daughters.

"Emotional biology" is a term for the basic ground of human emotions and emotional expression, which is not primarily a cultural aspect of a person (though expression can depend on a culture's attitudes of what is "appropriate" emotional expression), but is in larger part biologically guided by genetic personality, by gender in the brain (maleness or femaleness), by hormones, and by hormonal connections with the brain. Environment obviously plays a major part in emotional biology: emotions are stimulated, instantaneously, by the environment; and, extreme environmental stimulants, like traumatic child abuse, can "rewire" brain circuits, altering even the expression of genetic personality.

However, in the majority of children, who are not abused or constantly traumatized, emotional responses to life are mainly directed by their original genetic composition, which develops throughout the stages of human development, evolving into a noticeable emotional biology named "Chloe" or "Tamara" or "Davita." It wouldn't matter if they were brought up in Zimbabwe, Japan, Spain, or the U.S.; they would generally apprehend the world, experience their moods, and express themselves in similar ways no matter the culture.

In some cultures, of course, their emotional biology might hide in public but be very active in private (e.g., in Japan, public shame is associated with uncontrolled emotions, so girls are less expressive in public than they are in the U.S., but in private, Japanese girls can often be as giggly, or even as nasty, as their American counterparts). In some cultures, certain emotions would be more fully repressed than in others. In the U.S., for instance, females outwardly express more anger and dissatisfaction with life circumstances than girls and women do in China. Yet in China, girls and women often have more subtle ways of expressing their dissatisfaction. "Chinese girls use less words and more looks," a Chinese student of mine once told me, "but we mean the same thing American girls do."

Cultures, then, can affect modes of emotional expression, but they do not generally affect the emotional biology. While most girls will constantly experience the complexity of their emotional biology, none will want to experience it alone. And female emotional biology leads to immense complexities of relationship, and immense fragilities of connectivity—in this lies a great deal of the wonder of girls. It is important for us to have the courage to notice this difference from most boys. It is a difference that shows up not only in our girls' wanting to talk on the phone to their friends all the time, but even in our little girls' joining soccer teams as much to socialize as to play with the ball.

Female emotional biology is driven by and drives the intimacy imperative.

## The Biology of Femininity

At a lecture in Dallas recently, an elderly African-American woman came up to me and said, "You know, when I look back on my life, I don't remember what I accomplished exactly, even though I helped my husband run a company and then started one myself; what I remember are the relationships I had. It seems to me I can remember something about everyone I knew and loved. I just can't get enough of looking at my photos and reminiscing.

"Now, there were lots of times I just felt overwhelmed by my husband and my kids and by everyone else. I even went through a terrible bout of depression, but now I have six grandchildren and my three kids are such successes, and I have my friends (my husband being gone, rest his soul) and my body's not what it was but my mind is full to the brim, and it's the people I've loved and cared for who come back to me.

"You were talking today about femininity, female hormones, and our emotional biology and that's what I'm thinking about right now. I think that's what always mattered most to me: I led with my emotions and felt I had the right to. Everything I accomplished professionally was just fine, but it's the relationships I'm glad I had. I'm glad I was so emotional and so feminine."

When Gail and I lived in Turkey we had a friend, Necla Hanim, in her forties, a university professor in the dentistry program in Ankara, who grew up in a village near the Black Sea, then came to America (to

Cornell University) for studies. Often she and her husband and Gail and I sat talking about differences and similarities between American and Turkish culture. Once, when we discussed women's roles, she said, "I must tell you, I don't like the loneliness of women in America. I love my work, but it's just work, it's not my life. For me, my husband, my children, and my other relationships are always the most important thing. My work gives me the means to have a stable life. But my soul breathes in my work because it breathes in the relationships I have there."

For a number of decades, and for some very powerful and important reasons, it has been difficult for our culture to have a dialogue about women's rights and roles from the points of view Necla Hanim and the elderly woman at the conference suggest to us, in which intimacy is the highest personal priority because it brings the longest-lasting personal rewards, and professional work is important, but may not be quite as fulfilling. Many of us have intuited the truth of this prioritizing—and many women especially have envied those women who can live the priority—but we haven't come out and admitted it.

Our understanding of the female brain, and now of hormones, helps us to see the biological base for our intuition. Hormonal biology does not limit a girl or woman—it does not say, "If you value intimacies you can't value professional work." It does, however, inspire those of us who care for girls to shift our paradigm away from the more male vision of life—work first and relationships second, which for economic and ideological reasons women have been directed toward in the last few decades—to a more female vision of life: that human life is best served when all that we do and say in some way protects the sanctity of intimate bonds.

## FEMALE HORMONES AND THE INTIMACY IMPERATIVE

What the two women—one in the U.S., one in Turkey—described as their feminine reality can be understood biologically. There are four powerful ways in which female biochemistry guides your daughter toward intimate attachments, bonds, and relationships: the intimacy imperative.

* * *

*The Female Hormones Themselves.* Each of the dominant female hormones in itself directs its host toward varying degrees of intimacy-behavior. Often this happens simply because of the chemical makeup of the hormone itself and the interaction of that composition with other parts of the brain.

Estrogen, especially, is an "intimacy" hormone. It makes a woman feel good about herself, happy with existing relationships, and passionate about life. Some of this it does simply because as it attaches to estrogen receptors in the brain, it provides those signals. Estrogen also interacts with other brain chemicals, like serotonin, increasing the feeling of comfort with a home, a partner, a child, a relationship.

Other hormones as well ask people for intimacy (though unconsciously). Think of prolactin, which girls by fifteen have, on average, 60 percent more of than boys. In large part because of this hormone (and the larger tear glands it creates), girls process more sadness through tears than boys do (this is true not just in our culture but all over the world), and tears are one of the most powerful empathy mirrors in human intercourse. Humans are generally more inclined to give empathy (which increases attachment, intimacy, and bonding behavior) to someone crying than to someone walking away from them, or remaining stoic.

So a female hormone, as it interacts in the brain, brings its own inherent rewards of intimacy, its own craving for intimacy, to the female neural system; and it can produce a behavior that will enhance, rather than turn away, the intimacy and attachment of others.

We see this in children as young as a few weeks old. Brain systems, set up for sex-differentiated hormonal systems, already produce "female" and "male" intimacy behavior. Two-week-old girls, for instance, coo more, look parents in the eye more, and hold the eye contact longer than two-week-old boys. They are already asking for intimacy in a way a boy will have to learn.

*Interaction of the Hormones with Other Brain Chemicals.* As estrogen levels rise during the female cycle, serotonin also fills space between nerve cells—thus your daughter's neurotransmission, and her perceptions, moods, needs, and behavior become elevated, filled with more passion and enjoyment. Whatever intimate relationships she is in will tend to benefit from her increased adoration, comfort, and sense of safety. She just wants more of her boyfriend, her family, her girlfriends, her acquaintances, and she'll give more to her intimate attachment with these others.

Estrogen has a similar effect on acetylcholine, norepinephrine, and dopamine nerve cells. As neurotransmission fills with all of these, your daughter feels comforts with relationships and cravings for connectivity.

At certain times of the month estrogen drops and progesterone rises, causing the mood disturbances we already talked about. Simultaneously, progesterone binds to GABA receptors in the brain, and also interacts with serotonin, increasing intimacy "good feelings" and especially increasing constancy of need for relational reassurance ("Is our relationship doing okay?" "Are we okay?"). Often a girl gets the reassurance and connectivity her progesterone (and GABA-serotonin mix) requires by asking for it, or sometimes by seeming very sad and inspiring, thus, the love and care of her family and friends.

*When We Compare Female Hormones to Male.* Whenever we talk about hormones and intimacy, we end up comparing female and male hormones. We don't want to stereotype, but we can't avoid what's before us. Female hormones and the female cycle are different than male. Testosterone is a sex and aggression hormone. It spikes and troughs in the male bloodstream diurnally—daily—but does not have a noticeable monthly cycle.

Because estrogen, progesterone, and prolactin are individually and—when acting in concert with other brain chemicals—direct inducers of the yearning for connectivity, empathy, and conciliation; and because testosterone tends to direct its host to greater *independence* and *aggressive* activity—whose first priority is often competitive, not conciliatory or directly empathic—it's easy to notice how often girls will make the choice to try to reconcile, keep a relationship going, give up stubbornness and admit they are wrong for the sake of group cohesion, and conform to opinions that are presented aggressively in order to keep relational stability; the brain and its bio-chemicals are in large part creating this tendency *away from* independence and *toward* intimacy.

Thus, it is not only the existence of estrogen and other female chemicals that guides the female intimacy imperative, it is also the low amounts of testosterone in girls that enhance the imperative. As we mentioned earlier, when females increase their testosterone, they lose some of the intimacy imperative, becoming more ambitious, more independent, their self-concept less dependent on others' opinions of them, and their behavior more "male."

Saying this about hormonal differences does not mean that a girl cannot sometimes be one of the most independent people you know, or that a girl cannot aggressively pursue her desire to be the best basketball player on the court, a winner in everything she tries. Instead, we are saying that 1) more males around her for more years in a row, especially through adulthood, will tend to place the heaviest emphasis of their personal drive on hierarchical-competitive goals, and 2) males will find it easier at times to remain independent and stoic for months on end because they don't have an internal female hormonal cycle returning them, constantly, to the intimacy imperative.

If we want to look for one of the "male-specific" ways that boys and men push toward intimacy, one based in their hormones—one that contrasts, to an extent, with females—we would look toward what Macalester College professor Bob Obsatz, a male development specialist, calls "the sexualization of intimacy." Males, more than females, especially from age ten to whatever age they conceive children, attach more of intimacy to sex drive. Studies have even tracked word use among young males and females, finding that females use more words to create long-term bonds, and males use more words to create short-term sexual activity.

Every son wants love and affection, just like every daughter; every boy wants attachment and needs it, often desperately, as does every man. However, even down to use of words, hormones affect the imperative toward that intimacy in the sexes in different ways.

*When We Notice How Vulnerable Girls Can Be.* There is another way female biochemistry asks the world to notice its natural intimacy imperative, and one that every parent of a daughter has ached to better care for.

The female hormonal cycle creates natural mood instability and such a powerful wash of hormones that it is often not reasonable to think our adolescent daughter can handle what's going on inside her, or "act better," or "act the way we'd like her to." Her biosystem, her internal ecology, goes in and out of states of mild trauma.

One of humanity's highest goals has always been to give intimate love and attachment to those who clearly express or show their need for it. Females more often and more obviously evidence their need for empathy and intimacy than males. Girls ask for connectivity because it is connection, attention, intimacy, and attachment that help them feel, for many days a month, that they will be okay, they'll make it, they'll not be abandoned even though they become so difficult. A father of three—one girl and two boys—told me: "I see my daughter's fragility more often than my sons'. Her actions tell me when to give her more love."

His honesty resonates for many of us. Taken as a whole, the female hormonal system compels family, friends, and culture to constantly make the decision of empathy, of attachment, and of intimacy with girls. Girls cry, we hug them; girls talk, we talk with them. Mothers, fathers, husbands, boyfriends, coworkers are overtly challenged, by the nature of girls and women, to rise to highest ideals of patience, vision, and care. Instinctively a mother senses that even while her fifteen-year-old daughter, in Stage 4 of her cycle, will not generally say "I feel so lonely, so rejected, so worthless. Don't abandon me. Please, stay close," she is nonetheless feeling this within her drastic estrogen/progesterone floods and droughts. She wants more intimacy, even as she pulls away; and so the mother, father, or other caregiver keeps trying to reach out, perhaps seeking other ways to give intimacy than were given while she was happy in Stage 3. Now she may need more comfortable silences, or more requests from us (even as she says "No!") that she play basketball with us (physical exercise is a useful brain-mood stabilizer), or more small gifts, sweet cards, and special times. Generally, more than her brothers, or a husband, this daughter of ours will keep reminding us of the intimacy need because of the stages of her cycle. Hopefully, it is rare that we forget to reach out to her with hugs, cards, companionship. Her natural cycle is always reminding us to try as hard as we can to let her lead with her femininity, her emotional biology.

I hope in this chapter you've gotten an even deeper look through the looking glass into your daughter's inner life. In the remaining chapters of this book, while covering many aspects of raising girls, we will discover that every aspect is useful by the highest standard of attachment and love that our daughter, through her own internal process, is seeking to find and to deliver in her world.

As we integrate all this biological information into the practicalities of girls' relationships with mothers, fathers, other family members, other girls, and boys, and as we explore pressures our daughters feel in our culture, we will neither see female biology as a disease, nor avoid it. We will come from the theoretical base that our society cannot enhance or heal the lives of its daughters simply by pointing out gender stereotypes or encouraging "girl power." It must embrace the intimacy imperative girls live in. To do this, it must create a *three-family system* by which to raise every girl.

## The Three-Family System

In *The Wonder of Boys* I first introduced the term "three-family system." It is a term based on my study of thirty cultures worldwide. In this survey, I looked specifically for universal elements (both in our ancestral past and in the present) through which families raise the healthiest groups of children. I discovered that healthy children—both boys and girls—come, with highest statistical probability, from three-family systems:

- The first family is what our society calls "the nuclear family," a mom-dad family when traditional, but also a single-parent or blended family when necessary.

- The second family is what our society calls "the extended family," traditionally defined by grandparents nearby, but extending to include day care providers, mentors, counselors, coaches, and family friends *who become like grandma or grandpa or aunt or uncle.*

- The third family is what our society calls "institutions." Churches and schools are most traditional, but this family can include social service agencies, neighborhoods, community meeting places. For these institutions to qualify as third family, our children must have bonded with people and elements of these institutions in ways they would their own family members. For instance, a church or school is not third family just because a child goes there; she must have significant family-like bonds with adults in that community.

Children all over the world want to be raised in these three families. They yearn for the concentric circles of attachment. Most children who are disturbed or dangerous, or who have long-term psychological problems in adulthood, lack one or more significant bonds in one or more of the three families.

As parents of daughters, Gail and I are challenged to help create three families for our girls in ways that the female brain emphasizes: ways that protect our daughters' need to be protected and enlivened by constant, various sources of connectivity.

Enlivened by a mind that hardly ever turns off, my daughters are always in a state of interpretation, and experience heightened fears of abandonment and rejection. Their three families have to help them work with this state of mind almost constantly, especially once these girls enter Stage 2.

Children of large memories and intricate analyses, my daughters see things going on among their friends that often are not going on at all. They need the three families to teach them the codes of relationship, and even more importantly, be so stable as to give them safe environments in which to discover the codes themselves.

Structured for morality in some ways different from boys, my

daughters need the three families to teach them not only about themselves but about the confusing world of the male.

Touched by a baby's skin, or a doll's eyes, or a crying child in
ways a boy deduces, even enjoys, but does not as much crave, my
daughters need constant three-family safety, protection, and opportunity to give and receive intimate, hands-on care.

## The New Challenge

In Part II of this book, we specifically and practically explore what
girls need from their mom, dad, and other three-family members;
how to protect their emotional and moral development; how to
ensure rites of passage for them; how to inspire them to make a heroine's journey through life; and how to find meaning in their everyday
lives. We will explore parts of a whole—the whole is the creation of
the insurance that underwrites all other efforts: the stable, healthy
three-family system. In some cases, we'll call for a restructuring of
families, schools, and communities in order to provide girls with the
full life of love and discipline; in other cases—indeed, in many—we'll
recognize how well we're doing with girls. Overall, we'll enjoy the
possibility of enhancing girls' lives by the small change in everyday
experience that becomes, for our daughters, the large miracle of daily
love.

As we seek to be comprehensive by both exploring the specifics
and creating the whole, we will see how adaptable families are, how
if a bond is missing in the first family, we can create it in the second.
And we will, even if unconsciously, be making a commitment to meet
the new, twenty-first-century challenge of raising girls.

We will do this with an eye toward celebrating nature, but celebrating female biological design is not done to limit the options of
girls and women. Whenever I meet people who react to biological
information with "Aha, you see—girls and women should be obedi-
ent caregivers who give themselves up for their husbands and children," I know that they have not fully understood the wonder of
girls. Similarly, when I meet people who say "You're a throwback to

patriarchy," I know they too have not fully understood the nature of girls and women.

My daughters' biology gives them lots of options, in fact, it gives them, in many ways, more options than male biology gives males. In the next century, our civilization will gradually come to grips with this fact.

The world I envision for my daughters is one in which obstacles to meaning are removed. If my daughter finds great meaning in climbing to the top of a corporate ladder, so be it. If she finds meaning in caring for children, so be it. If she finds meaning in both, so be it. I trust her internal world to guide her. My job, and her culture's job, is to help her know that world, and protect it vigorously with close and intimate bonds.

In the next section of this book we will explore more practically what a girl needs from the people who love her. We'll divide practical information into separate chapters—for instance, one on mothering and one on fathering a daughter—but let's agree that all of us are in partnership with our girls. Mothers, fathers, extended family, and schools need to work together. Some of the things I give responsibility for to the mother, in this book, can be given to the father, and vice versa. Our girls strive to live in the web lines that connect moms, dads, and everyone else. Let's explore what girls need from home, school, and community so that they can feel, as they move between their caregivers and within their community, that they are living the wonder of girls.

# PART II

## What Girls Need

*"A child's life is like a piece of paper on which every passerby leaves a mark."*

—Ancient Chinese proverb

# 4

# THE ARTFUL MOTHER

## WHAT GIRLS NEED FROM MOM

*"Opening and closing the gates of heaven*
*Are you able to play the role of mother?"*
—Tao Te Ching

Gabrielle Lauren Gurian came into this world on a wintery day in February, with labor beginning on Valentine's Day night. Gail and I had enjoyed a quiet dinner, shared loving cards, and then gone to bed. Gail woke up around 2:00 A.M. Her water had broken.

Gail and I were both thirty-two years old. We had read all the books, talked to elder family and friends, prepared for both the worst and the best. Gail's body was ready to evict this little living thing—Gabrielle, like many firstborns, had already passed her due date—but Gail confessed, on Valentine's Day, to trepidations. There was nothing in the world that compared to becoming a mother, she said aloud. It was exhilarating and frightening, both. "Will I be a good mother?" she worried, with all her heart.

Now it was the middle of the night, and we called our physician's service. The decision was made to come into the hospital the next day, as contractions were still far apart. We tried to sleep a little, then got up, showered, and went in to begin what would turn out to be, indeed, a most frightening adventure.

Gabrielle was born safely, but not until forty hours later. By the time she was born, there had been more medical personnel in Gail's room than two young, inexperienced, not-quite-parents-yet could have imagined possible. Gail had experienced hypertension earlier in the month, but as the birth became imminent, her blood pressure shot up to frightening levels. At about thirty hours into the birth, an emergency caesarean section was planned. "If the epidural doesn't lower her blood pressure," the doctor said, "we'll have to do a C-section right away." At that point, there were nine hospital personnel hovering—three doctors, a midwife, nurses, and other techs. Then, suddenly, the epidural worked, lowering her blood pressure. Gail returned to the path of a nonemergency delivery. There was talk now of a possible vaginal birth.

But ten hours later, after dilation did not go beyond 9 (it hovered at 9 for eight of those hours), the doctors were back.

"We have to get this baby out!" they said, and the C-section transpired.

As Gail's supporter, I was in a trance of exhaustion, commitment, fear for her and the child, and anticipation. Just before they gave the baby to Gail, I cut the umbilical cord, one of the most significant events in my life. Gail, though groggy from medication, and I, lost in both the grandeur and the bloody reality of the moment, could not stop ourselves from crying.

As Gail recovered, as the baby slept, as friends came and went, I wrote a letter to Gabrielle, telling her about the whole experience, and wondering how she would experience her parents. Gail awakened, asked what I was doing, and upon hearing my reply, smiled. "Yes, tell her everything. Tell her I'll never make anything more important to me than she is." Already, in those moments, the mother's bond with her child was asserted.

I knew that Gail's fears—"Will I be a good mother?"—were already diminished, for now Gabrielle was here, and Gail had already begun to care for her. Gail had become a mother.

## A Mother's Love

Long before our first child came, the light of motherhood was in Gail's eyes. She enjoyed holding babies. We often joked about how, in Ankara, Turkey, where we lived before having children, she cared for the stray cats along our back doorway, and even the ants that emerged, every night, in our kitchen sink. Every morning I watched her help the ants out of the sink on a piece of typing paper, to save their lives.

Gail's body and mind sought and found small beings to care for. When she said, toward the end of our second year in Ankara, "It's time to go back to America, our home, and have children," she assumed her right to become a mother of her own children; she knew it viscerally, and I, as a man, knew that her internal call—her "biological clock" so often joked about in our culture—was in fact a sacred thing, a voice of spiritual importance. Gail and I knew that clock to be, indeed, biological—oxytocin, estrogen, nerve chemicals—but also mysterious: a child, yet unconceived, calling to her from the world of the unborn. My role was to say, "Okay, let's do it," and protect and nurture her right to motherhood *above all else.*

In this chapter, and in others, we want to pay special attention to specific individuals and family systems in which mother and father are not both, at all times, present. While we know that in a book like this one we cannot deal with every type of family, we also know that every type of family exists, especially now, as we enter the new millennium. While most of what we discuss in this book can be applied to any parenting situation—for instance, nearly everything in this chapter is useful to both intact families and single mothers—there are specific needs in specific families, and we will hope to address some of these as well. Much of what we'll discuss begins with the mother.

From the mother, a daughter receives not only life, but an absolutely loyal mirror of herself. A mother cajoles, cries, laughs, convinces, dresses, bathes, listens, directs, praises, shows her disappointment, adapts, and is omnipresent.

A mother's sounds are to her infant what the best poetry is to a sophisticated adult, or the song a teenager will not forget long into old age. A mother's eyes carry a piece of her daughter's soul, and that brings to the relationship of mother and daughter an intrinsic understanding of each other, and at some point, the need to pull away.

To mother a daughter is an act of great love, for the mother gets the chance to be of service not only to this new life but also to all the unbidden memories of her own girlhood. To mother any child is the supreme act of self-sacrifice, for there is little room for a mother's ego when a child's soul is so constantly beckoning for love and attention.

Mothering is a sacred profession that has, in our day and age, been relegated to a sub-profession; hence, mothers live today in an unavoidable tension, a juggling of selves, and at times, a kind of shame. Given the way nature is, right before our eyes, calling most women, no matter their culture, to mother children at a certain stage of their lives, the tension mothers feel today is a sadness they carry along with their passionate, intense love of their children.

Gail, after returning to the U.S., continued in her career as a family therapist, leaving her job at the American Embassy in Ankara for a job with Catholic Family Service in Spokane, but she felt sometimes desperate tension between the natural need to have children and the demands of a career. She knew that if she stopped her career to be a mother she would be inadequate in the eyes of some people, but if she continued her career while being a mother, she'd be inadequate in the eyes of others.

Ever since we had our two children and Gail moved to part-time employment, she has lived in that tension of self, and she knows it is very difficult not to pass on the self-recrimination to Gabrielle and Davita. Gail and I were startled one day to hear Gabrielle, at eleven, come home from school and say, "I think maybe it won't be all right if I become a mother." We asked her what she meant. She talked about a conversation she had had at a sleepover. Her friend's mother was talking to the girls about how hard it was to work as a legal secretary and take care of children. She talked also about what she gave up to have children.

"She wanted to be a lawyer," Gabrielle told us, "but she couldn't because she had children. I think maybe it won't be all right if I have children." Feeling this mother's regret and confusion, Gabrielle was asking, in her own way, if it would be all right for her to become a mother.

This moment sobered us. We worked hard to make sure not to overreact to it, because it was more an exploration of feelings and of the future for our daughter than a plan for life. We told her that there was another way to think about being a woman, a way to think about natural stages of a woman's life, and to value herself based on what she does in various stages of her future. We told her the final arbiter of her womanhood might not be the business world she moved in and out of during her life. We talked to her about how important it was to let her own body, mind, self, and family tell her what to value.

When she asked, "But which is better, being a mother or being a lawyer?" we felt a twinge of real sadness for the pressure already put on her at a young age. We answered as we believe, "Being a mother is more important than being a lawyer in our family's value system, but you don't have to see them as better or worse. If you want to, you can do both at different stages of your life." In conversations over the next couple of days, Gail and I sat together in order to decide how to explain women's roles to our daughter. Then, that weekend, we described to Gabrielle a nature-based model for looking at motherhood, one we hope will help you as you talk about motherhood (and experience it) with your own daughters. All our daughters will face the tension that mothers today face. One of the primary things they need from our culture as a whole, from mothers, and from others who support them, is a model for seeing women's lives that allows for the absolute sanctity of mothering.

## A Season for Mothering

When we do not think about girls and women as children of nature, it is not difficult to embattle their psychological development in a lifelong choice between seeking status in the workplace and fulfilling the need to care for children. When we think about the material presented in Chapters 2 and 3, the intimacy imperative inherent in a girl's neuroemotional development and a woman's life path, we see other possibilities, for inherent in female nature is not only an imperative to intimacy but also the natural cycle of life, a cycle that unfolds in *seasons* of womanhood.

*There are natural stages to a woman's life, and every daughter wants to know what they are.* While there are certainly more stages to a woman's life than the four in this model, and while there are exceptions to everything said here, to live only the exceptions and caveats is to rob our daughters of real-life discussion in the family of basic human nature. And so we propose to them these four stages in the motherhood process:

STAGE 1: Before a woman has children, she is experimenting with love relationships that, even if she's unconscious about it, live or die for her in large degree based on how she assesses the man as father and husband material.

STAGE 2: Once she has children, caring for them becomes *her highest calling*——her nature wants to organize life around care of her children.

STAGE 3: As her children grow and detach from her, she will find herself gravitating back to the primacy of other pursuits, and developing new sides of herself, personally and professionally.

STAGE 4: Once her children are grown, she may well return to experimenting, trying on new professions and selves.

In teaching this model to our daughters, we are teaching them some "subtexts," which we have to take responsibility for in our dialogue with them.

1. That our understanding of female nature shows us a primal need among most females to be mothers and to be supported, for a period of many years, by husband, extended family, and culture in performing the duties and experiencing the unique love of mothering.

2. That to fully mother, a woman may, throughout her moth-

ering years, keep up a profession—in the cases of many, even most women in our economic system, this may be necessary, and very helpful—but she will regret her life if her profession is pursued to the detriment of fully experiencing motherhood.

3. If she does choose to work professionally—part-time or full-time—during the season of mothering, she will need to make sure her children have a "second mother" (this could be an at-home dad), one or more day care providers, a nanny, and/or grandmother or auntie, who nurture the child with her, with consistency of attachment to the child.

In teaching these things, we teach our daughters to plan their mothering years toward the highest possibilities for themselves and their families, but never to sacrifice the care of the child to any other social goal. In developing this womanist philosophy, we are not agreeing with the conventional idea that the predominant issue facing a family is economics. The issue we are addressing is not one of economics (we trust that our daughters will make the best economic decisions they can make during their mothering season); we are coaching them to be smart about their economic base, but not to believe they must give up their nature—their desire to put mothering above all else—just because they live in an economy-based culture that measures soul not by how a woman shows compassion and shapes her babies into adults, but by her professional and financial success.

In teaching this philosophy and this logic, we are realistic that it must not boomerang, and end up making mothers as restricted as they were in the 1950s. The womanist philosophy, concerned heavily with the natural stages of a woman's life, is useful to girls and women because it is a path to freedom, not social constriction. It is a middle ground between the old view: a woman must stay home—and the feminist view: a woman must conquer the workplace.

In the womanist view Gail and I teach our daughters, a woman can do both *during the season of life in which her nature guides her to do each*; and the essential job of a civilization is to protect *both* the woman's right to professional success during those seasons of her life and her right to mothering during its season. Civilization is measured, in this view, by how it bends over backwards to assure the success of a woman of balance, and ensure the possibility that a mother can mother her children fully.

There are two other subtexts we teach our daughters. Each is somewhat controversial, yet each needs to be discussed.

The first subtext is that for the stage of life called "mothering" to be fully respected, our culture will have to focus more heavily on what a *mother* needs than what a *woman* needs. Mothering will have to return to center stage in dialogues about women's lives. Especially among feminists, it will have to move out of the background, and into the foreground. Debates about glass ceilings are an example of this.

Most mothers who work professionally while raising children will experience a glass ceiling. Because they honor motherhood above all else during the motherhood season, they end up working part-time, or working full-time but compromising in some ways to stay closer to their children; thus, they may not advance in professional hierarchies as completely as many men. Feminism has held up the destruction of the glass ceiling as a panacea for women. This panacea will not generally be reached by mothers in our womanist, staged view of a woman's life.

But the woman will gain back the sense that she is a mother above all else, and need not feel judged for missing a corporate ladder. As Gail said to me while we worked on this chapter, "If I can become an old woman with the knowledge that I raised my girls really well, I'm willing to give up being a CEO or getting every promotion."

For Gail to become fully sanguine with herself as a mother who mothers first and finds corporate success second, she has needed the support of her husband, friends who join her in putting mothering first, and some good luck in being able to work part-time while mothering. She has made the conscious choice to approach her life and its demands from a nature-based point of view rather than an economy-based social dialogue. It is one of the most intriguing, and tragic, elements of our culture that to give up the tension a mother feels today as she strives to give her love, she must choose between nature and nurture.

A second controversial subtext in our womanist, staged perspective about which we are honest with our daughters involves their differences, as girls, from boys. We ask them to consider the idea that a man's life is simpler than a woman's. (We should note again that we know we are generalizing—that many women never have children and many men don't fit a simplified explanation.) A boy grows into puberty without a monthly reproductive cycle—instead, he experiences a diurnal hormonal cycle that helps him perform in a socially productive (or destructive) way. His connection with reproduction is not as intimate as an adolescent girl's.

When he becomes an adult, he is generally on a path of social production that he will follow, even as he changes jobs and careers, throughout his life. Should he engage in reproduction, he will hopefully devote himself to his children but his life path can differ in two crucial ways from his wife's:

1. He will not experience the hormonal, biochemical bond with his children his wife has. His bond will mainly be social and psychological. To think of it as a "lesser" bond is incorrect. It is, however, a bond of different quality. Not to note this reality is to rob the mother of the special quality of her bond with her offspring.

2. The presence of the child in his life will usually not (though there are certainly exceptions) impinge as severely on the continuation of his social production as it will almost definitely impinge on the social production of his child's mother.

In discussing this with our daughters, we are asking them to notice and contemplate, while they are growing up, a basic truth about human nature: that the natural demands of reproduction are, in terms of personal time and ego sacrificed, more severe than the social demands of production. We ask our girls, while adolescents, to face this truth and make decisions about men, marriage, work, and their future life with an understanding of basic human nature in tow.

"There is a season in your life when you will probably want to have children," we teach our daughters. "In preparation for that season, here are two crucial things you must decide:

1. "WHAT will you sacrifice in order to be a mother? You need to prepare for this sacrifice, lay the groundwork, create the home, put things in order for years before. You don't want to try to do this alone, nor until you are ready from an economic and emotional standpoint.

2. "WHO will be the father? You have to select very carefully, with not only romantic love in mind, but also how the man 1) will support you during the seasons you devote to childcare, and 2) how he himself is suited to father your children."

We teach our daughters that once they have a child, nothing is more important than the nurturing of that child. We believe that if girls know this, they are freed of a great deal of psychological confusion. They now have the highest standard by which to create their world during their mothering years. They can judge whether they want to work full- or part-time, when they want to return to work, what workplace conquest they might give up in order to cut work time back to part-time or whether to be strictly a stay-at-home mom. They can make these judgments without feeling that they've become second-class, or a "non-professional" who has "given up" what is really important—full-time career work—in order to mother children. They hold to the idea that it is first-class, once a woman has children, to be a mother, and workplace activity is valuable, but secondary. Then, when the mothering stage ends for the woman, workplace productively can return to its ascendancy in personal self-image.

In teaching this philosophy, we are not teaching our girls to envision a life of unhealthy dependence on a man, or one in which they must give up all workplace activities during their children's years of maturation. Nor are we saying that their husbands couldn't stay home with the children for a few years while our daughters worked outside the home. The womanist philosophy we teach allows for *every* possibility, while presenting girls with a staged blueprint for life to hold up against the chaos of those possibilities.

We teach our daughters the primacy of mothering even knowing that they may end up having to work full-time once they become mothers; that they may make difficult marital choices or suffer eco-

nomic hardship; that they may face abandonment or divorce. While
we teach our children to be realistic about the sufferings life can and
will give them, we still teach our daughters the ideal of motherhood
because it is motherhood that they will remember on their deathbed.
Should they choose during their childbearing years to have children,
it is their children, grandchildren, and great-grandchildren who will
surround them during their elder years, when they've matured
beyond either the season of childbearing or of profession. They will
know they've truly lived because, during the season of life set up by
nature for having children, they devoted themselves to being who
they truly were: mothers fully capable of giving a mother's love.

## From Mommy to Mom: Mothering a Daughter Through Childhood and Adolescence

Being a mother today involves experiencing the sacredness of one's
work, and passing on the confidence of that sacredness to daughters.

While we must all work to help this transpire in our cultural
rethinking, it is also done very practically, every moment of the day.
The mother is the artist of her child. Let's talk now about *how* to
practice the art of mothering—and thus, how to get the most out of
our daughters as we provide the mothering they need. Much of the
material in this chapter will be divided into the four stages of a girl's
development as discussed in Chapter 3.

Because our girls each mature at a different pace, let's agree to let
these four stages be highly adaptable to your family's reality. You as a
mother intuitively know your daughter's stages of growth. Let your
intuition be your ultimate guide.

I hope that as this chapter proceeds, you'll find answers to some
of your toughest questions as a mother of a daughter. I hope, also,
that dads will read this material, as they are so crucial in helping a
mother artfully and effectively mother a girl. Some areas of emotional, moral, and spiritual development will be reserved specifically
for Chapters 6 through 8.

## COMMUNICATING WITH YOUR DAUGHTER

Mothering a daughter is a constant communication. If you're not talking to your daughter, you're listening to her. And if neither of you is speaking, nonverbal communication carries constant messages.

There are a number of tricky communication areas mothers get into with girls. Keeping healthy communication going is, after understanding your daughter's nature, perhaps the most important thing in the mother-daughter relationship.

As this chapter progresses, you may notice that there is an undercurrent running through it: helping mothers build bonds with daughters that allow for constant, healthy communication.

## The Artful Mother in Stage 1:
## Birth to Five Years Old

In the first few years of life, communication (much of it nonverbal) is a key to attachment. Making sure mother and daughter are attached is absolutely crucial, for it is upon that attachment that the health of the girl's future, and the mother-daughter relationship, greatly relies. If there is a sacrifice to be made in the family toward ensuring this attachment, now is the time to make it. If a father must work harder so the mother can take more time off, it is his sacred duty to do so. If a mother can take maternity leave for more than two months, or work part-time, or take the baby to work, or find another innovation to stay *in close proximity to her daughter and physically hold and cuddle her and communicate with her frequently throughout the day,* she must do so. Not only does the mother biologically yearn for this, but so does the child; and many, if not most, of her daughter's later problem areas, should those arise—like self-cutting, eating disorders, depression—will be either primarily or secondarily caused by inadequate attachment in the first three years of life, or at least exacerbated, a priori, by that inadequate attachment.

Secure attachment of mother (in some cases, at-home fathers play the role of "mother," as do grandparents or other caregivers) to daughter was ensured in previous cultures because mothers could carry their infants on their chests or backs while they worked at gathering tubers, at the marketplace, or as they planted and harvested in fields.

*Our culture is very different: It is not "nature-based," but rather, "economy-based."* If mothers work, they generally cannot hold their babies on their chests or backs for long periods of the day. They cannot coo at them, talk to them, be available to be smelled by them, to be tasted at the breast, to be seen, eye-to-eye, to be heard. Among primate infants (including humans), *infant attachment to the primary caregiver* (usually the mother if she survives childbirth) *is one of the primary indicators of later success as an adult,* both in forming attachments and intimacy, and in finding a respected place in social networks. But our society, focused so heavily on economic success, forgets this.

*Becoming Attached* by Robert Karen, *Oneness and Separateness* by Louise Kaplan, *The Earliest Relationship* by T. Berry Brazelton and Bertrand C. Cramer, *The Motherhood Constellation* by Daniel N. Stern, and *A Secure Base* by John Bowlby are crucial reading for any mother (and anyone who supports her) who feels uncertain about the importance of mother-infant attachment, or simply disbelieves its importance.

Mother-infant attachment is a very serious matter. Some researchers argue it is the foundation of a civilization. It is certainly the basis for all later mother-child communication.

## THE QUESTION OF CHILD CARE

In our contemporary reality, it is often not possible for working mothers and their daughters (or sons) to be attached to each other twenty-four hours a day, seven days a week, after a few months of maternity leave. Among our ancestors, this was sometimes the case as well. In most of these cases, the mother had died in childbirth. A "second mother" took over. Children were born into a three-family system that was strong scaffolding against even this terrible tragedy. A grandmother or auntie became the child's mother.

Even when the mother was alive, she generally shared mothering attachment with at least one other woman (again, usually a grandmother or auntie).

As industrialization took over our economic system, and mothers began to have to work away from their infants and toddlers, they felt secure that the attachment needs of their children were being covered because they left their child, for a few hours, with a relative who was experienced and cared about the child by nature of blood connection.

In the United States, however, far more than in any other culture, this mother/second mother-of-the-same-blood was not possible for many, if not most, families. Mothers lived far away from blood kin. The day care industry filled in the vacuum left by families having to move from city to city to find meaningful, well-paying work.

While there are many innovations today available to mothers who need to work (fathers staying home with infants and toddlers is one of the most interesting), including wonderful day care centers, the reality most mothers face is that, if they are going to work, they will give the care of their child to a stranger. That stranger may well not be paid very much, and will seek other, higher-paying employment when she can. This is especially the case in large day care centers. These individuals are not able to bond completely with infants and toddlers.

Thus, the mother today is hit with a double whammy her great-grandmother, or even her mother, may not have felt. She yearns to be with her child (weeps as her daughter weeps every morning at the day care door), and yet can't be; yearns to give her child to someone she loves and trusts, but often cannot.

As our society comes to better understand female nature, basic attachment, and the intimacy imperative, the culture of day care will change to better support mothers. It will change in three crucial ways that can be your guide, as a mother as you choose a day care:

1. Day care centers will become smaller, or large day care centers will construct smaller units of care within them (e.g., two infants for each adult caregiver, or eight toddlers for two caregivers);

2. Day care providers will be paid the wages of teachers, so they can make day care a profession; thus, staying for years and attaching to children over long periods of time; and

3. Day care centers will become like an "aunt's" house or

"grandma's." Owners, providers, volunteers will bond with parents, form a caregiving adult community that allows for parents to see their children as often as needed, to "drop in," to share adult lives and bonds within the community.

These kinds of day care centers already exist, and can be a mother's best friend. In them, a mother and father, during their first visit, will notice many adult caregivers but not an overwhelming number of kids; order rather than chaos; cleanliness, brightness—not only on walls, but on the caregivers' faces; an employment record that shows caregivers at work in the location for a year or more; and an open-door policy.

In our children's early years, Gail and I utilized part-time day care, finding a center, Pavlish Playhouse, that fit the description I've just given. It was a wonderful place of attachment and early childhood learning; our daughters' lives are the better for it. Gail made the final choice of what day care we would utilize, and became friends with Marianne Pavlish, the center's owner, and Jennifer Anderson, one of its long-term employees. Our daughters consider these women to be like their aunties.

Should you, as a mother, need to work away from your infant or toddler child, and should other innovations be unavailable (stay-at-home dad, grandmother, nanny), this kind of day care is not only "an okay option," it is a very good one. Good day care centers and preschools can, like a grandmother or auntie, enhance a child's chances for happiness and success. A child can be raised by a first and second mother through the crucial brain development years of birth to about five years old.

## PROVIDING DISCIPLINE IN STAGE 1

Perhaps the most discussed topic regarding birth-to-kindergarten-age girls, after the issues of attachment and day care, is the issue of discipline. Should you as a mother have intricate logistical questions about how to care for your infant daughter's health, feeding, and other survival needs, I highly recommend the books by Arlene

Eisenberg, Heidi E. Murkoff, and Sandee E. Hathaway entitled *What to Expect When You're Expecting* and *What to Expect in the First Year*, and continuing from there.

Should you have equally intricate questions regarding love, affection, and stimulation, the books on attachment that I referred to earlier—especially the work of T. Berry Brazelton—are very useful.

On the issue of discipline, let's focus here on specific discipline techniques, then the issue of spanking.

Discipline is most effective when it is part of a *discipline system*. This system is set up among primary caregivers (mom, dad, child care), and hopefully applied, in terms of core values and procedures, in extended family, school, church, and other parts of the three families.

Discipline is only in small part about punishment; in large part, it is about building character, testing self-esteem, and teaching social skills that will ultimately create a *self-disciplined* adolescent and adult.

As your daughter moves through the stage of life from birth to about kindergarten, you are constantly ordering her life. While you follow her lead a great deal of the time (you give her your breast or, if necessary, the bottle when *she's* hungry), you are also taking charge (disciplining) by creating, for instance, a sleep schedule for her. (For parents having specific troubles with their child's sleep patterns, I recommend *Solving Your Child's Sleep Problems*, by Richard Ferber.) This sleep schedule can be part of a discipline system if it fits with the other discipline techniques you use.

If, for instance, you force your two-year-old to learn to potty train, but you also let her stay up till whatever time at night she wishes, the inconsistency confuses her development. Her mind is chaotic enough already as it grows in leaps and bounds. For *basic* training of her *natural* impulses (sleeping, eating, going to the bathroom), it seeks consistency and builds self-discipline by knowing what to expect and how to achieve what's expected, not just in one area—potty training—but in all areas.

The consistency we are discussing here—consistency of expectations, consistency of consequences—is the bedrock of building self-confidence and self-discipline in your daughter. It is the bedrock also of the specific discipline techniques that work most effectively in raising a girl.

TECHNIQUE 1: *Change the Environment.* When your daughter is doing something that shows lack of discipline (it's just plain wrong!)—pulling the cat's tail, let's say—you change the environment by taking the cat away.

TECHNIQUE 2: *Verbalize the Wrong.* As much as you can, verbalize what your daughter has done wrong at or near the time she's done it. "Pulling Kitty's tail hurts her. It's wrong to do."

TECHNIQUE 3: *Showing, Rather than Telling.* Sometimes, beyond saying "No!" or "Don't do that!" or "That's hurting Kitty!" we need to show our children the pain they cause. This is most needed if your daughter is repeatedly doing something wrong—again, pulling the cat's tail. After a third time, you can change the environment, verbalize, and you can lightly pinch your daughter, showing her what it feels like to have a "tail" pulled. She'll generally get the point (and, of course, this cannot be a violent pinch, or it is abusive).

TECHNIQUE 4: *Distraction and Diversion.* Well into the toddler years, you can distract your daughter in order to command her. You yourself may have practiced this artfulness, or seen other parents doing so: Your daughter won't come into the house from the car, preferring to linger in the snow; you could try commanding verbally, or even yelling, but it is more artful to say, "Come help me call Grandma, would you?" Your daughter can't wait to help.

TECHNIQUE 5: *Negotiation and Choices.* If you want your toddler to do something and she says "No!" you might try asking her again, then you might try negotiating. This builds a child's brain. She has to think to negotiate.

Of course, you'll want to save this artful gesture for a few special times in a day. More frequently, you can use the tack of asking her again, then on the third go-around, giving her two choices (no more). "You can either put that book on that shelf, or you can sit on your bed, which do you choose?"

TECHNIQUE 6: *Give Her a Moment.* Interestingly, studies show us that boys need more time than girls to process a demand, command, or recommendation. So parents of sons notice, even more than parents of daughters, that they can tell a child to do something and their daughter will do it a little quicker. Nonetheless, the brain development of all Stage 1 children does not include much capacity for instantaneous action. Often, if you give your daughter a half minute or a minute to fulfill an expectation, she'll do it. If you want her to do it right away, you may be creating needs for punishment that grow not from wrongness of her action, but incompleteness of your own understanding of what her brain can do.

TECHNIQUE 7: *Time-Out and Loss of Privileges.* In most cases, your daughter will need no more than the loss of a privilege (or toy), or a time-out (one minute for every year she is old, sitting alone in a designated "time-out" chair) when she is refusing (after three tries) to do as told, or otherwise not meeting your expectations for discipline.

These, then, are fundamentals of a discipline system. For many parents, spanking is a fundamental question of discipline.

## THE QUESTION OF SPANKING

Nearly every month I receive an e-mail or letter inquiring about spanking. In nearly every case, the parent who writes wants to make sure to discipline in a way that does not harm a daughter's emotional safety. I too have spent a great deal of time both agonizing over this issue and studying it.

To answer the question of spanking, let me start with our household.

Our daughters have rarely been spanked, yet there have been moments when they've received a swat on the bottom, and they learned what they needed to learn at the moment. In each of their lives, they've been swatted in this way probably ten times total. Perhaps hundreds of times they've been in time-out, lost privileges, spent time in their rooms.

Gail and I belong to the group of families that utilizes other techniques for discipline, erring on the side of not spanking because it is our suspicion that there are more peaceful, authoritative methods of discipline available to us; we can accomplish discipline while best protecting our daughters' emotional development.

This suspicion was recently corroborated by the American Academy of Pediatrics, which, after decades of study, released these findings:

- Spanking children under eighteen months of age may cause injury and the child will rarely, at that age, even understand why she is being hit.

- Spanking can alter parent-child relationships, making emotional bonds more difficult.

- Repeated spankings may not only cause more aggressive behavior in children, but may also lead children to become more physically aggressive with parents, especially in adolescence.

- Spanking is a kind of all-or-nothing technique. Because relying on it makes other discipline methods less effective with children, spanking itself can become the only, or the major, way to solve problems.

- The more children are spanked, the more anger they report as adolescents and adults.

- The more children are spanked, the more likely they are to hit children and spouses when they are adults.

- Spanking has been associated with higher rates of violence, substance abuse, and crime.

Will a few swats on the bottom once in a while harm your daughter's emotional life? Probably not. There are times when we look back at our own childhoods and say, "I remember that time I got spanked for such-and-such. I really needed that." On the other hand, given the potential emotional consequences of physical violence in any relationship, as much as we can avoid or control spanking the better.

There are some "spanking rules" we can follow. If we spank, it is best to leave the child's pants or skirt on—making your daughter strip naked or "pull your skirt up" before being spanked is unnecessarily humiliating and thus can be emotionally damaging. If we spank, we want to make sure not to hit anywhere but the bottom, to use no weapons or belts, to wait as much as possible until our own anger or rage has calmed down, and to both explain why we are doing what we're doing, and make sure to reconnect with our daughter, emotionally, afterward.

## TEACHING MANNERS

Throughout your daughter's life, and beginning in her toddler years, she wants and needs to learn manners. By nature she wants to keep relationships and social intimacies stable and friendly. While she won't be afraid to fight, manipulate, cajole, and exploit others at times—all children experiment with these things—it would be inconsistent with her nature to think, "Teaching her manners just forces her into a feminine mold," or some other "anti-manners" philosophy. Girls love social manners; manners make them feel safer.

- By the time your daughter can walk, she can walk with you to see friends to the door.
- She does not need to consistently interrupt adult conversation.
- She needs to learn the magic words "Please" and "Thank you," as well as "Excuse me."
- She does not need to run through the room where adults are talking.

These are basic manners. At times, if you or others have not given your daughter enough loving attention, she'll act out by running through the room, or interrupting. If this is happening, your daughter needs conversation and discipline, and your awareness that this behavior signals that your daughter is feeling a lack of attachment and needs reattachment (about five or ten minutes of mother-daughter alone-time generally does it).

## THE IMPORTANCE OF CHORES

From as early as she can begin picking up books she's dropped, or cleaning up after herself, your daughter wants the sense of accomplishment that both spontaneous and ritualized chores give her. Spontaneous ones are ones that just happen—she drops something and you ask her to pick it up (even though you're tempted to just do it yourself). This builds a sense of responsibility in her. Ritualized chores are, for instance, cleaning a section of her room once a week at three years old (probably with your help) but then by five, cleaning her room (even if imperfectly) herself once a week.

## THE BEGINNINGS OF SPIRITUAL LIFE

Raising a girl is so much easier when parents have the help of unseen aids and authorities. Not only does spiritual life make a girl (or boy) feel safer in the world ("God's in charge so I'm okay"), but it also fits parental authority into a higher authority.

Neurobiology, as I understand it, consistently supports the importance of spiritual life (everything from reading the Bible or other sacred stories, to talking with nature, to going to church) in child development. The human brain, especially in life's early years, is growing tissue and moving neurotransmitters in the four lobes at the top of the brain, the lobes in which "consciousness" and "higher understanding" take place. Your daughter's brain yearns to expand into nature, the unknown; yearns to think that "God has a plan," or "Where do dead people go?" or "Are there angels?"

Church and other faith-communities, as well as spiritual stories in books, make for greater bonding and expanded self-discipline in all children, even in toddlers, who we may think aren't "getting it." A parent or parents with a spiritual bent may well raise a brighter, calmer, more self-confident, and more loving daughter because they shared the unknown world with her.

## MEDIA USE

We will discuss television, movies, and other media in greater detail later in this chapter, and also in the Appendix. For infants, however, it is crucial we say that the American Academy of Pediatrics, after decades of research, recommends no visual media for children two years old or younger. The human brain, until nearly two years old, can be negatively affected by the quickness by which images move on-screen.

While one *Barney* show here or there won't hurt your infant daughter, a lot of TV use will. A day care that relies on TV to babysit is a potentially dangerous place, as is a home in which infants and early toddlers watch a lot of television.

I hope in this section we've covered some of your basic questions. Issues like discipline will come up again in the next chapter.

Now, carrying with us the assumption that most themes and techniques introduced for a previous stage will, with modification for maturity, fit a later stage, let's look at crucial developmental issues your Stage 2 girls might present to you, and nature-based strategies and techniques you can use to raise these girls.

## The Artful Mother in Stage 2: Six to Ten Years Old

When your daughter becomes of school age, you find new challenges. Here are some issues that many mothers ask about. They have certainly come up with my own daughters. Because *The Wonder of Girls* hopes to provide basics of nature-based child development, but cannot, in this space, provide minutiae, let me recommend a year-by-year resource by Louise Ames and others at the Gesell Institute. The series begins with *Your One-Year-Old*, and continues through *Your Ten- to Fourteen-Year-Old*.

## DEALING WITH LYING AND STEALING

When Gabrielle was five, she took candy, on the sly, from a grocery store shelf while shopping with Gail. Gail discovered it after she got home, marched Gabrielle back to the store, made her apologize and pay for the candy, and let her eat no candy for a week. Gabrielle did not steal again; she was absolutely mortified and shamed in front of the store clerks.

A friend told me about her daughter, eight, who lied to her about nearly everything for about a week. My friend remained patient, for she was going through a divorce and knew her children would act out. But finally, after a week, she exacted punishments, and compelled the behavior to change.

Both Gail and our friend were faced with an emotional-moral dilemma. Gabrielle faced shame in front of the clerks, and our friend's daughter needed emotional outlets for her stress, yet both parents chose to compel "the right values" rather than protect short-term emotional equilibrium.

So often this is needed as you face lying, cheating, or stealing. Gabrielle's action, and the actions of our friend's daughter, were developmentally normal, both as experimental behavior and as a stress response. Yet they must still be dealt with, right away. Time-outs, loss of privileges, or loss of allowance are good punishments. Our friend made her daughter, who lied, pay a dollar per lie (she received five dollars a week in allowance) to the mother. Quickly, she lost three weeks' allowance. This cured her of lying.

## HOLDING CLEAR AUTHORITY

A teacher in Missouri told me this story:

She had taken her daughter, nine, to a birthday party at a house with a swimming pool. When it was time for the birthday girl and her friends to get out of the pool, the birthday girl became whiny. It took nearly ten minutes to get her out. Her parents cajoled her, threatened her, begged her. The teacher confessed, "It got so bad, the parents were embarrassed, and so were we." The mother apologized, later, when the kids were playing with unwrapped gifts, to a group of moms: "I have such trouble being hard on her. I want to protect her independence and self-esteem. But she's so . . . so stubborn."

Often these days we fear "crushing a girl's self-esteem" but act against what she is, by nature, asking for. This mother wanted most of all to raise an independent girl, not one who would be intimidated by others. She was trying to protect her daughter from having what we've called "the malleable self" by letting her daughter, from early on, develop her own authority and not be malleable to others' authority, even her mother's.

In following this course, she missed the fact that a child learns to be an authority by modeling after others *who hold clear and competent authority*. It is the child raised by people without strength who becomes weak. It is the child raised with high expectations who becomes independent. And it is the child raised to act well who acts well—including acting well when faced with others who are strong, later in life. Girls don't "become independent" and "have high self-esteem" because they act out, to the shame and embarrassment of others, when they won't come out of a swimming pool. *They have high self-esteem because they act appropriately, and feel good about doing so.* They have high self-esteem because they esteem their parents and caregivers. The teaching of self-worth and self-esteem is, thus, not an individual effort of a stubborn girl, but a group effort accomplished in a web of relationships in which authority and expectations are clear, and the child rises, proudly, to meet them.

Each of us has been those parents cajoling their daughter. Each of us has feared that we would "crush the independence" of our daughters if we "became too authoritarian." The mother, and we ourselves, have nothing to be ashamed of. We must do all we can to give our girls the lease on their own lives. But it is crucial, as we do this, we don't forget to what a great extent their sense of their own worthiness comes from meeting expectations, not from controlling their parents.

## DEALING WITH WHINING

One way to measure success as parents is to watch the tenor of whining in your girls. Every girl whines, but how much is too much?

In our home we practice a No Whining policy. Whining is considered improper behavior, and ultimately unsuccessful. Not only is it off-limits in our family, when it does occur, we try to point out how obviously unsuccessful a girl who whines will be. To do this, Gail and I have to remain very strong in not giving in to those things that are whined for.

We believe that whining is bad form and unsuccessful because we feel it is the kind of manipulativeness that does not ultimately help a girl find equality in the adult world. What is gained, in adult relationships, by whining, generally backfires. Gail and I came to this realization from our years as marital therapists. Because we could observe many marriages, we were in the position to notice that while there are enjoyable games and eccentricities in all marital relationships that sometimes involve jesting, cajoling, even whining—for the most part, couples work because their communication is *honest and aboveboard*. Workplaces are successful for the same reasons. Whining can manipulate events successfully, but the souls of the adults involved know they've been manipulated. The cycle of manipulation just goes on and on, and can fracture attachments.

Mothers (and fathers) who work hard to shut down most of their daughter's whining create a happier home. There is an exception to this: when a child is very hungry or very tired. In that case, the whining occurs because we haven't fed her or put her to bed (or made sure she does these things herself, if appropriate). It is also important to remain patient through that particular kind of whining that comes especially in a girl's early adolescence, when life is a complete misery, for hours and days on end.

Yet, still, in most cases you can be clear to point out the whining, and send your daughter to another room if she can't stop.

While living a "just don't whine" policy, it is useful if you teach the alternative: "use logic." Require your daughters to logically explain to you why they want something and how the thing they want will help *not only themselves but also one other person, place, or thing*. "If I get that bicycle, I can give my old one to the Goodwill and someone will get to use it." Making this work can be a real thinking challenge for your daughter, whose mind is growing these days in leaps and bounds. For Gail and I, as parents, it is crucial that our children think of others even while thinking of self. Success and happiness grow not only individually, but as a reward for attachments and the compassion of being with others continually in the web of life.

## TEACHING YOUR GIRLS TO ENJOY THEIR NOBLE FAILURES

A teacher in Missouri told me about a third-grade girl who cried whenever she lost at a game and puffed up, almost rudely, when she won. The girl's parents confirmed that at home she was mean when she lost at board games. While at school the teacher talked to the girl about her problem, she had little room to provide the girl the needed discipline. At home, she discovered, the girl's father found his daughter's competitiveness "cute," not understanding that it was hardly competitiveness, in the pure sense of that word, for if a child cannot lose well, she is not a competitor—she is a tyrant.

When the teacher was able to help the father see this, she, the mother, and the father began a team effort of teaching sportsmanship, and giving consequences. At home, as soon as the girl became belligerent in a game, she was sent to her room. She was compelled to apologize to everyone involved on her return to the game.

Within a few weeks, she became a better sport. And now she was able to see that failing can be noble, for the teacher reported, about two months into the girl's new regimen, hearing the girl lecture another, "It's okay to lose. You learn a lot by losing."

Your daughter's noble failures are everywhere. Failing is, indeed, more than okay. Losing is crucial. The mind learns by losing, by failing; and especially by loving mothers (and fathers and others) who help a girl understand why she failed or lost, and how to adjust, then to succeed gracefully.

## MONITORING MEDIA IN STAGE 2

Davita came home one day when she was eight and told us her eight-year-old girlfriend had just shown *The Matrix,* a violent sci-fi film, at a sleepover. This was the second time Davita had slept over at that house, and the second time she had seen a film dangerous to her brain's developmental age (the first had been the also violent *The Mummy*). It was time for Gail or me to call her friend's parents and explore with them whether Davita would be able to go to their house again.

"Mommy," Davita mourned, "I love going to Stacy's house!" She had wonderful times there, but she was being exposed to material we considered immoral for her age group. I volunteered to make the call, but since Gail knew the other mom pretty well, she took on the duty.

The world of stories (media, books, movies, MTV) is a world in which our children wander relatively aimlessly. Until our children have completed the lion's share of their brain's emotional and moral development (by about sixteen), we cannot be too vigilant about what stories we find worthy for them. When they are seven or eight, their brains cannot abstract well enough to integrate the violence of *The Matrix* into the compelling moral scheme of the movie. Thus, the movie does their development—at that age—more harm than good. At that age, books and movies need to be "harmlessly imaginative"—i.e., without demeaning sex, violence, or immoral messages, and they must have *uncomplicated moral conclusions.*

In the end, Gail could not extract from the other family their promise that "what the older kids watch won't be watched by the younger." So Davita had her girlfriend over to our house for an overnight, but no longer the other way around. Gail felt like an ogre insisting on this, and yet would do it again in a heartbeat. Not just the growing nature of our daughter's body, but also of her brain is Gail's (and my) charge to protect and nurture.

In another instructive incident involving the media, Gabrielle wanted a magazine with Christina Aguilera on the front cover. We were at a coffee shop with her grandma and grandpa, getting our morning coffee. Gabrielle told us how much she liked Christina, how pretty she was, how great her songs were. Next door to the coffee shop was a video superstore. The magazine cover stimulated Gabrielle to want to go there and buy a CD of Aguilera's. She had been asking for this CD for about a week now, in various ways.

Because Gabrielle knows how important media literacy is to us, she said, "If I tell you what's right and good about this music, will you let me buy it?" She asked with those mischievously upturned eyes that every parent recognizes in a daughter who wants something and will try everything to get it!

Gail said, "Okay. That's a deal. You explain the moral values and logic of the lyrics to us. Then we'll look at getting the CD."

Gabrielle sat down with Gail, me, her sister, and her grandparents and explained that Christina was like a genie in a bottle. "There's a boy who only talks about himself, and Christina says, 'I don't want to be with you if you don't open the genie in me.' The song is about what a girl wants, and what she wants is to be seen for who she is, not to be stuck in a bottle."

Gabrielle, at ten, worked very hard to explain these values and the character lesson in the song to her family, and she was rewarded with the CD. Her mother told her how proud we were of her for listening to the messages of the music, and for organizing her thoughts so she could explain them to us.

Gabrielle was learning media literacy—an essential skill for all children today. And she was taking responsibility for the music she listened to. While doing all this, she was absorbing, consciously, the stories of a role-model—Christina Aguilera, her media friend—into her own self-development journey, rather than not thinking out her relation with the media friend and thus simply attaching her malleable journey to Christina's.

In matters of story, television, music, and the movies, we parents (and, often, mothers, who spend more time seeing what the girls see) are as much the arbiters of self-discipline in pre- to middle adolescence as our daughters themselves are. Our girls look to Mom for help in developing a language for the overstimulation of media imagery.

The development of self-discipline, especially in Stage 2, is a process of imagination. We parents have the responsibility to help our daughter not just absorb images into the imagination, but organize those images into a particular value system. In doing this, we are helping her make adult self-discipline out of the billions of stimulants she experiences.

A nature-based approach to parenting begs parents to disallow televisions in Stage 2 children's rooms and to disallow unsupervised Internet access there as well. To the extent your daughter spends her time in her room watching TV or in chatrooms, she is equally disconnected from her family—and it is her family she needs the most.

## The Artful Mother in Stage 3:
## Eleven to Fifteen Years Old

Girls come to puberty in this age group; they are filled with bursts of different feelings and ideas and are hungry for a mother's love. Let's start this section by looking at how to artfully communicate with girls in their matters of feeling.

### HANDLING AN ANGRY GIRL
Does this kind of exchange sound familiar?

"I don't care what you think."

"Honey, I wasn't trying to impose anything on you."

"You always think you know me."

"No I don't."

"Yes you do!"

"Why are you so angry?"

"You never understand!"

"What?"

"You're worthless!"

"Caroline! Don't talk to me that way."

"Oh, forget it." Your daughter leaves the room.

What happened? There was no anger a moment ago, was there? And usually, five or ten minutes later, the anger will be gone again. A mother can't help but wonder what she did to bring this on, and how to help her daughter feel better.

A useful approach to angry exchanges like this is to treat them like detective stories, to look for clues. This approach helps a mom keep the distance she needs on outbursts like this, and helps her turn the moment into a teaching moment. Sometimes the anger is mainly a neural and hormonal stimulant, having little to do with interactive reality, and requiring no real response. That's good to remember throughout Stage 3.

But in Caroline's and her mother's exchange are wonderful clues to a daughter's state of mind. Her angry demeaning of her mother— "You're worthless"—is probably also anger at herself. She projects onto her mother the worthlessness she herself may well be feeling. So often, when an adolescent girl gets angry, she is experiencing not only the turmoil of her own hormones and feelings, but this sense of worthlessness, meaninglessness, not belonging, not understanding. She is living a chaos of internal and external life, feels clueless, and bursts. She doesn't like the feeling, so she projects it onto Mom quite often, whom she trusts, who she knows, at some deep level, will understand her.

In this way, a daughter's anger with her mother is often a veiled compliment. The mother of an adolescent girl must find in herself a great patience, and keep a broad perspective, in order to see the compliment, feel the trust, and engage in communicating through, with, and then beyond her daughter's anger.

A mother can deepen her daughter's trust in her by noticing the hidden clues, and reflecting them back. Before this can be done, it is usually important that respect be returned to the relationship. "Caroline, I don't mind your being angry, I don't mind your telling me I don't understand, but I do mind being called worthless." It is generally not useful for any child to diss her mother significantly and get away with it. In fact, it's probable that, over the long term, the more a girl tries to verbally attack a mother's core-self and gets away with it, the lower the girl's self-esteem (core-self development) will be. If a girl destroys her image of her mother, she is to some extent destroying herself.

Just what moment the mother chooses to exact an apology is a matter for her intuition. Some mothers will try to get it while the girl is still outraged. This generally increases the rage, but sometimes does not. Generally, if a daughter has cooled down, she will feel bad about attacking her mom. She will feel better as her mother helps her to explore her own feelings of not belonging, of being in chaos, of not understanding herself, of feeling low and worthless.

In taking this approach to a daughter's anger, a mother uses the anger as a sacred and important part of a girl's growing up. Certainly there are times to teach her to withhold her anger. Learning to control oneself is part of being mature. Certainly there are times to just let her scream, punch a punching bag, or ventilate till she's done. And certainly there are times to worry about why a daughter isn't getting angry. But in all these a mother can often best help her daughter by holding a mirror up to the anger, and showing her daughter all of what is there.

When a daughter's anger becomes overwhelming, it is absolutely appropriate to take time out for oneself. ("I can't keep talking to you like this right now, Caroline, I'm too angry. I'll talk to you in a half hour.") If leaving the room isn't possible—for instance, you are on a long road trip in the car—then sixty seconds of silent time is appropriate. And there is certainly nothing intrinsically wrong with getting angry oneself. A mother doesn't have to be a saint. She can match her daughter's anger when she has to.

At the same time, how a mother handles anger, and the depth to which she takes her daughter's hand through the anger, will do a lot to develop a girl's personal maturity and strength.

## HANDLING YOUR DAUGHTER'S SADNESS

The female brain and hormonal systems, especially during Stage 3 of childhood, are very vulnerable not only to angry outbursts, but to sad moods. Certainly the male are as well, but not in the same way as the female. When adolescent male systems get angry, they tend to "*act it out*" more than girls—express it in physical movement, punching, sport, fighting, violence, and other physical dominance behaviors—and they tend to use fewer words in their angry interactions. When adolescent males are sad, they tend to use less words, and again move toward actions—like smoking, taking drugs, high-risk behavior, and violence. The tendency of the male neural system is to stop traumatic feelings before they distend—before they expand—by repressing them, or by quickly releasing the tension the feelings cause.

The tendency of the female neural system is to distend—expand— the neural processing of the feelings. Thus females use more words, carry on more conversations, write more diary entries, and so on. While some of this male-female difference is probably socialized into boys and girls, even that socialization did not rise in a vacuum: Our brains and hormones set it up.

Thus when girls are angry, they often talk more than boys, extending the feeling rather than repressing or quickly releasing it. When they are sad, they extend the feeling more often, also. We see this at both ends of the depression spectrum. At the highest end, we find that more females than males have more depression for longer periods of time. At the lowest end—short-term sadnesses—we also find more females than males extending the time of the sadness.

This creates particular challenges in the mothering of both boys and girls. With girls, we often find ourselves trying to navigate diffi- cult waters of sadness for a longer time than with boys. Some of these times of sadness are not clinical depression; some are. We know the ones that are clinical depression (many adolescent girls will expe- rience clinical depression at some time between ten and twenty) because they do not come and go in cyclic ways (i.e., connected to hormonal flow), they last more than two months, they often follow a significant stressor that has increased the stress reactivity in the brain (e.g., a death, the loss of a boyfriend, a trauma at school, a divorce, a life-change like moving to a new city), and no matter what we do or say, and no matter what our daughter tries, she cannot shake these "blues." When we are faced with this challenge, seeking professional help is generally the best medicine, along with increased love, affec- tion, caregiving by nuclear and extended family, and vigilance about our daughter's healthy eating, lifestyle risks, and mood swings.

*A Parent's Guide for Suicidal and Depressed Teens*, by Kate Williams, is a crucial resource for a mother who feels her daughter is clinically depressed, as is immediate attention from a mental health professional. We will delve deeper into female depression and mental illness in Chapter 6.

What about the sadnesses other than long-term, clinical depression? What are effective ways to react to the moments of pain, grief, sadness, tears, and melancholy our Stage 3 girls go through?

- Quite often, words have to end; she needs to be hugged, touched, given a backrub, offered a silent drive in the woods or a bike ride.

- Often words have to begin, but in a way not yet tried. For instance, rather than asking your daughter why she's sad, telling stories of your own sadnesses as a girl can be powerful. Adolescent daughters need to hear about their mothers' griefs.

- Body movement is important to encourage—get her exercising, playing her favorite sport, walking with you while you talk. Physical exercise helps stabilize hormones and brain chemicals.

- Vigilance about food intake is crucial. While it may appear that eating chocolate bars helps "cure" her sadness—the cure only lasts a few minutes, then the sadness can deepen. Refined sugars are a food that fills the body—in a transitory way—with uplifting neural reactions but then leaves it depleted, so the sadness and feeling of emptiness (or angry agitation) can get worse twenty minutes later.

- Often sadness is a good time to continue educating girls about their own hormones and cyclical feelings. "You're just hormonal" is generally less effective than "Sometimes I really know I'm a woman when I have feelings I never invited, that don't seem to come from anyone doing anything. I just watch them, like a river, passing by."

- Often there is a clear cause for the sadness, and helping a girl find it in her own psyche is a cure. For a girl to be able to talk to her mother about nearly anything, her mother must, in these cases, be a good listener.

- Often Mom has to play the role not of fixer or friend but of liaison. For instance, maybe this is a sadness Mom can't help with, but she can alert Dad or Grandma or the godmother or a teacher or coach who can help her daughter.

- Just as in your daughter's anger there is so often a clue to her inner state, so there is in her sadness; and often that inner state is one of self-blame. She feels inadequate, feels she has acted badly, wrongly, ineffectively, stupidly. So often, along with the self-blame is the lionization of someone else—her best friend, the boy she's seeing, a teacher, or her mom or dad. She feels terribly wrong and the other becomes a god in her vision. A great deal of sadness in adolescent girls is the shame felt when she sees herself as wrong and the other as right.

It is very useful for a mom to be cognizant of this, and to try to help a girl think out whether and how she is blaming herself and/or putting the other on a pedestal. When a girl deserves some blame, a mother shouldn't flinch from helping the girl say "I see what I did wrong." At the same time, an artful mother remembers her own adolescence, and how immensely self-reactive she was. This perspective can help her guide her daughter toward the kind of self-care that every person needs.

## HANDLING HER PULLS TO AUTONOMY

The journey of adolescence is a journey of individuation—and of new aloneness. When we were innocent children, beloved and cared for by our families—when, for instance, we were babies in our mother's arms, or seven-year-olds who always knew Mom (or Dad) would pick us up after school—we did not know aloneness. As a girl enters preadolescence, then puberty, then full adolescence, then becomes a young woman, she learns what it means to be alone. She craves the aloneness as much as she fears it. She is no longer protected from the human condition: the sense that each of us is, in some mysterious way, alone; and learning how to manage that aloneness—that individual, irrepressible identity—is the source of our strength.

The adolescent girl's journey to individuation—there are so many words used for it: independence, autonomy, separation-from-Mom (and Dad)—is a journey into self-trust if it is a journey well mentored by three families. We want our daughters to become autonomous. We want them to learn to trust themselves. It is the primary goal of adolescence. If we have to put up with some strange adolescent behavior, angers, little rebellions, experimentations, and even scary risk-takings, we'll complain, cajole, guide, and let go in our continuing commitment to our child.

But making the journey of adolescence with girls today is sometimes very difficult as many of our girls are pulled in Stage 3 toward gross rebellions ("I don't have to do anything you say or want and you can't make me") rather than small leaps of independence ("I'm gonna sneak a kiss from Dave even though Mom will kill me"). Today, the media and some peers teach our Stage 3 daughters not to "work with and around us" as individuating children have always done in the past, but inculcate into adolescent thinking the idea that not only parents, but also all elders and all previous generations, have little to teach, and must be "killed off" (have their authority removed) in the developing psyche.

As a result, parents are frightened by the journey of individuation, and they are relatively unsupported as their daughters make the journey. Mothers feel embattled. Their daughters are being influenced on all fronts, and mothers often feel unprepared and alone as they try to hold on to a girl's innocence, yet help her establish her independence.

Judy Ford, along with her daughter, Amanda, is the author of *Between Mother and Daughter: A Teenager and Her Mom Share the Secrets of a Strong Relationship*. Judy recently began an article in *American Girl Magazine* with the following real-life dialogue:

MOTHER: You're late again, and you didn't call to let me know.
DAUGHTER *(tosses her hair)*: So?
MOTHER: I was worried.
DAUGHTER So don't worry next time. Give me a break.
MOTHER: You never used to speak to me that way.
DAUGHTER *(turns to leave)*: Me? You never let up!
MOTHER: *Wait.* I . . . *(watches daughter walk away)*. What happened to us? We used to be close.

That is a poignant reminder of how it can be for mothers. In Ford's studies, she discovered that the median age for this kind of deep mother-daughter discomfort is fifteen. Ford also discovered that even the most rebellious daughter carries, in some part of herself, a deep need for connection with her mother. Even in homes where mothers have been brutal to their daughters, and from which daughters have had to flee, there is almost always in the daughter a yearning for the mother.

If you are facing a communication meltdown in your relationship with your middle-adolescent daughter, here are crucial ways to try to heal your relationship.

### Handling Major Communication Breakdowns

- If your daughter is not in danger, let time be the best healer. Maintain basic rules, provide discipline when rules are broken, but do not expect life to become comfortable in the house for a number of weeks.

- If your daughter is in danger, confront her and enlist the aid of father, extended family, and professionals as needed. Do an intervention if necessary (see the book *Tough Love* for methods of family intervention), involving the whole extended family.

- In whatever your daughter's circumstance—whether she is in danger, in gross rebellion, or in more subtle independence behavior—remember that she often feels alone now. Remembering this can aid your intuitions as you relate to her.

Judy and Amanda Ford suggest these "healing messages daughters need to hear":

MOTHER: We don't get along the way we used to. I feel sad about that. I wonder if you do, too.

MOTHER: I can listen better when you talk to me respectfully. And I will speak respectfully to you.

MOTHER: We're working on a new kind of relationship as you grow up. Things are changing for both of us.

MOTHER: It takes both of us to make this work. I want you to know I'm willing to do my part.

*Is Adolescent Rebellion Necessary?*

It is important for mothers not to go into adolescence expecting aggressive rebellion. The human individuation process is normal—in the thirty cultures I studied, I found that all young people enter a difficult journey to independence in Stage 3. However, most young people do not *rebel.* In other words, in most cultures, as well as in most homes in America, young people "find themselves" while still remaining respectful of their parents' worth. They find themselves in order to first join, then modify their society, not to destroy the safe relationships and practices established within it. They work around their parents, and sometimes take risks against social rules, but they remain committed to the sacredness of their family and society.

Rebellion—the attitude that "I am fifteen, I'm an adult, what you say means nothing"—is the view of only a few of the world's adolescents, and certainly not their right. Our culture overemphasizes it for a number of reasons: America was born, two hundred years ago, in nation-state rebellion; some children are raised by abusive, addicted, or otherwise dangerous parents and cannot become stable adults unless they leave these parents behind; and the middle to late twentieth century, what we like to call "the sixties," which shaped a great deal of our popular culture, grew from a heartfelt need by young people to rebel against the corruptions and restrictiveness of elders who held on to old, dangerous beliefs about colonialism, racism, and war that we no longer needed.

Rebellion is something of a national American pastime. But it is not necessarily what your daughter wants or needs. The openness and depth of your communication with her between about eight and thirteen years old will, to a great extent, shape how rebellious she becomes. The more attached she is to you and your extended family, the less she will need to bond with rebellious kids. The more respectful you are of her and she of you the less she will become accustomed to being disrespectful. The more time you take to understand her and help her understand herself, the more accustomed she will become to relying on you. This reliance is a good thing to develop. By the time she is fourteen or fifteen, she will try to work around it herself, while still remaining attached. Thus she will do what she is meant to do during adolescence—learn how to be alone while still knowing she is loved. Ultimately, this is the best kind of self-trust.

### Changing with Your Daughters.

To remain close (even while separating) to our daughters during adolescence, we are challenged to grow along with them. This may mean changing from being ultra-authoritarian, if that's how you were ("Do what I say when I say it") to "I'll pick my battles" and "Sure, we can negotiate about that one."

It will also mean giving your daughter new *freedoms* and new *responsibilities* in nearly equal measure, and making sure to talk about each as it comes. It's important to talk about why new freedoms are coming, and why new responsibilities are necessary. We often think our girls are "getting it" without our engaging in conversation with them. But are they? Think about how many times you have to repeat some simple instruction, or expectation, to your adolescent daughter. Does it make sense to think that a lot of the deep things in life are getting through without equal repetition?

As family practitioners, Gail and I have found that the more time the nuclear and extended family spends with their daughters—and the greater the intimate networking in the family systems—the easier the adolescent journey for mother and daughter. And this implies the help of the father, which we will discuss in the next chapter.

## THE ISSUE OF PRIVACY

In my practice I counseled a single mother whose daughter, thirteen, insisted that her room was a private place, and wanted a lock on the door. This insistence was both a literal and symbolic outcome of a family that had not raised her in a clear discipline system. The father had, after the divorce, moved to another city, seeing his daughter infrequently. In the mother's house, where the girl primarily lived, she had been allowed to do and say a lot of things her mother now regretted. But because she had been given inconsistency and too much freedom too early (and with added stress of the divorce), she had hit puberty with the sense that "I've run my own life thus far, why shouldn't I run it even more privately now." She felt alone, that feeling felt safe, and she wanted to increase it by ensuring it with locked-in privacy.

Not only did family counseling help resolve a number of issues, including the girl's tacit aloneness, but a lock was not allowed on her door, and her room was not considered off-limits by her mother. Even in the face of trauma, like parental divorce, the issue of privacy is relatively cut and dried.

A growing child has no inherent right to absolute privacy. The child lives in the parents' house and lives off her parents. While common-sense privacy is essential, a great deal of self-discipline grows in all of us, including our daughters, because we cannot get away from each other totally—we must learn to interact constantly.

## THE BATTLE OVER CLOTHING

I received an e-mail from a mother worried about her daughter's clothes. The girl was fourteen, and had taken to wearing—like some of her friends—scanty clothing. She wore too much makeup with it, so that she appeared to be a vampire. Her budding breasts pushed out, and her tight shorts showed every curve of her buttocks. When Mom and Dad confronted her on her clothing, she accused them of being old-fashioned, cried that she'd be out of sync with her friends, and got so angry it scared them.

As it is so often, understanding girls lies in a mother's intuition. At the end of the mother's e-mail was the key to how to approach the girl.

"I think this isn't just about clothes," wrote the mother, "but it's about her safety. I think her clothes put her at risk."

The girl saw her clothing as a matter of personal, independent self-expression. Her parents saw it, viscerally, as a matter of safety. Both daughter and parents were right. But in the end, the mother's intuition had to rule the day.

Clothing is an expression of self. And it can put a girl in danger.

I advised the parents to ask the daughter what "independent self" she was expressing. In our correspondence I learned that the girl hemmed and hawed, finally admitting she wore the clothes not to be independent, but to be just like her friends. She thought she was "being independent" by wearing scanty clothing. In fact, she realized she was just being one of the girls.

Her parents also talked about the possibility of rape with her. Her mother revealed to her that her aunt (her mother's sister) had been raped when she was twenty-three. This led to a very tearful discussion between mother and daughter. They worked out ways for the girl to dress differently—as independence behavior; she chose colorful blouses, patched pants, loud shoes, even retro-turtlenecks. Within a week, she felt just as independent wearing safer but still expressive clothing.

"Now I wonder what the crisis was all about," the mother ended her last e-mail. "She's as happy as a clam."

The crisis, this mother knew in her bones, was about growing up, and the rite of passage that clothing can be. Adolescence is a series of minicrises, milestones of passage, in which a girl learns who she is, what she's worth, how to reveal and communicate herself by overdoing things until those who love and care for her use her actions as springboards for the continued teaching of self-discipline.

A great deal of this "overdoing things" goes on in Stage 3, which is one reason that most cultures in the world give Stage 3 girls an organized, planned, and staged event (or more than one) in which to do this kind of development: rites of passage.

## RITES OF PASSAGE

Planning rites of passage for a daughter's adolescent journey is a crucial part of the mother's role in her daughter's life, beginning at around her daughter's tenth birthday, and continuing through first menses, and even beyond, into later adolescence.

Meg Cox has written a wonderful book called *The Heart of a Family: Searching America for New Traditions That Fulfill Us.* In it, she tells the story of an organized rite of passage for her niece's thirteenth birthday.

"My niece, my sister, and I walked down to the beach in the evening. We drew a circle in the sand and lit sparklers and candles around it. Then we stood in the middle and toasted my niece and spoke about the awesome woman she would become. My sister and I asked her what she wanted to know about growing up. She asked how it was for us when we were her age. We gave her thirteen gifts, each of them symbolic. There was a globe, because she will explore the world; a book about strong women; a clock, because time is hers to use wisely; and so forth. All of us were deeply moved by this ritual of passage we created for her."

There is a veritable movement in America—a culture that has nearly lost definable, healthy rites of passage for youth, and discovered that youth will create dangerous, unhealthy ones if healthy ones are not provided—to not only resuscitate good, traditional rites of passage, but also to create new traditions, like Meg Cox described. In our home, we have created our own, as well as enjoyed institutional rites of passage through church and synagogue communities. We have also encouraged our daughters to involve themselves in school-based rites of passage, and organized rites of passage, with friends (camping trips, rafting trips, ropes courses).

One of the most valuable lessons I learned as a child who lived around the world was the importance of rites of passage. Boys and girls are both hungry for these occasions during which questions of heart and soul become conscious, and the child hears her parents' voices clearly, as well as the voices of other mentors and ancestors. These are times of ordeal—like a camping trip that gets rained out or a ropes course that frightens the girl initially—also times of exhilaration, camaraderie, and joy. They are times of self-knowing, and they are times of self-doubt. But because they are organized, ritualized, mentored, and protected, they are, by nature, times of healthy growth. And because they form lasting memories, our daughters remember them as moments of personal transformation and maturity.

Rites of passage in your family can take place with your family alone, say when your daughter is ten: She and you (and Dad) can write a letter to one another, answer questions, ask questions, speak of the past and future, of expectations and purpose, give gifts, and build family symbols. Rites of passages can take place in the extended family, in the church (or synagogue, in the case of a bat mitzvah). Others can take place spontaneously, on field trips or camping trips. In all

cases, a mother's hand will probably be felt—whether as the one creating the rite of passage, or driving her daughter to Hebrew class, or vol-
unteering at school, or worrying while her daughter is gone for the
first time in her life for a whole week at camp.

Rites of passage in tribal cultures always have a biological, or
nature-based, undercurrent. They are connected to a girl's various
internal, biological rites of passage, like the appearance of breasts,
her growth spurt, her first menstruation, her first sexual intercourse.
While we are not as "biology-based" as our tribal ancestors were, we
gain by honoring their basic premise that a girl's biology is an important part of her need for rites of passage. First menstruation, for
instance, is something to celebrate in a rite of passage. Even her first
date is a rite of passage. In our home, Gail has suggested that, when
our daughters become sixteen, I take them on their first date, enjoying with them a beautiful occasion, talking honestly with them about
whatever they need to know from me, and showing them the respect
they ought to expect from boys whom they date. Gail got this idea
from another family, whose daughters are now grown, that practiced
this rite of passage with great success.

There are many ways to enjoy rites of passage—daughters can
help mothers (and aunts, and fathers) construct a rite of passage ritual or ceremony. And, of course, our daughters will discover many
rites of passage without us, as they struggle with and enjoy their own
growth in spheres we do not touch. We can hope that as they take the
risks of adolescence, it is with the foundation of the rites of passage
their families, and those who love them, spent the time, energy and
spiritual focus to create and nurture. There is a wonderful organization—ICA Journeys (www.icajourneys.org) that provides rites of passage and assists families.

## The Artful Mother in Stage 4:
## Sixteen to Twenty Years Old

By about sixteen, your daughter will have nearly completed the lion's
share of her brain development, and she will have gained, therefore,

about sixty to seventy percent of the life skills she needs not only to manage her own cycles and systems, but also to manage where she fits in society and family. As you mother a girl in late high school and college, you generally notice:

- greater maturity and strength
- a focus on a few primary interests
- more interest in males and sexuality
- a more independent young woman
- precious moments of connection with you and reliance on you, but not necessarily every day

Many of the issues that we discussed regarding Stage 3 girls can also still apply in Stage 4. And if there has been significant emotional and other trauma in Stage 3, your daughter can seem immature in Stage 4, and can be involved in high-risk behavior (see Chapter 6).

No matter where your daughter is on the maturity spectrum, she will be asking four questions of life and of you.

## THE FOUR QUESTIONS EVERY ADOLESCENT GIRL IS ASKING

There are four primary questions in every adolescent's life, and no one can quite help a girl answer them all like her mom can. This is even true in Stage 4 when many moms feel pushed out of their daughters' lives or feel their parenting work with their daughter is basically done. It's not done! Stage 4 is a time of heightened self-questioning for the daughter, and heightened opportunity for the mother to be artful.

The four key questions of this stage (that began, less overtly, in Stage 3):

1. Who am I? The question of Identity.
2. Can I trust myself? The question of Autonomy.
3. What are my core values? The question of Morality.
4. What is love? The question of Intimacy.

As you practice the art of mothering with your middle-to-late-adolescent daughter, and as you feel confusion, fear, regret, uncertainty about what to do, let these four questions focus your communication and understanding.

### The Question of Identity.

Girls, even before adolescence, are asking themselves and their world, Who am I? At adolescence, their questions about who they are become like a sacred text in their mind. Their changing body, hormones, and brain forces them to read this text, but like any sacred text, much of its language seems foreign, or at least lined with complex metaphor; by middle adolescence, they are getting far better at reading the language of the text. Yet, still, people who have read the text before, over and over, are needed.

When a mother learns everything she can about female biology and nature, she is intuitively equipped to help her daughter become a woman; she is knowledgeable and wise about female identity and can speak the sophisticated language of the middle-to-late teen. In order to understand female identity, adolescent girls need, as a base, the information in Chapters 2 and 3—information about human nature. In former times, grandmothers, aunties, and godmothers proffered this female-identity information, making sure fifteen-, sixteen-, seventeen-year-old young women knew it (and themselves) well. Nowadays, quite often, the mother has the singular responsibility of interpreting, throughout a girl's adolescence, that sacred text for her daughter.

Identity is also, of course, a matter of more than hidden nature. It is a matter of knowing one's ethnic lineage, religious heritage, likes and dislikes, personality type. It is a matter, too, of beginning to gain a deep sense of why one is alive in this world. In survey after survey, middle-adolescent girls reveal that their mothers are their primary role models. Our girls want to hear their mothers' stories (even if for a few months, or years, they act like they don't). Our girls need to talk to Mom about what a woman is, what Mom is, and who the girl is becoming—issues we discussed in the first part of this chapter. They are judging their mother's identity to form their own. An artful mother enjoys the process with her daughter, admitting where she's felt tensions, anxiety, inadequacy as a woman trying to make it today.

A large part of the female identity search is involved with "belonging" among other girls, and "attaching" to boys. Mom is often the best guide through the identity information that belonging and attaching brings to a girl. We will explore these two themes much more deeply in Chapters 6 and 7, helping mothers, dads, and others to complete their conversations about identity with adolescent girls.

### The Question of Autonomy.

The same artful mother who perhaps began the conversation about autonomy when her daughter was ten ("You're getting older, you're making some of your own decisions." "I liked how you made that decision on your own." "What do you think?"), now becomes the mother who says:

"You think you can't do that on your own, but you can."

"It seems to me you feel afraid like I did, afraid of love and of sex, afraid you'll lose yourself in David; I'm here if you need me."

"When I was your age, I was afraid to drive, but look at you—so bold!"

"Do you know why you did what you did today?"

In Stage 4, the mother's role in the autonomy process includes previous roles, but expands to helping a nearly grown daughter grapple with deep questions about personal responsibility, personal power, and personal freedom. The father helps a great deal with this, but at the same time, he is not female; there is intuitive wisdom about how a woman manages her freedoms and responsibilities that only a woman can share with a daughter who is now a young woman.

### The Question of Morality.

Chapter 7 of this book deals with character development and provides you with many tools for helping your adolescent daughter answer the deep questions about her values as she develops into womanhood. She is constantly asking why she believes something, what she believes, what is right, what is wrong, how she should act, how much she should allow herself or another to act at the edges of her values, what moral risks to take, when she must sacrifice one value for another.

In our house, we carry on moral discussions at the dinner table—about current events, or a moral issue that arose in one of our daughters' school days, or a moral issue Gail or I faced. Sometimes we get into loud debates. We try to support our conversations with references to sacred texts—the Bible, the Koran, the Gita—even while realizing that we ourselves, as individuals, are responsible to provide the final word in our lives. We try to talk from personal experience when we can, sharing our stories, learning more about our daughters' unfolding moral stories.

Morality development is crucial to the raising of healthy girls, yet high schools, for many years, have had to shy away from many moral issues, and families have been too busy to raise them. Religions hold less sway in family life than they used to, thus one of the primary moral storytelling agents has decreased in strength; kids who have gone to church, synagogue, temple, or mosque in childhood and early adolescence often stop going by Stage 4. And with extended families in disarray or disconnection, that grandparent or aunt or other moral interrogator is gone.

Yet our girls are very moral creatures asking very deep moral questions. To discuss these questions with a growing girl is often difficult—for instance, when the subject is "Should I have premarital sex?"—but mothers who become comfortable with moral conversation celebrate the positive interpersonal universe, the joy, that mothers and daughters can feel when a daughter believes her mother understands her internal world. To not engage in moral conversation is to let a daughter know that the mother cannot be fully trusted, for she does not understand what it means to be a growing girl.

### The Question of Intimacy

In Chapters 6 and 7 there is a great wealth of practical material for helping girls navigate the worlds of intimacy. Let me just mention a few points here. Romance novels constitute 40 percent of all books sold to late-adolescent and mature women. Have you noticed that most other novels written by women—from Oprah books to comic novels like *Bridget Jones's Diary*—involve girls or women grappling with issues of relationship? Girls and women want to know how to be intimate. By the time they enter Stage 4, this question is primary to them, and it will be throughout life. By the time your daughters become menopausal, they will have explored the intimacy imperative their nature drives them to explore, and resolved many of these questions of intimacy that rise in Stage 4 so passionately:

"Will I ever be loved the way I yearn to be loved?"

"Do I need a man?"

"Is there *one* Mr. Right for me, or are there many?"

"Will I always fear rejection and abandonment?"

"Will I ever feel comfortable, with a man, about who *I* am?"

"Will women be my friends or competitors?"

"Will I find a man to look up to?"

"Given how different women and men are, can I find peaceful understanding with men?"

An artful mother does not always wait for her daughter to raise the question of intimacy. She reads her daughter's signals—the sadness or elation after a date, the sudden obsession with a certain perfume, the Internet surfing to certain sites—and sees her daughter's hidden, very natural questions.

She asks:

"What are you thinking about these days? Anything you want to share?" (The sharing may not come until a day or two later.)

"How aggressive is John being with you?" (Even if her daughter cries, "Oh, Mom!" Mom knows that her daughter knows she is available to talk to.)

"If I were going to do things differently with your dad, you want to know what they'd be?" (A daughter might say "No" at first, but especially if the mother is sharing as mature women do, the daughter's curiosity may win out.)

A mother's focus on questions of identity, anatomy, morality, and intimacy is a way for a family to guide its daughter through adolescence—these questions provide a railing, so to speak, as a daughters crosses the deep and sometimes frightening canyon between childhood and adulthood.

A beautiful resource for mothers of all adolescents, especially those in Stage 4, is a book called *You and Your Adolescent* by Laurence Steinberg and Anne Levine. I highly recommend it. Many parents have told me they use it as a support for many of the crucial issues they need to focus on with their daughters.

## THE CO-ED SLEEPOVER: A MODEL OF STAGE 4 MOTHER-DAUGHTER ATTACHMENT

"Mom," your seventeen-year-old daughter smiles, "I want to have a sleepover. With guys too."

You might cringe a little. You try to smile back, thinking, "I'm not ready for this. How do I say no?"

It is intimidating to think about young women and men sleeping together in the basement, or the living room, or all over the house. They've got pajamas on, but . . . well . . . anything can happen.

It's intimidating but also a beautiful opportunity—an opportunity to be the center of your teen's "attachment community." Why not let your house be the one where healthy interactions occur? Why not be the parent who is attached so well to her daughter that she trusts her (and lays out good ground rules)?

Here are some agreements that make a co-ed slumber party work for the whole family and community. If these are negotiated and made clear to (and by) the teens before the party, there are generally few problems:

1. The party happens in one large room—no sneaking off to small bedrooms or attics.

2. Mom and Dad are not going to leave, and the party isn't totally private from them. Parents have the obligation—for teen safety—to walk in now and then.

3. The list of guests can't be a long one. This isn't an event that just anyone is invited to. Your daughter can keep a list and check people off when they come in. No uninvited or "spontaneous" guests can come in unless everyone agrees.

4. The young people need to stay at the party—they can't go in and out of the house as they please. This is mainly done to make sure alcohol and drugs aren't being brought in.

5. Household liquor, guns, and any other harmful items are locked up.

6. Set a curfew for the party. Lock the house (say, at 12:00 A.M.) and set the burglar alarm. If a guest tries to leave, he or she will be embarrassed by the commotion. If you have no burglar alarm, announce that you're going to be sleeping in a location outside the party room, but not far away.

In deciding to have a party of this kind, your intuition is the most trustworthy as to:

- whether your daughter (and her friends) are ready, and
- whether your daughter (and her friends) are trustworthy.

If you decide they are, and if you make sure everyone verbally covenants to the necessary agreements, things should go well, and you have provided a home that is a place of family fun, healthy peer interaction, and attachment.

## MAINTAINING A FAMILY TEAM

An undercurrent in the discussion of the co-ed sleep over, and indeed throughout this chapter, is the idea that the mother is a dominant figure (sometimes *the* dominant figure) in making sure a three-family system is in place. This system is just as crucial for middle teens as earlier-stage girls, and just as rewarding.

When a seventeen-year-old goes to a soup kitchen with Mom, Dad, and the rest of the family to serve the hungry, she enjoys the family team quality.

Even at eighteen, she yearns for Mom to say, "Let's all watch a movie together Sunday night."

She still hopes Mom will take her shopping with Grandma, or with a woman friend.

She still wants to get together at family reunions.

The more we've maintained a three-family team environment from birth, the more she'll yearn for the developmental safety of a family team even as she becomes an adult. Nothing can be healthier for her (assuming, of course, she lives in a safe family, which most families are). She wants to become a young woman who can always trust her family.

At the Gurian Institute, a parent volunteer, a retired physician, sixty-five, talked of her family's yearly team activity. She, her husband, and her daughters (even during their first summers after college began) traveled to an underdeveloped country with Doctors Without Borders. Her daughters acted as volunteer nurses while their mother fulfilled her duties as a volunteer doctor and their father, a computer expert, helped with computer systems in rural clinics. For this family, these "team" activities are a constant source of conversation and nostalgic memory, even though the girls are now out of college.

"Mother's work is never done," the saying goes. Not only is it a true statement, but even more true is the statement that "an artful mother's work is never done." A mother who does more than the minimum as she commits herself to raising happy and successful daughters often sees before and behind her only what is left undone.

Yet she has actually done more than can be measured. I hope this chapter has provided you a skeletal framework for enjoying the art of mothering, of communicating with, cajoling, guiding, enforcing, listening, worrying, and finding exhilaration in your daughter's development.

One area we have not covered is stepmothering. Let's talk about it now.

## How to Be an Artful Stepmother

Perhaps at the heart of the stepmother's difficulties (and joys) in raising her stepdaughters is the question of how to handle her stepdaughter's needs for love, attachment, and intimacy. Girls who experience their parents' divorce and father's remarriage often do not know how to explain their own attachment needs to their new "second mother." In our therapy practice Gail and I have noticed how often girls· must act out their needs—through behavior and psychological problems—instead of speaking them aloud, because they have not attached well enough yet to the stepmother for words to be trusted.

This situation was brought home to us when we were asked by a blending family to help them with their twelve-year-old daughter, Justine.

The mother described her daughter this way: "She is suddenly so angry, and complains a lot, and has no self-esteem. No matter what I do, she seems to be regressing, becoming a belligerent little kid again. Her little brother is a year old and she's twelve but sometimes I can't tell them apart. I think she might be developing an eating disorder— she's so thin, but she complains of being fat."

The father said: "She doesn't go between our two houses very well. And she says a lot of the kids are mean to her."

The stepmother said: "She definitely doesn't like me. She sees me as the enemy. Plus, she's not very popular, which makes her unhappy, and she's under a lot of pressure from peers and the media. There's a lot of pressure to be thin."

The stepfather said: "She's trying to bond with me, I think, but I don't know if it's going well. I give her a lot of distance, let her make up her own mind. But it's hard, because we have to have some discipline in the house, right?"

The girl herself said everything her parents and stepparents said, in her own way, and with her own language.

What no one said, except the stepmother, during a particularly powerful session, were these words: "She's having all these troubles because her parents divorced." Her stepmother said it in sympathy for the child, not judgment of the parents. It was the obvious, the bull in the china shop, and needed to be said. Once it was said, we were all able to focus on the core problem that divorce creates in a child: Secure attachment with two parents becomes insecure attachment with at least one (generally the father), and, at times, thinly stretched attachment with the other (generally the mother, if she has to spend more time in the workplace away from children now). Furthermore, there is proposed new attachment to two unasked-for parents (stepparents), both of whom the child may resist fully attaching to in order to hold on to a semblance of her earlier sense of safe attachment to her own parents.

Adolescence is a journey of separation from attachments, one that has a set developmental pattern. An adolescent girl takes her time separating from attachments, and chooses new attachments (mentors, coaches, friends, boyfriends). When divorce occurs, as it generally does just before adolescence, the normal pattern of attachment and separation often dissolves. Now the girl is forced into attachments she can't, many times, complete, and forced away from attachments she desperately needs.

"She's angry, she's regressing," the mother said.

"She doesn't go between our houses very well," the father said.

"She doesn't like me," the stepmother said.

"I don't know if she's bonding with me," the stepfather said.

While they spoke of many other things—including her fear of getting fat, mean kids, media imagery, gender stereotypes—each of these parents knew, even without knowing, that the key problem here was the divorce and the girl's new, difficult episode in her journey of love.

My role in helping them was mainly to take their knowledge— which the stepmother was the first to bring to the surface—and add to it insight into the attachment needs of the girl.

So we did a profile of what had happened in her life over the last two years, then a profile of what each of the four adults would have needed from parents and stepparents if they had been in the girl's shoes.

Here is the profile that emerged:

In the last two years, Justine's parents had divorced, her mother had remarried, her father had remarried; she had been forced to spend half her time in a house she didn't know with a woman she didn't know, and a stepsister she didn't know, and half her time in a house she did know with a man she didn't know; she had begun puberty, she had moved to middle school, and her mother had just had a new baby.

Once we realized this profile, we understood how insecure her whole life had become. All four parents were able to see that this girl had gone from attachment safety to gross insecurity. We then put ourselves in her place and wondered what she would need. Every parent realized some area of major change she or he needed to make in order to help this girl.

Justine's mother saw the need to change work hours, and to spend more time with her daughter.

Justine's stepfather saw the need to take on a greater wage-earning burden, and to give discipline duties, for a while, to the mother.

Justine's father saw the need to spend more time with his daughter.

Justine's stepmother agreed to challenge herself to enjoy the girl's activities more, engage in them more, if the girl would let her. And this stepmother made a further sacrifice, one that inspired all of us.

She was a newlywed who wanted from her husband a lover and friend, not the burden of a twelve-year-old girl. But she made a gesture that showed the kind of sacrifice a stepmother needs to make in order to help a young woman, who has by fate become her protégée, her "niece," her godchild-by-proxy. She agreed to call off the remodeling of the house (in which she had decided to make the bedroom her daughter now used—a room next to the master bedroom—into a study, and move her stepdaughter to a bedroom in the basement). She now agreed to consummate this remodeling in a year, or even in two, whenever Justine began to feel better.

This gesture was her powerful way of saying to this father and daughter, "I will not put a distance between you." The stepmother was going to be giving up some of the privacy she desired with her new husband in order to save his child's developing self.

The role of the stepmother is often this kind of a role—she often must make immense sacrifices of privacy, self, and intimacy in order to be a good stepmother. The life of the stepmother (like the stepfather) is too little written about, understood, or celebrated in our culture. If you are a stepmother, *The Courage to Be a Stepmom,* by Sue Patton Thoele, does a nice job of unraveling key secrets you can use in everyday life.

As Gail and I parent our daughters, we hope that should we divorce, or should Gail die and I remarry, that Gabrielle and Davita will gain a stepmother like this one, insightful, willing to bend, and able to become, as our daughters let her, a second mother. Should they not let her be this to them, then she will have the added struggle of rejection in her life, as many stepmoms do. We hope all stepmoms make it a priority to gain the support and counsel (beyond what the new husband can provide) that can help her retain her strong self-image despite the very difficult position she is in.

## If Your Daughter Were a Parenting Expert . . .

I asked my daughters and their friends to pretend to be parenting experts and tell us what they wanted most from moms. I asked them this question about fathers as well, and have absorbed their answers into the next chapter. On mothering, they gave many answers, most of which you've already thought of. Yet again, they are both kind and courageous answers that bear repeating:

1. Listen to me. I don't always say it just right, but I mean something important.

2. Talk to me. I want to know what you think, even sometimes when I say I don't.

3. Be consistent with rules and consequences. I don't really mind, even if I complain.

4. Laugh with me. There's nothing like a sense of humor. And cry with me too.

5. Be a parent first and a friend second. I have lots of friends, but not a lot of parents.

6. Be a good role model. It's hard for me to be honest and open when you're not.

7. Pick your battles. And let me win some.

8. No one's perfect, so let me make mistakes. It's how I learn.

9. Respect me and I'll respect you. It's all about respect.

10. Tell me you love me at least once a day.

If it fits into your family life, you might ask your daughters and their friends to list ten pieces of advice they'd give their parents. The results will lead to interesting discussions. And of course, you then have the right to say to them, "If I were still a girl . . ." and name the top ten things you would want a growing girl to keep in mind about being a daughter!

Let me end this chapter with a humorous look at mothering, which I received via e-mail. The author's name was not included, but I salute her!

## Looking Back on What Our Mothers Taught Us

My mother taught me about *stamina:*
"You'll sit there 'til all that spinach is finished."

My mother taught me about *contortionism:*
"Will you *look* at the dirt on the back of your neck!"

My mother taught me about *the circle of life:*
"I brought you into this world, I can take you out!"

My mother taught me about *weather:*
"It looks as if a tornado swept through your room!"

My mother taught me to *appreciate a job well done:*
"If you're gonna kill each other, do it outside, I just finished cleaning!"

My mother taught me how to solve *physics problems:*
"If I yelled because I saw a meteor coming at you, would you listen then?"

My mother taught me about *hypocrisy:*

"If I told you once, I've told you a million times: Don't exaggerate!"

My mother taught me how to be *psychic:*

"I think you know what's gonna happen when your father gets home!"

And, my mother taught me *logic:*

"Because I said so, that's why!"

Mothering is truly one of the most difficult jobs on earth, and requires more courage than anyone ever measures. Perhaps the greatest courage is required when a daughter leaves home, and becomes a woman. In some ways, a mother expects her son to leave her; but between mother and daughter there is often almost the same heartbeat. And then the daughter is gone. For this final act of courage every mother deserves our blessing.

Gail's and my daughters have not left home yet, but we know one day they will. As I, their father, help Gail, their mother, I know I am observing, and am a part of—one of the most sacred alliances in human development: the mother-daughter relationship. As my daughters enjoy their adolescence and begin their letting-go, I wonder all the more about what role the father plays in their lives.

That is the subject of our next chapter.

# 5

## THE GIFTS OF THE FATHER

### WHAT GIRLS NEED FROM DAD

*"A father is the first and often the longest connection a daughter will have with a man."*

—Charles Scull, Ph.D.

*"It is the wise child that knows her own father."*

—Ancient Indian proverb

Davita Kathryn Gurian called to us before we even knew her. Both Gail and I thought we were going to have another girl. We pretended this feeling must be wrong: "We have a girl already," we rationalized, "surely this will be a boy." Yet, first Gail, who knows well the humming of her own blood, then I, for some reason I cannot explain, knew a girl was coming. We had planned on the name Davita, the Hebrew feminine form of the word "Beloved," and we prayed for a safe delivery.

Unlike our experience with Gabrielle, this caesarean section was planned in advance; Gail's was a high-risk pregnancy, her whole term in the care of an Ob-Gyn rather than our primary care physician. Gail contemplated taking the risk of natural childbirth, but she and all of us who supported her agreed with her decision to "do the safer thing." Davita's birth experience went smoothly, and our family changed yet again.

This time, as I held the surgical scissors over my newborn, snipped the umbilical cord, then handed Davita to the nurse for the three-step journey back to Mom's arms, I felt less fear, less exhaustion, and less confusion than with Gabrielle. But I felt no less love. This is a miracle in having children: that there is always love for the new child. As Gail and the baby rested, I sat down to write Davita her "Letter from Your Father." This one included less about the drama of birth than did Gabrielle's. This one was filled more with promises from me, as her father. I remember thinking, as I wrote it, "I get another chance. Any dumb mistakes I've made as a dad so far, I can redeem."

For me, as a father, there has always been the intensity of wanting to do well. My daughters have been my sacred trust. Most fathers, I know, have felt feelings like mine as their children are born and grow.

And we fathers also sense that a father's heart is a little different from a mother's. The mother carried the child and, generally, spends more time with the children than does the dad. A father's sense of the sacred trust is generally a *man's* trust, not a woman's—a trust similar in its humanity but perhaps different in its character. Like a mother's love, a father's love is beautiful and, so often, mysterious.

## A Father's Love

A father's love can make or break a girl. Just as there is no way to understate the importance of a mother in a girl's life, there is no way to understate a father's. He is the hero of her childhood and often a wall she pushes against during her adolescence. He is often both the rule-maker, laying out laws of discipline and competence, and the rule-breaker, helping his daughter take risks, push the envelope, and explore uncharted worlds. He often exists at extremes in her psyche, at poles of authority and then playfulness, immersion and then absence. A daughter forms in her own mind an impression not only of the real father she lives with, but also the ideal father who spends so much time away from her.

A father who is honest with his daughter about his own flaws becomes her confidant. A father who remains stoic becomes her enigma to solve. A father who distances himself too greatly from his daughter becomes a burden she carries into life. A girl must know, with all her big heart, that she is loved by her father. No matter his style of fathering, a man who supports his daughter's progress can become her oracle. He carries from his closeness with her an abiding—even if unconscious—sense of prediction about how his daughter will turn out.

There is no perfect way to be a father—there is only the demand that the father give his love unceasingly. Fathers adore their daughters, but in their adoration is often some distance, and complex expectations, which can shape a girl, for better or worse.

If a father dotes too much on a girl, without asking her to prove herself worthy, she can often become one-dimensional, able to prosper only in relationships where this doting is re-created.

If a father does not give her approval as she needs it, she can often become an adolescent and then a woman desperate for approval, especially men's approval.

If a father gives his daughter too little conversation, she is not generally harmed, but if this lack of conversation is combined with a lack of physical affection, a lack of activity together, and a general lack of his presence in her life, a daughter is likely to learn too little about how to love, and too much about how painful love can be.

If a father rejects his daughter too much or judges her too harshly too often, she learns she is inherently inadequate.

If a father does not listen to a girl's changing self, if his finger is not on her pulse of development, if he is merely the imposer of morality, not the mentor of her own growing self, she will, as she can, reject him, and not only will her own soul feel a constant hole, but he too will realize, one day, that he could have charted a happier course for himself and his family.

If, on the other hand, the father provides discipline and moral training, while inherently respecting and trusting his adolescent daughter's own mind, he will keep his daughter for life, and also develop a friendship with an adult who loves him dearly.

If a father grows along with his daughter, he will grow new branches on his own growing soul.

If a father always finds time to cuddle, listen to, toss in the air, dance with, run alongside, coach, comfort, and protect his daughter, he will give her the gift of life he is built to give.

If a father withholds nothing, teaching his daughter the life skills she needs to know, he shows an active kind of respect for variety in a girl's developing self.

If a father competes with his daughter in games but, especially when she is young, lets her win her share of races, he is showing her both his own humility and her potential.

As a father does all these things and also provides for his family, in a partnership worked out carefully with the mother, a man shows his daughter the greatness in every man.

And as a father helps a daughter enter the worlds of sexuality, romance, and then marriage, a man becomes more than an arm to walk down the aisle with—he becomes, in his daughter's mind, fearless; for what could take more courage than to acknowledge, as a man, a daughter's budding sexuality, and then lead her on her journey into the bed of another man.

The father's work is sacred work, work diminished in the last few centuries, and work, once fully revived and revisioned, that has the potential to ensure that the wonder of girls will not only flourish, but find ultimate equality in our complex society.

## Father Attachment

Fathering is a commitment of the heart of manhood to the future of human civilization. It is done one child at a time. Mothers and fathers bond somewhat differently to their children—this is nature's way of giving children the best of two wonderful worlds at once.

A father does not secrete high doses of oxytocin, progesterone, or estrogen—biochemicals that hormonally bond offspring to the chemical host. Therefore, men do not have as deep a biological bond with their children as do their mothers. The male body requires greater reliance on both emotional and *social* bonding systems in order to complete the father's attachment to his offspring. He has to bond emotionally with his child, and he has to be aided in ongoing connection to offspring through social strategies like social status, social pressure, marriage, and role-modeling.

David Blankenhorn, in his classic book on fathering, *Fatherless America*, acknowledges this reality by writing: "Men, more than women, are culture-made." Margaret Mead, years earlier, discovered: The most telling way of judging a civilization is by observing its ability to socialize its men into healthy, attached, and effective fathers. Fathers, perhaps more than mothers, must learn to father.

That a man is not biochemically bonded to his offspring in the same way as the mother provides the base, in nature, for both the difficulties and the high achievements of being a father. He must be attached and yet he always remains detached. He is most often a doer—one who is always in action for his children. But many of his actions—especially if he works far away—do not show daily attachment to those children. Nature has given men their own particular challenge as fathers, and has done so for millions of years.

Perhaps the father's most difficult challenge today lies in being able to bond with his daughters. We are a culture that has experimented with turning away from nature as its base of operation. We have neglected to focus attention on the natural part fathering plays in girls' lives, and we've done so with grave results.

## OUR FATHERLESS DAUGHTERS

Nearly half of our daughters will be raised without their fathers in the home during a year or more of their childhood. David Blankenhorn culled statistics and studies from our own and world cultures. When girls are raised without substantial father-bonds, they are more likely to:

- be sexually abused, molested, and raped
- experience other physical violence
- divorce later in life
- receive lower grades in school, be suspended or expelled
- experience child abuse and domestic violence
- have more trouble getting along with peers

- display emotional and behavioral problems
- get in trouble with police
- live in poverty and economic insecurity
- find and stay in lower-paying jobs as adults
- bear children while they are still children

According to the February 2000 Economic Report to the President, children without fathers are:

- twice as likely to do drugs
- 53 percent more likely to commit suicide
- five times more likely to grow up in poverty
- 63 percent more likely to run away
- twice as likely to end up in jail
- four times as likely to require professional help for emotional problems

That these kinds of statistics are true whether the children live in the U.S., England, Syria, India, China, or any other culture should not shock us. Human children, whatever the culture, need to be fathered as well as mothered.

The situation is even worse in cultures where the father's absence is not filled by extended family. Of the thirty cultures I studied for this book, I found that the absence of the biological father—whether to death, divorce, or to work outside the family's proximity—did not cause as severe a crisis for the children if a "second father"—grandfather, uncle, mentor, stepfather—"fathered" the child, in healthy ways, for at least a year or more. This finding has been corroborated by research done by Big Brothers and Big Sisters of America, a nonprofit organization that provides mentors to motherless and fatherless children. When Dad is gone, *and* there is also little or no compensating male presence from the extended family, our daughters don't bond with healthy elder males, and they suffer.

Ironically, while we live in a time when fatherless daughters are becoming more of a norm, we also live in a time when fathers want to bond more fully with their children at birth and want to father them more fully than in centuries past. Suzanne Levine, author of *Father Courage*, points to a new study by the Radcliffe Public Policy center which found that 82 percent of men in the twenty-one to thirty-nine age group deemed a family-friendly work schedule to be "very important," and 71 percent said they would be willing to lose some pay in order to spend more time with their children. The study also found that three times as many working men took advantage of paternity leave in 1999 than did in 1994. The fight for paternity-leave laws paid off, and fathers are using those laws to be with kids. Fathers want to father now more than ever.

In this chapter, as I present you with research, anecdotes, and practical suggestions for how to best father a girl, I do so knowing full well that while fathers want to bond with their children, in many circles today, fathering is a declining art; many fathers are, as family systems break down, losing the ability to be close to their daughters. All practical suggestions are somewhat weak if the father receiving the suggestions is not bonded to his children.

Thus, I will present material and suggestions to you that have, as their ultimate goal, *the general and specific increase of the father–daughter bond in not only our families, but the culture as a whole.* While there are many ways to father, I will present some of the basic gifts a father brings to his parenting, gifts that grow from and build healthy father-daughter bonds in a family system (even if divorce has occurred).

## Gifts of the Father

As a family therapist, who generally sees not the happy families, but those facing stress and difficulty, it has nonetheless been my experience that in the vast majority of cases, the fathers of our daughters are not only good dads, but they may well be better dads than we realize. It is with this positive and optimistic attitude that I'll approach this practical exploration of the gifts fathers can and must bring to their daughters' lives.

In exploring these gifts of the father, I am assuming one gift already: that especially when the mother is in the child-bearing season, the father will, if at all possible, make the personal sacrifices of time and energy necessary to provide the lion's share of financial support for the family. In some families, the mother's job will pay more; in some families, the father will make his contribution as a stay-at-home dad. There are interesting and inspiring exceptions in modern society. In whatever way a father can, he yearns to give the gift of providing for his family, and his family yearns to accept it.

## THE GIFT OF PRESENCE

"Are you coming to my recital, Daddy?" a girl, eight, asks.

"Of course, sweetie."

"Okay." She cuddles up on Dad's lap.

A month later, she comes to him as he sits at his desk: "Are you coming to my open house at school, Daddy?"

"I think it's next Tuesday, right?"

"I guess so."

The father confirms on the calendar that it is, but shakes his head. "Sorry, sweetie, I have to be gone."

From her face he can see her heart sinking, and he feels terrible.

Perhaps a father's harshest self-recrimination (and that of a mother who works away from home) comes when he sits in his car, or on an airplane, or in a hotel room, knowing that he has missed one of his daughters' life moments. Like most fathers who miss these things, he wants to give the gift of presence constantly to his girls, but cannot.

He would like to be able to provide service to the world, make a living, and fulfill intimate obligations to his children all at once, but he cannot. He yearns to give the gift of presence to his girls, but bows to reality, and must withhold it.

Yet this very withholding, quite often, can inspire insight. Perhaps driving to a business meeting one day, he feels an awakening (coming from the very natural guilt he's experienced as he disappointed his daughter, and coming too from pressure others have put on him to be more present to his daughter). He thinks, "I have to find a way, no matter what, to give the gift of presence to my children even when it's the most difficult thing to do." And so perhaps he comes home that night with a plan, a how-to, a piece of evidence of his leadership. Here is what the plan might look like:

1. He will from now on make sure the monthly family calendar is planned so that he is present for at least two-thirds of his child's major life occasions. If this means cuts in pay, he explores that option.

2. When he knows he can't be available on a consistent basis—perhaps for a six-week selling trip to another country—he facilitates a godmother, grandparent, or other extended family member to be available and present as needed.

3. He speaks to his children by phone at least once a day, and e-mails frequently. Thus, he commits to making his children an integral part of his workday.

4. He keeps channels of communication and romance open with his children's mother on a daily basis as well. He knows that she needs his gift of presence as well.

5. He allows himself only one broken promise a year. If he is making promises of presence to his children and breaking them consistently, then he will consider himself an inadequate father, and immediately do something about it.

6. When he's home, he is emotionally available. If he has a particularly exhausting job, he will need to work out rituals with his family regarding how he returns home, revives himself, then gives his presence. He may need to take a relaxing walk or meditate before walking in his front door.

7. He finds other fathers to support him by talking to him, playing basketball or racquetball with him, relaxing with him, and also challenging him. He specifically tells his friends he needs help to be a good father, and will help them as they may require. By doing this, he creates a male kinship community for himself (and for the betterment of his family), one that all dads need.

A girl who knows that her father is always near can forgive him some missed recitals, and knows his long arms will gently enfold her when she needs them. A father who has, through a daily process of presence, opened his arms in this way to his daughter can feel adequate about his fathering, even if he is not able to be present in every moment of a girl's life.

## THE GIFT OF INDEPENDENCE

In a new and very moving book by reporter Bonnie Angelo, *First Mothers,* the lives of the mothers of presidents are revealed. We learn, for instance, how Sara Roosevelt nurtured her son's self-confidence, and how the optimism Franklin Roosevelt brought to tough American times was partially his mother's optimism. We learn how Martha Truman saved her son's life when he was little, hitching up the family wagon and driving him fifteen miles to the doctor.

We also learn something quite intriguing about fathers: not the fathers of Harry Truman, FDR, Gerald Ford, Jimmy Carter, and the seven other presidents whose mothers Ms. Angelo profiles, but about the grandfathers—the fathers of the presidents' mothers. *Ms. Angelo discovered that most of the women who shaped our country's presidents enjoyed a close bond with their fathers.*

These women were, as daughters, "papa's girls." By papa's girl Ms. Angelo does not mean "daddy's girl": a girl whose father gives her everything she wants, especially in a material sense, and in turn "wraps him around her finger." Papa's girl means a relationship between father and daughter in which the father encourages the daughter's independent thinking. All eleven presidents grew up in difficult financial and family circumstances, their mothers challenged to make ends meet. Ms. Angelo believes these women came to their ability to raise brilliant children in difficult times because they had received *the gift of independence* from the most important men in their lives: their dads.

A teacher at the Gurian Institute told me this story. His daughter, Melanie, was seven when the family moved to a house about two blocks from a park. Melanie made a friend a few houses down whose parents let her ride her bike, alone, to the park. Melanie's dad and mom did not want a seven-year-old, even with her friend beside her, going to a park unsupervised.

A few months went by and she turned eight. Now the dad said to his wife, "Honey, let her go. She and Carly will be together. It'll be all right." The dad told me, "It was just something deep inside me that said, 'She's gotta do it!' "

In the father was the visceral push to help his daughter be independent. In his wife, still, protectiveness outweighed. Father and mother haggled for about a month, then finally Mom gave in. Melanie was allowed to go to the park with her friend, and only with a friend—never completely alone.

This family's haggling over a daughter's independence is quite natural; as it is natural for so many men to be like this father—independence-minded himself and, so, oriented toward bestowing the gift of independence, as it becomes appropriate in his eyes, on his children.

Studies continually show that girls who are raised by fathers who help them find their own independence will generally do better in the workplace, and grow into more self-confident women. Beyond social self-confidence, girls who grow up to be independent and personally responsible find the mothering process, as they have children, less a burden on their social self-confidence. They are better able to "take time for themselves" when they need it, better able to create boundaries with their own children, more confident at providing discipline.

Some rules of thumb apply to providing independence-training to daughters. Fathers can involve themselves in many, if not all, of these (as, of course, can moms):

1. Use athletic structures to aid in independence-training. Whether or not a father can coach his daughters in a sport, he can certainly encourage his daughters to enjoy at least one athletic activity. Even while learning teamwork, girls learn independent action through athletic challenge.

2. Let girls do lots of little things independently, like chores, before they are given big gifts of independence. A girl who wants to ride to the park alone but has to be nagged to do the evening dishes may well need Dad to talk to her about the relationship between the privilege of independence and the duty. Duty comes before privilege.

3. Follow the girl's own natural spirit of independence. Little is gained by forcing independence on a girl who is not ready. If it looks like forcing will be required, first try the soft touch of talking to her about why she is inordinately afraid of a particular freedom.

4. It is crucial for a dad to be fearless about admitting a mistake concerning a girl's independence. Sometimes a father gives a freedom too quickly, and must pull it away. His daughter wants to go on the Internet unsupervised, promising she's trustworthy, but then she goes to sites dangerous to her. It is a father's duty to make her wait now, perhaps for a month, before trying the privilege of independence again.

5. Model healthy independent behavior. Every father has to be a follower in certain parts of his life, but there is always some way in which he can lead. Girls watch their fathers lead and gain a model for their own leadership.

6. Provide clear discipline and structure (to be discussed in more detail in a moment) in order to provide independence. Often people forget that the natural way of the mind's growth is evolutionary; in other words, it grows by struggling with problems. A child who grows up with only the loosest rules and little authority around her often ends up being less independent and less sturdy in life because, as a child, she did not have to struggle in order to free her mind.

7. Help facilitate the independence of the mother. Girls who see their mothers taking care of themselves learn the sanctity of independent self-care. Girls who never see their mothers acting for themselves are more likely to grow up cowed by life. Fathers who help mothers find "soul-time"—time for personal renewal— reap the rewards of happier and healthier daughters.

## THE GIFT OF ADVENTURE AND LAUGHTER

Recently, I received this e-mail from a father of three girls:

*"In our house, adventure and laughter go together. Groucho Marx once said, 'A day without laughter is a day wasted.' I always liked that comment. With my kids I kind of add to Groucho: 'A day without adventure is a day unfinished.' I'm the kind of dad who loves new things. My experience with my girls has taught me that a girl's moods go better when she's having adventures, and laughing at foibles and fumbles along the way.*

*"I'll give you an example. This Sunday, I got my daughters to help me repair an antique rocking chair. I am not very handy, and the girls know it. Disaster in the making! Anyway, it didn't take long before I had bruised both my right and left thumbs. Ingelisa, my nine-year-old, was sympathetic. She volunteered to hold the nail for my hammer.*

*"'Don't hold someone else's nail,' I taught her. I told her about a day during my boyhood when I held a nail for my brother's hammer and nearly lost a thumb. Ingelisa, Judith, PJ, and I kept working and still made a mess of things. This was a great little adventure for all of us. We laughed a lot, I can tell you."*

The dad knew his girls and knew that adventures could be little things as well as big. He sounds to me like a master of the little adventures girls love.

I spoke with a minister recently who confessed that there were times he had to make spirituality an adventure. "My girls are so used to hearing about God and the rituals of prayer and practice, sometimes I have to get them away from church.

"Sometimes when we're on vacation and we're in another city, we don't go to the church there. Instead, we go to a natural place, a park or a river. We spend an hour searching for rocks, crawdads, and others among God's creatures. We splash each other, and get our shoes wet, and laugh. We end with prayers. Our silent prayer time there, in the presence of the cascading water, is a divine outdoor adventure, different than our everyday 'Church' Sunday."

Children love adventure, and sometimes it's the father's job to make adventure part of their lives. Girls love to laugh, and sometimes it's the father's job to be the joker. Nearly any family can get in a car and drive somewhere and discover something, and quite often, if Mom wants a rest, Dad can have father-daughter time for these adventures, moments when he and his daughters branch out on their own.

In all these adventures (and the humorous misadventures they entail) there is a great deal of Dad saying with or without words, "I believe in you," "I know you can do it," "You're a young woman who *will* know herself and *will* make her mark." There is also a lot of the kind of team building that will help her, throughout life, to know how to socialize, how to compete, how to accomplish, and how to enjoy herself wherever she is and in whatever she does.

Some father-daughter adventures are athletic ones. I, like many dads, have coached my daughters at soccer. This is often a humorous misadventure! I am not the greatest coach. As the girls get older, they advance in both soccer and karate with other coaches; my role in the adventure is to drive them around, support them, and help them through disappointments, not as a coach, but as a companion. Whenever possible, especially when they were young, I tried to let them beat me at things, like running or scoring goals, but as they got older, the adventure became "how to beat Dad," rather than, "Dad will let us win."

As a father provides his daughters with adventures, with fun, and with games, there can be one very practical downside to watch for. It occurs often among divorced dads. Dad only sees his daughter a few days a month and wants her to be happy with him. He chooses to just have adventures and games with her—no rules, no restrictions. Every divorced dad needs to be vigilant about this very natural tendency to just want to be a daughter's friend, for a girl who only knows her dad as fun and games does not fully know her dad. She will not learn everything he has to teach, and the constant sense of game and adventure will, finally, wear thin for her, because it is her nature to need more from her father than just "happy times."

## THE GIFT OF AFFECTION

Once, as my daughters and I left the parking lot to enter an ice skating rink, I saw a father in police uniform, about 260 pounds and all muscle, holster empty but belt on, holding one of his daughters, about four, to his chest, and another, about eight, by hand. Both girls glowed in his affection. He looked like the sort of man who did not hug much—a grim-faced fellow with straight blond hair cut nearly in a crew style, serious, hard-working, diligent, and true, but not very emotional, not very expressive. Yet I sensed that he was also the kind of man who, when he did show affection, touched his daughters with warmth; from their happy faces I saw that this man's daughters knew he always, and unconditionally, loved them.

Often fathers are not sure if they are meeting the minimal requirements for providing affection to their daughters; sometimes girls' emotional needs are mysterious to dads. Hopefully, the blueprint that follows will be helpful. If you as a father provide it, you can be stoic like the man appeared at the rink, and yet more than completely bestow the gift of affection.

1. Create rituals for your girls. Driving to the store with your daughter once a week, or doing the yard work or fixing the car together, or doing sports together—each provides structured, ritual opportunities for sharing affection, whether physical, with "high fives" slapped hand to hand, or verbal, with critique and encouragement shared, or silent, as two people who love each other join together in work. Bedtime reading rituals, church time, breakfast and dinner time, school plays, and recitals can be ritual times of verbal and even physical affection.

2. Mirror affection physically. Give back physical affection when a child reaches for it.

3. Provide approval consciously and constantly. There is nothing for a daughter quite like hearing from her father: "I'm so proud of you."

While it is important for a father to provide discipline, critique, and even show disappointment in his daughter, it is even more important he shows his approval for jobs well done. Whether with hugs, words, or just a simple nod that says, "Yes, you did it, girl!" a father ought to approve of his daughter most of the time. If she is involved in high-risk, immoral behavior, then this equation changes; yet even then, he needs to find things to like about her.

Especially if he is not the kind of man who hugs his daughter, he must find the words, even if only a few, to let her know when she has done well. When he compliments, he might be aware of whether he compliments only one element of her—say, her physical beauty. She needs him to compliment her mind, body, soul, and heart at different times, and in balance.

4. Provide lots of father-daughter physical activity. We have often seen fathers who scare mothers by tossing their toddler daughters up in the air over and over until the child is laughing hysterically. By nature males tend to be more physical and spatial in their play style than females. Generally, fathers do not endanger their daughters with their roughhousing, and the affection shared is vital. Again, especially if a father tends toward verbal and physical stoicism, play is a great outlet for letting love glow in the dance of father and daughter.

5. Enlist mothers to help. Moms can help build affection between fathers and daughters by pointing out to girls the gifts of love dads give. This is especially important in homes where fathers are not too expressive. "Your dad may not always say it, but he sure loves you, and I'll give you an example." Some men more than others need women to help them fully display themselves to their children. If you as a father are this particular kind of man, it is especially important you return the gift of revelation Mom offers by showing your daughter how valued her mother is, in the ways her mom needs you to.

6. Stay close through adolescence. Fathers often lose the ease with which they give affection as their daughters hit adolescence.

This is natural: A girl becomes harder to be around, and sometimes men are also frightened by a daughter's budding sexuality and hormonal moods. At the same time, it is natural for the father to find new ways to keep close to her.

Will Glennon, author of *Fathering,* interviewed hundreds of fathers for his book, discovering, "Early adolescence is exactly the moment when Dad steps back. Even the good dads who were there when she was little do this. Girls are being severely and unnecessarily handicapped."

Heather Johnston Nicholson, research director of Girls, Inc., an organization that studies and assists female development, corroborates Glennon's conclusion. Her studies have found that girls who enjoy loving relationships with fathers throughout adolescence "show more confidence in themselves and achieve more in school." She also points to studies that have found these same girls are more likely to go to college, something most fathers today hope their children will do.

Part of the father's blueprint for giving affection is to never stop giving it. As his daughter grows breasts and becomes self-conscious, he cannot be as intimately physical—but now he can develop athletic rituals with her that don't involve a lot of touch. He can play tennis or another sport with her. He can teach her to drive. He can still call on her to help him make repairs. He can sit and listen to her, sometimes even when she is boring him to death.

7. Fathers give affection by the sacrifices they make for daughters. Girls need fathers to help them understand these father-sacrifices. Early in my relationship with Gail, she told me about her father, Dean, with whom I've now become good friends. He confused me at first because he is a very silent man and I'm a talker.

I asked Gail, "What was it like, being brought up by so stoic a man?"

She said, "I always knew he loved me, even though he didn't speak much." She listed many things about him that gave this sense, ending by saying, "I always knew he would sacrifice anything for me."

In the end, no matter the style of father a girl has, she needs to know he will give up anything for her safety, and her good life. That is the ultimate gift of affection.

## THE GIFT OF DISCIPLINE AND SELF-RESTRAINT

Often you might hear people say, "Moms are better at discipline than dads." Equally often: "Dads are better disciplinarians than moms." In the human conversation we tend to take shortcuts as we both remember and discuss being parented. Sometimes these short-cuts are accurate, but so often, the application of discipline in a child's life is more complex. Since giving discipline is a crucial part of a father's love, it is fair to say that a man's daughters cannot fully feel loved or be loving if they do not experience love as not only a glow of affection but also as discipline—the teaching of self-management of feeling and behavior. This discipline is provided, of course, by Mom, Dad, and others in the three families working together.

There are some interesting differences in how moms and dads generally provide discipline. Mothers tend to provide discipline and compel self-restraint by talking to daughters about what they are feeling. Girls learn, through interaction with Mom (and by watching her), how to manage their feelings in microscopic ways.

Fathers tend more to teach self-restraint by imposing it. Men tend to be more macroscopic: We generalize more. "Now, honey, you know that's whining, and whining gets you nowhere with me."

Both the masculine and feminine ways of teaching self-restraint are generally good ways. From Gail, my own daughters learn how to process their feelings better than from me. From me, they learn how to control their feelings better than they do from Gail. Both "processing" and "self-control" are equally important to a growing child. Maturity is measured both in terms of how well a person *knows* her own feelings and how well she *controls* them.

For girls especially, the issues of knowing and controlling feelings are very much a matter of juggling the demands of the female mind. The female brain experiences so much sensory-laden and emotion-laden material in a given moment—because of more emotion stored in the hippocampus along with memory, because of more blood flow through the emotion-charged limbic system, because of larger tear glands than males, greater socialization toward emotion, and greater left hemisphere word-emotion association. Helping a girl to both process and control feelings is essential, and often the father is the person more geared toward "control."

Some females may notice that often the father is more geared toward "enforcing rules" and the mother toward leniency. (As always, there are many exceptions to this.) A mother may joke with the kids about how much less chaotic life would be for them if "their father was not around." At our own dinner table conversation about this recently Gabrielle smiled and said, in her wry way: "I think we'd get away with a lot." Gail and I often return to the idea of microscopic and macroscopic in order to try to undertand what Gabrielle so wryly observed.

Mom, who typically does more of the hands-on child care, is often so involved with the *microscopic elements* of raising her daughters that she can't attend as closely to the *structural elements*. She is thus likely to say, "Don't do that again . . ." "I said, 'Stop that!' " "If you do that again, there will be a consequence," and say these things many times in a row. The positive result is that her daughters exercise their muscles of autonomy and "get away with stuff," the negative result, however, is that Mom gets overwhelmed, and her daughters forget where their developmental boundaries are.

The father, who is typically less microscopically involved with children's lives, tends to pay more attention to structural elements; he tends to impose territory and boundaries. "If you do that again there will be a consequence." He may say this in a deep, resounding voice, and much of the time the unrestrained child behavior does not happen again. His daughters are "forced," by his attentiveness to structure, to stay within the boundaries. The disadvantage to his masculine discipline style comes when it is either extreme or abusive, or when he knows nothing else but to impose structure.

Once during a family discussion about discipline, Davita said, "We're more afraid of you, Daddy, than we are of Mommy." This was an insightful comment for a seven-year-old, one that both hurt me in my deepest heart, and one that satisfied me. While I do not abuse my children, it hurts a parent to know their child fears them. Yet, I knew by her comment that things were okay in my house; that what used to be called "the fear of God" existed in my house—a basic respect for authority and order; and that Gail was receiving, from me, assistance a father can and should give. When, after this conversation, I asked Gail about Davita's comment, she admitted, to my surprise, a certain relief. "Actually," she said, "I'm glad they're a little afraid of you. You should see how different it is when you're not here. They're just wild. When you're here, life's easier."

In our home, we are fortunate to provide our daughters with a mama bear and a papa bear—two different styles of parenting toward discipline and feeling-management that we believe will end up creating an emotionally healthy—both emotionally expressive and emotionally restrained—adult woman. We know too that in many homes, it is Dad who lets his child get away with more unruly behavior and Mom who is the macroscopic disciplinarian.

Every home has its own structure, so I hope you'll modify the following discipline tips to fit the parent best suited to pursue it. Some of them were presented in the previous chapter, on mothering. I present them to you here, in this discussion of a father's gifts, because often it is a helpful division of labor to make sure Dad imposes many of these boundaries on children.

1. Discipline is really not an issue for daughters who are eighteen months or younger. The developing brain cannot yet fully process—whether experientially, verbally, or in memory—how the act of discipline (especially something like a swat on the bottom) pertains to the personal behavior. Especially fathers who physically punish infants must immediately educate themselves on how that beautiful little mind is growing.

2. Altering a child's behavior—which is the primary reason we punish—of girls eighteen months to about four years old can

often be accomplished by distracting the girl, or making up a game by which to accomplish the task the girl is refusing. It's worth trying these options before punishment.

3. Discipline of a daughter can almost always be accomplished through time-outs, taking away privileges, and other nonphysical strategies. Spanking might happen once or twice a year (see Chapter 4), and a swat on the bottom two or three times a year, but no more is generally necessary.

4. Whining is something to help a girl phase out by the time she's about five. It is useful to remember that whining behavior is generally not emotional behavior. In other words, a dad is not hurting his daughter's emotional development by helping her to stop whining. Whining is generally a manipulative strategy. The exception to this occurs when a daughter is whining relentlessly because she is hungry, or because something is going on emotionally that she can't yet name. In these cases, the whining masks something very important. Otherwise, whining is generally a kind of behavior to "cure." Generally a week or so of stern comments (with follow-through) along the lines of "You may not whine about that anymore" handles the problem.

5. While sibling rivalry is normal, nasty fighting is not allowed. (See Chapter 7.) If nasty fighting, name-calling, sibling competition, and getting-each-other-in-trouble is invading safe, comfortable family life, it becomes a prime issue for discipline.

6. One of the greatest allies to discipline and self-restraint is high expectations for performance, including performance at small things, like doing chores. Often fathers need to be vigilant about supporting chore schedules. Just as often, fathers need to have high expectations for a daughter's behavior, school work, and rela-tionships. A great ally in making sure chores get done (as well as other important actions) is ritualized life. Often Dad's deep voice needs to remind his daughter to clean her room *before* she goes out to play, or do homework *before* watching TV. The more ritual-ized the daily and weekly events in a girl's life are, the more natu-ral self-discipline becomes.

## THE GIFT OF THE BODY

Fathers often, and for very natural reasons of embarrassment and confusion, neglect to fully care for a daughter's sense of her own physical development. Often, it is as if we are looking at someone right in front of us, but not fully looking.

A great deal of an adolescent girl's self-image is based in her body image, as we will explore more fully in Chapter 6. There are intrinsic biological reasons for this, reasons which have existed since the beginning of human development. Budding breasts, the female figure, waist size, length of legs, facial beauty, even hairstyle are all issues of biological self-image for girls, especially as their bodies, guided by genetics and hormones, enter puberty and become attractive to males. Female culture is the most influential element on female self-image during a girl's pubescence—moms, other women, girls, girl-oriented magazines. This female culture often unconsciously strives to shape girls toward attractiveness to males. So even though boys, fathers, and other men may not be the intimate guides of the female body, women are guiding its development in large part based on their assumptions of what males want.

In this very complex nurturance of a girl's body and self-image, our daughters need stable male influences—men they trust to whom they can turn for wisdom. This is especially true in our present era, in which the media bombards girls with conflicting messages about body image, and in which hormones used in food and pesticides are affecting female puberty and body image relentlessly (see Chapter 6 for more information).

A hundred years ago a father might protect the budding bodies of his adolescent daughters by holding shotguns to potential suitors. Now, we can protect our daughters' bodies by fully fathering their bodies. What does this mean?

1. It means embracing their bodies with our attention, good communication, and our wisdom. We don't turn away from our girls, we don't stop hugging them for fear of touching their breasts. We talk to our girls about how complex our adult male feelings are, and how mindful girls should always be of the way

boys and men think. We stop hugging only when our daughters want that. We listen to our daughters' fears and joys surrounding their changing bodies.

2. We help our girls develop a plan for how they will show their bodies during adolescence. We help them figure out how they want to dress and why, what they gain and lose by showing off breasts and upper thighs. If we have to err, we err on the side of modesty, championing more clothing rather than less. Here we must be artful as fathers. We talk, we cajole, we convince, we listen, we compromise. We apply to our communication with our daughters the same negotiation skills we would use in a complex business deal. Our goal is not totalitarian—but it is not blind. We are men who know the realities of the sexual lives of adolescent boys, and our story, our wisdom about constructing a body-plan for adolescence is crucial to keeping our girls safe.

3. We help our girls develop a "dating and mating" plan for adolescence. One of the biggest mistakes we've made as a culture over the last few decades is the elevation of romantic language to the primary language of adolescent cross-sex bonding. "Do you love him?" we ask, as if 1) a fourteen-year-old girl necessarily knows what that means, or 2) the answer to that question is more important than "Is he good for you?" or "Do you know what you're doing?" Adolescent girls may often claim to care only about love and romance, but they themselves need and want help in understanding males, and making practical—not romantic—decisions about boys and young men. We will discuss this much further when we deal with sexual morality in Chapter 7.

Gail and I won't allow "alone-dating"—boy/girl alone—until our daughters are sixteen. We are honest with our daughters about matters of the body and sex, as well as abstinence and birth control options. We very much like the book *Beyond the Birds and the Bees*, by Beverly Engel, as a parent resource for dealing with adolescents and sexuality.

*One Father's Story: When the Father Has Not Given the Gift of the Body*

Personally and professionally, I realized the pain fathers can feel when working with a particular family in my therapy practice.

There had been a divorce and custody of the two girls went to the mother, with the father allowed mainly weekend visitation. The second daughter, who was eleven at the time of divorce, became a very difficult adolescent. By the time she was fourteen, she was sexually active. By the time she was fifteen, she had a boyfriend she had discovered on the Internet, who lived in the same city. They saw each other nearly every day. When the girl's mother threatened consequences should she sleep with the boy in her home, her daughter ignored her. Her daughter would not even respond about whether she used birth control. When the mother pleaded with the father to become involved, he confronted his daughter, who said, "What do you care, you're never around." He had no authority in her life, and her mother had lost her authority, overwhelmed as a single parent.

"It's my body," the fifteen-year-old told me when she and I discussed her situation. "It's mine, and I can do with it what I want."

This girl went from being a developmentally appropriate early adolescent—modest, self-protective, and appropriately immature—to being a body-oriented, sexually promiscuous fifteen-year-old. While there were many reasons for this shift, one of the primary reasons was her loss of her father's authority. He was no longer a healthy mediator between her and male culture. He was no longer the "protector" he could be—armed not with shotgun, but with wisdom—as she moved into the world of boys and men.

The active father gives his daughter the gift of sexuality in ways she desperately wants and needs. She relies on him to stand with her in good relationships, and stand between her and dangerous ones.

## Helping a Daughter Manage Peer Relationships

We've focused on specific gifts a father gives his daughters. One more gift, very broad and very important, requires our attention, especially in today's adolescent world of confusing peer relationships.

Generally a father does not have to *consciously* help his daughter manage the relationships in her life unless they become relationships that disturb her or the family. Generally, she learns to manage her own relationships by trial and error, and of course by watching the examples of Mom, Dad, and others.

However, one of the most difficult situations families face is when their daughters become involved in unhealthy peer alliances. How can a father help his daughter and his family when this happens, and how can he help prevent it?

As with so many things we've discussed, the father, mother, other elders in the family, and community are working together. Fathers, who can tend to think their adolescent daughters "are grown-up girls, so they don't need me," or "girls, not boys, so I don't really have a role," can find out how essential they are to their daughters by practicing the art of fathering in the following ways. Every child will probably, one day, form a peer relationship parents don't like; but in most cases, if a dad does these things, his daughter should be generally protected.

1. As a dad, be as involved in school activities as much as possible. When you can't be, make sure you are fulfilling your responsibilities as a father to create a family environment in which Mom, another family, and extended family members are constantly active in your daughter's school life. The more active the family is in the girl's schooling, the better able it is to help guide her toward healthy friendships, and see unhealthy alliances for what they are. The majority of these are formed in school.

2. Let your daughter know that no matter what her age, if danger enters a relationship, you will contact the peer's parents. It is worth remembering that no growing child has an inalienable right to a completely private friendship. When a child has a friend, the family has gained a friend. When a child enters a dangerous relationship, the family has come to dangerous ground as well. Letting our daughters know that we will always help them, even when they are afraid of losing the friend, shows how much we care.

Out of respect for our daughter, we must contact the friend or peers' parents carefully, and with full disclosure to our daughter, especially as she is becoming more independent during adolescence and the teen years.

3. Set aside time every week to have your daughter's friends over, to get to know their parents, and to socialize with adults in your daughter's friendship circles. Make your home a peer-welcoming place. Take your daughter and her friends to activities they would enjoy. When a father knows his daughter's friends, his daughter feels more bonded with her father, better able to manage friendship issues, and better able to talk to Dad about any peer problems.

4. Engage your daughter in conversation about how her relationships are going, especially as she grows from early-to-middle adolescence. This is a difficult time. Our daughters generally want to know we are there for them as they navigate social waters.

5. Create and enforce reasonable rules for your daughter's and her friends' behavior in the home and surrounding environments. When your daughter is seven or eight, these rules will probably be relatively benign—no running through the living room while adults are talking, pick up after yourself, don't leave the screen door open. As your daughter starts getting older, old rules can be renegotiated. Yet there must still be *core rules* that your daughter knows she *and her friends* must abide by.

When a boy is going to come over to do homework with your fifteen-year-old daughter, for instance, it is appropriate to say, "In this house, until you are sixteen, you can't have the door closed." Your daughter might gripe (more than once), "You don't trust me!" but before you know it, she may also be saying, "You know, Dad, I'm glad we had that rule, because remember that guy, Paul, who used to come over—I think he wished the door was closed for more than studying." A father's wisdom does not always prove itself in the moment, but quite often, in a daughter's memory.

6. Lead your daughter to community and spiritual activities where she can meet healthy young people. Keep her directed

toward church, synagogue, mosque, and other religious communities. Keep her directed to family groups, uncles, aunts and cousins, or to co-ops and other non-blood extended family groups. Show her volunteer service groups in her early adolescent years. Help her join and enjoy skill-oriented communities like athletics or 4H or Girl Scouts or band or clubs, where she can meet peers with whom she forms healthy friendships.

One major advantage of getting her involved in these activities is the decrease of her time spent in front of TV and other media. The more she's with real people, the less attached she becomes to media imagery that promotes unhealthy alliances. Girls who don't bond with their own families and communities do often bond with the media characters, stories, and images. While these images are sometimes useful to those of us raising children, they are generally not based in a creator's or producer's desire to raise a healthy girl. Media programming is based in the desire to use visceral neural images to guide girls toward the consumption of products that, most often, girls don't need. The more a father guides his daughter (and joins with her) in active social life away from the media's neural programming, the more likely that a girl will grow into healthy social relationships.

Creating orderly environments for growing girls, encouraging community involvement, and being an active father will, along with active mothering and family time, make a life for a growing girl that keeps unhealthy influences, and friendships, to the minimum. However, some will arise, and here are some steps of leadership to take:

1. Clearly think out whether the friend is unhealthy or not, and exactly why. If you can, discover reasons (it's often useful to write them down) that are quite concrete ("On June 10, Maggie came home at 12:00 A.M. though she had an 11:00 P.M. curfew, then again on the 17th, 25th and 26th, and each time she was in Jeb's car. . . ."); check these with your daughter's mother or another caregiver you and your daughter trust. The concrete

items need generally to be *actions*, not just "What I don't like about so-and-so is . . ." A peer's clothes, for instance, are not generally an issue for intervention. A father who jumps to conclusions—blaming his daughter's friend for what might actually be his daughter's problem or attacking externals like clothing—will alienate his daughter. Clearly determining cause and effect, then getting a second opinion, helps a father avoid these pitfalls.

2. Bring the issues to your daughter in a nondomineering way (especially if she's in middle-to-late adolescence). Focus her attention on the peer's *behavior*, and her active participation in it. Begin the conversation with positives—how much you love your daughter, what you like about her, what you like about her friend—then be unflinching in presenting possible consequences of her dangerous actions, such as drug use.

3. Even if a confrontation ensues, find a way to get your daughter to talk about why she likes the friend, what she is valuing in her relationship with her or him. Through this, and through tears and anger, it is sometimes possible to help her see that she is valuing another person above herself.

4. Work out a deal regarding this friend. "Let's give it another week to see if you can solve the problem with your friend." Help your daughter, by using methods like role playing, to find the skills to talk to the friend. Let your daughter know that you will have to contact the friend's parents by the end of the week, if your daughter and you, together, are not satisfied with what is happening.

5. Contact the friend's parents if necessary, especially after the allotted period. Engage the help of other community members if needed—for instance, counselors and teachers.

6. As a last resort, and only after an open policy of conversation and action has been tried, forbid your daughter to see the dangerous friend. If you are in a position of having to resort to this tactic, especially with a teen, be ready for many weeks of family confrontations. Recently, I helped a father, mother, and

family negotiate a situation in which the daughter, fourteen, was forbidden to see a boy, sixteen, who was a drug user. The girl was very attached to the boy—"I'm in love with him"—and for three months, the family was torn up. The daughter was grounded many times. But when the boy ended up arrested, and as time healed wounds, the family reconnected.

In this particular case, someone had to hold the hard line, and the father chose to be "the bad guy." It was immensely painful for him. He thought he had lost his daughter forever. But his fear for her safety compelled him to hold the hard line, and he ended up "being right." The whole family was hurt by this for months, and being right was little satisfaction, but at least the father was able to look back and say he had done his best.

## Fathers, Daughters, and Divorce

Most of what we have explored regarding the gifts of the father apply to any father, including divorced, single, or stepfathers. And yet, as every single or blended family knows, there are some core issues unique to that family circumstance.

A divorced father told me about his seventeen-year-old daughter. He and his wife divorced when she was twelve, one of the most difficult times (puberty) for a child to experience the dissolution of family. This girl became very angry, mainly at her father. She blamed the father (though in this case it was the mother who initiated the divorce). The father was in the military and was gone from the home for many months of the year. The daughter focused on this as her initial reason for anger, but in the months after divorce, she had no focus: just constant rage at Dad. Finally, he decided to give sole custody of her to her mother, and now she lives with her mom and stepdad.

This father said to me, "Mary Ellen is a good kid, and one day she's going to talk to me again, but for now, what else could I do?"

This father's sacrifice is one of the supreme sacrifices men make for children. Every day fathers are divorcing and being divorced, and they are trying to hold on to attachments with children, and many, finally, are having to just let go. The pain of the divorced father today is not fully understood. This father's pain affected every day of his life. "To tell you the truth," he told me, "there isn't a day goes by I don't think about Mary Ellen. Every day, it breaks my heart."

Our culture has embraced divorce without embracing enough the specific needs of the players in the divorce—mother, father, or children. Each of these figures in the family triangle suffers immensely. For fathers, the greatest suffering is most often the suffering of increased distance from children.

Yet our daughters adore us and need us. Here are some keys to maintaining attachment with your daughter during, and after, a divorce:

1. Make maintaining a close relationship number one on your priority list. If and when it looks like marital reconciliation with the mother is not possible, move a large share of your emotional efforts to maintaining intimacy with your child.

2. Forgive the child's mother as quickly as possible for whatever wrongdoing or grievance you feel. Do it for the sake of the child. Forgiveness of the mother allows for a better relationship with her, and thus a closer relationship with the child.

3. Fight for joint custody when appropriate, and show the court you will give up work hours if you can to spend more parent time with your daughter.

4. Continue to advocate for courts and our culture to understand that a father who must work to pay child support cannot be penalized by being cut out of joint custody.

5. Join a support group through your church or other community agency as soon as the divorce process begins. A man who goes through a divorce without structured emotional support generally has more trouble maintaining attachment with his children.

Vivian Gadsden, director of the National Center on Fathers and Families in Philadelphia, adds this short, important list of tricks for staying close:

1. Agree on a time every day to call or e-mail your daughter. This could be at breakfast or bedtime. You might make the agreement to "tell about our days" as the starting point of the father-daughter time.

2. Keep up with your child's interests. Ask questions and listen to answers. Remember the names of her friends.

3. Only make promises you can keep.

This last tip is so important. A broken promise can devastate our daughters, and our attachment with them.

In a letter a divorced dad wrote: "I have worked harder at being a dad since my divorce than I have at any other thing." So often divorced dads feel this and need our support.

Important references for any dad going through divorce include *The Divorced Dad's Handbook*, and *Divorced Dads*, by Sanford Braver and Diane O'Connell, and *Vicki Lansky's Divorce Book for Parents* by Vicki Lansky.

## The Stages of "Dad"

Let me end this chapter with a touching and somewhat humorous note sent to me via the Internet. Many thanks to the author, who did not name herself.

*Four Years Old — My daddy can do anything!*

*Eight Years Old — My daddy knows a lot!*

*Twelve Years Old — My daddy doesn't really know quite everything.*

*Fourteen Years Old — Naturally, Daddy doesn't know that either.*

*Sixteen Years Old — My father? He's a dinosaur!*

*Nineteen Years Old — Dad's okay, just clueless.*

*Twenty-five Years Old — Well, he might know a little bit about it.*

*Thirty-five Years Old — Before we decide, let's see what Dad thinks.*

*Forty-five Years Old — Wonder what Daddy would have thought about it.*

*Sixty-five Years Old — Wish I could talk it over with Daddy.*

How does a father of daughters measure his life? Certainly it must be in whether his daughters find happiness.

As a father, I would be satisfied by this humorous age-staged measure of a happy relationship with my daughters. If when I'm gone they will say, with genuine affection, that they missed not only my presence, but also my wisdom, I think I will smile forever.

# 6

## INNOCENCE AND EXPERIENCE

### PROTECTING THE EMOTIONAL
### DEVELOPMENT OF OUR GIRLS

*"Help! I'm on an emotional roller coaster!"*

—Gabrielle, twelve

*"I don't think a parent ever feels like she's done enough to pro-
tect the emotional development of girls. It's a mountain that
we never finish climbing. But I wouldn't have missed climbing
it for the world."*

—Terry Bridger, teacher of twenty-five years,
and mother of three girls

Jasmine, fifteen, walked into my office dressed in blue jeans, a
black leather jacket faded at the edges, a nose ring, and multiple
earrings. Her hair looked like it had not been combed or washed in a
few days, yet it looked styled—this, I knew from my own daughters,
is "the messy look." Jasmine wore a blank expression, her face plas-
tered with makeup so it looked like a mask, her eyes twinkling inside
it all, but her demeanor so accustomed to extremes of emotion—
either withholding how she felt or expressing it inappropriately—
that she had chosen, even if unconsciously, to just appear numb,
especially with strange adults in authority.

Jasmine and her family had been referred to me through an interesting coincidence. One of the teachers, Patty, at the Gurian Institute

in Missouri had mentioned to me that her sister lived in Spokane, and had a daughter who had gone through hard emotional times the last year. Patty talked about her niece who, at eight or nine, seemed to enjoy life, navigating well enough its ups and downs, but by thirteen, had been depressed, angry, and numb.

When Jasmine walked into my office with her mother, the building of trust was helped generously by the fact that I knew her Aunt Patty in Kansas City. As I finished the "family" portion of the initial interview and asked to speak to Jasmine alone, I noticed in conversation with this teenager a striking similarity to her own mother—she criticized herself a great deal.

In the mother, the self-criticism was overt: "I can't think of what her father and I have done wrong, but whatever it is we'll fix it." In the daughter, the self-criticism was less based in taking personal responsibility and more in her demeanor and manner. Her heavy makeup and earrings created a teenage persona that attempted to change herself from the girl she must have thought she was—not flashy at all; not rebellious; not seen, heard, nor listened to—into a young woman who would be noticed. It struck me that she was also a little like her aunt in Kansas City, who wore a black leather coat.

When I called this latter fact to her attention, Jasmine shrugged approval of my insight, and spoke of her aunt whom, she confessed, she had once thought she'd like to live with. Jasmine tested my trust as our conversation began and, finally, paid me the ultimate compliment a therapist can receive after a first session with a troubled teenage girl: She said she would come back.

Jasmine is like many of our daughters in perhaps a hundred ways, but one in particular stands out for me: She is emotionally fragile. Every human being is emotionally fragile and yet there are certain ways that adolescent girls are particularly fragile, and require our special attention if we are to feel we have done our best for our daughters.

1. Like many adolescent girls, Jasmine had enjoyed sports (volleyball, in her case) at eleven years old, but by fourteen felt "I wasn't ever going to be good enough, good like some of the other

girls, so yeah, I quit. No big deal." Her self-confidence was fragile; an all-or-nothing kind of self-concept.

2. Like many adolescent girls, Jasmine had enjoyed a pleasant, communicative relationship with her parents at ten years old but by fifteen often refused to talk to them about why she was crying, or angry, and what was happening in her life. She experienced her primary relationships as fragile alliances. While some "leave me alone" is normal, it can also signal fragile trust in oneself and others. Jasmine had this fragile self-trust.

3. Like many adolescent girls, Jasmine's hold on previous security routines and people was fragile. She had enjoyed a normal early adolescence in terms of eating habits, school, and family life, but now ate only junk food (often refusing family meals), did not do homework—grades dropping from A's and B's to C's—felt oppressed by family gatherings, and thought most kids "sucked." The more emotionally fragile an adolescent feels, the more a pattern develops whereby she will tend to ensure her fragility by breaking apart structures that used to keep her happy.

Jasmine clearly needed help. She, I, and her family began with some questions.

Following are ten questions for any parent whose daughter, like Jasmine, is going through the emotional fragility of adolescence.

1. Given her genetic personality and who she is by nature, can her emotional development during this time go better?

2. How much of her emotional fragility is normal for any girl her age?

3. How much will time heal through the normal adolescent process of emotional trial and error?

4. To what extent are parents responsible to heal her?

5. To what extent are other family members and friends responsible?

6. To what extent is the girl herself responsible for her emotional development during early-to-middle adolescence?

7. To what extent is her situation a result of difficulty she is having in fulfilling the intimacy imperative?

8. What external factors—like pollutants from media, bad nutrition, and social pressures—are stimulating her toward less self-trust?

9. In what way is there a long-term gain in both human fragility itself, and in the way a girl and young woman is experiencing it?

10. How does her tumultuous emotional development lead her to develop character and a sense of deeper meaning as a human being?

Jasmine's emotional fragility had gone somewhat beyond normal, though there were many normal components to it. When I gave her and her family a list with these ten questions to ponder, they were surprised to find that the word "self-esteem" did not appear on it. Jasmine's family had been talking mainly the language of self-esteem with school counselors and parents. I was nudging them not to devalue that language per se, but to create other language for Jasmine's emotional life too.

Why didn't we spend a lot of time on the question of how to raise Jasmine's self-esteem? Her self-esteem was certainly low, and her therapy over the months sought to help it rise, but unlike some of my colleagues in the field of psychotherapy, I've found that *starting* with "self-esteem" often makes sure that girls, their families, and their mentors avoid some of the *deeper* issues of a girl's female emotional development.

## Girls and Self-Esteem: A Different View

Parents and professionals today live in a time that is almost obsessed with protecting girls by "boosting their self-esteem." Measurements of whether a girl has "high self-esteem" or "low self-esteem" are generally based on a girl's assertiveness in the world around her, even though assertiveness is only one measure of self-esteem, and can be quite deceptive. Advocates for girls, early in the 1980s, seized on the phrase "low self-esteem" to describe a girl or woman who was not functioning at peak levels of social or business efficacy. A number of books came out to help all of us cherish our daughters better by helping them have better self-esteem. Mary Pipher's *Reviving Ophelia: Saving the Selves of Adolescent Girls* showed us deeply troubled girls, each a victim of very low self-esteem. At the more practical end of the spectrum was Carol Eagle and Carol Colman's *All That She Can Be: Helping Your Daughter Maintain Her Self-Esteem*.

The "self-esteem" research has obviously been of great help to us, but in our practice and work Gail and I do not spend a great deal of time with it or with its language, because in so many cases we have found that the emotional issues a girl faces only get dealt with superficially when a family, or the girl herself, is focused on her "low self-esteem."

## MYTHS ABOUT SELF-ESTEEM AND GIRLS

To some extent, the self-esteem dialogue has been a limiting one rather than a liberating one, and it has lacked, in certain crucial areas, simple common sense. Here are some myths that bind it, and some commonsense facts that liberate our girls to find deeper meaning in life.

MYTH 1: Self-esteem is mainly a socially controllable emotional state. Girls' self-esteem is mainly controlled by outside forces—the "culture." Our culture—patriarchal—exists, in this myth, to damage girls' self-esteem.

FACT: While there is no doubt children (and girls in their particular way) experience cultural pressure and damage, a girl's self-esteem is often an internal biological process, a flow of energy moving outward, inward, outward, inward. It is certainly influenced by culture, but it is not as much a victim of culture as people have argued. To link it with culture only, and not the hormonal cycle, is to cut girls and their families off from one of the primary ways girls develop meaning and emotional growth: through their own natural rhythms, *which always include periods of self-esteem drop*, for between one and two weeks during the female hormonal cycle.

MYTH 2: Self-esteem drops, especially in female adolescence, indicate deep trouble in a girl's life. The normal, healthy state of being for girls should be "to be like they were at seven and eight, feeling good about themselves." The AAUW (American Association of University Women) studies in the early nineties identified the adolescent female self-esteem drop as one of our worst social problems.

FACT: Girls' self-esteem drops are normal and, even further, it is crucial that girls (and boys) experience self-esteem drops. The drops are normal biologically and neurologically as the child's brain, body, and psyche are, during Stage 3, becoming adult. As children transform, they feel overwhelmed by the adult world; self-esteem drops as the psyche experiences, in trial and error, the pressures upon it. Furthermore, these self-esteem drops are crucial in developing adolescents as the child's psychological method of combating the inherent narcissism of adolescence. Self-esteem drops are experiences of humility every adolescent needs, and as a society we should want our children to go through them so that our children become mature and healthy adults.

MYTH 3: Paying attention to a girl's self-esteem is more important than other themes in her life. To be a good parent is to care first about our girls' self-esteem.

FACT: Paying attention to female *character* development (which includes self-esteem)—paying attention to a girl's assessment of herself on *moral and spiritual* grounds (subjects of Chapter 7)—are just as important, yet less discussed these days. A landmark study out of the University of Minnesota discovered that positive spiritual connections was one of the three most important ways to help girls move through adolescence. "Boosting self-esteem" was not in the list of the top three (the other two were family bonds and school life).

To talk about self-esteem without talking about character, God, and spirit is to be disengaged from the nature of our daughters.

MYTH 4: Girls experience worse self-esteem drops in adolescence than boys.

FACT: Though this was a popular argument for over a decade, it has been thoroughly debunked. The Horatio Alger Institute, Judith Kleinfeld, Christina Sommers, myself, and many other researchers have shown how deeply *both* boys and girls experience self-esteem drops. They experience them, of course, in *boy-specific* and *girl-specific* ways, but to advocate that girls are the primary victims of low self-esteem and that boys are relatively immune to emotional fragility polarizes a culture and confuses parents of boys and girls.

## Protecting Innocence, Guiding Experience

Given the myths surrounding self-esteem language, Gail and I find that while some of our job as therapists involves protecting girls' emotional development through boosting self-esteem, in fact, about 80 percent of the emotional work we need to do with girls involves four other factors which generally and intrinsically take care of self-esteem issues. These focused strategies both protect a girl's innocence and guide her nature experience:

1. Helping girls and families understand how to find *meaning* in their emotional biology. In almost every case, we find that families and communities do not know enough about the internal world of adolescent girls, thus we become teachers of biology, neurochemistry, and what is normal about adolescent self-esteem drops, mood swings, peer relationships, family life, and developmental stages. We hope that in Chapters 2 and 3 we've helped you fill in information gaps. In this chapter, we'll more directly look at issues of female nature and culture that specifically chal-

lenge female emotional development—stresses it usefully and painfully—through the journey into adulthood.

2. Helping girls and their families understand how an effective *three-family system* (as we've described it in Chapter 3) is the best protection for a girl's adolescent emotional development (and self-esteem care). In almost every case, we find that an adolescent girl *within a three-family system* who needs therapy is struggling from an overt personal trauma (attack on self) from *within a three-family system*:

- abuse, sexual abuse (most sexual abuse is not stranger abuse but within family/community);
- a mental illness—e.g., clinical depression, anorexia, substance abuse—that her family system is not able to handle effectively; and/or
- an overt family trauma—divorce or other breakdown of family and extended family relationships.

We generally find that the best way to protect the emotional development of any girl, even if she has been abused, is mentally ill, or is going through her parents' divorce, is one and the same: *Build and rebuild attachments within the three-family system she can inherently trust.*

3. Helping girls take *personal responsibility* for their own emotional life. Maturity is a journey of adversity and courage in which an adolescent learns through experience how to both effectively *express* emotions—speak, yell, cry, smile, act out—and effectively *repress* emotions—hold back, wait, delay reactions, choose rational rather than emotional responses. She must learn both emotive strategies while navigating tumultuous personal, family, and peer relationships throughout adolescence. So often, parents and communities hold to myths about the female journey to maturity—for instance, they think repressing feelings is necessarily a negative thing ("I don't want to crush my daughter's voice by telling her to stop cursing in our house"). Or they think that growing up should necessarily be easier for their daughter than it

has been for any generation ("My daughter is struggling to find herself and I do everything I can to make her challenge easier for her because I don't want her to go through hard times like I did"). These myths, as often as not, confuse a girl's process of self-discovery, both her discovery of how to express her emotional fragility in ways suitable to her own nature, and in ways to hold back her vulnerabilities when stoic strength is needed.

4. Helping girls focus their emotional development on issues of *character, morality, and spirituality*. In most cases, we discover that families and communities think of emotional development as more important than character, moral, or spiritual development, hoping for emotional cures to what may be larger character and spiritual issues, and receiving little help in contemporary life for the linkage, so deeply human in all generations, between feelings, values, and soul. We strive to help families and young people focus on character by opening them to the possibility that "character" (the subject of Chapter 7) is a good word for thinking about "self," "emotion," "feeling," "values," and "spirit" all in one.

If 80 percent of our work is not on "self-esteem," certainly 20 percent is. Gail and I join our colleagues in pointing out pollutants to female emotional growth—media imagery, bad nutrition, toxins in food and fertilizers, toxic peer pressure. Because our therapy practice and approach to parenting is nature-based, any toxins—media, food, or social pressure—which directly skew normal female brain function is a crucial area for therapy. In helping girls, we strive to work in a wholistic approach to female emotional fragility as described in this chapter.

## The Malleable Self

During one of our sessions, Jasmine licked at her lip ring and lowered her head. For a few seconds she studied her hands on her lap. I had just asked her how often she felt she simply lost control of herself— Every hour? Every day? Every week? Initially she thought I meant, "did drugs or something crazy, lost her temper and screamed at someone . . ."—in other words, she thought I meant, "couldn't control her emotions or actions." She had already discussed this kind of loss of self-control in an earlier session. "No," I'd just said, "I don't mean that: I mean, how much of the time do you feel that you're not yourself. Your 'self' is just over there, or it's far away, but it's not where you are, and you watch it making decisions you know you'll regret, thinking things you know are 'crazy,' or just feeling like you should give up and let other people, maybe a boy, make you feel good?"

She licked her lip ring, looked at her hands, then looked up. "You're talking about, like, when do I feel like I'm nothing and anyone could make me into anything, like maybe I'm like clay?"

"Yes," I said, realizing that my own description was actually more confusing than hers. "Yes. When do you feel like that?"

She let out a teenage girl's chuckle—disdainful, needy, and full of grief. "I feel like that all the time."

And so it is, to some extent, for every girl as she enters and moves through adolescence. She is malleable, feels malleable, and often feels malleable all the time. She faces life-experience with great vulnerability.

While all children at different times experience this malleability—this feeling of being like clay that anyone can shape into anything they want—girls feel it with a constancy less common in boys. Our daughters' brains register emotions differently than do the brains of boys around them. This difference means, as JoAnn Deak, author of *How Girls Thrive*, puts it, "Girls feel anxiety more keenly or react to it more readily." The male brain lateralizes brain activity, while the female brain spreads it out throughout the brain. Boys will more often focus life development on an emotional course and follow it; girls are more susceptible to endless emotional ponderings, and emotional compromises. Often, in specific situations, the greater amount of blood flow in the female limbic system will be obvious: A boy will make an emotional decision quickly, the girl will keep changing her mind, keep working through her feelings. Female hormones increase the issue of malleability for females. Testosterone, the male base, is often what one mother called a "stubbornness" hormone—not as malleable. Estrogen, progesterone, and the complex female hormone base creates not only an inherent malleability in the female psyche, but also cyclical fluctuations in that malleability: For instance, when a girl's estrogen is high, she tends to be more independent; when it is in depletion, she is more susceptible to weeping when a friend forgets to call her to come to a party. "But honey, it's no big deal," we might say. It is not a big deal, and yet in her natural flow, her whole self, so fragile at this particular time, is malleable and thus wrapped up in getting that invitation.

It is crucial, when we worry over the emotional development of our daughters—and every parent does!—that we give nature credit, and feel ourselves in the flow of that nature *along with our daughter.* When we see the lion's share of her experience of emotion, fragility, and malleability as *natural,* we immediately encounter the most natural "solution," "cure," or better yet (since those two words imply what's natural is a problem or disease), "way of supporting her growth."

## THE ANNE FRANK PRINCIPLE

A girl develops, over a multiyear period (from about nine or ten to about fifteen or sixteen), a self-designed ability to handle the malleability that she learns is natural to her, by building an emotive self from within the protective scaffolding of her intimate attachments. As she becomes a woman, she navigates her own malleability, shaping it, learning to use it when needed to manipulate life situations, and learning to understand how it shapes her decision-making.

Parents (even during adolescence) and extended family mentors (especially during adolescence, whether blood kin or not) are most effective in dealing with a girl's inherent fragility and malleability. Gail and I have found that in nearly every case in which we've provided therapy for girls and families, improvement in their emotional development has depended on *improving family bonds.* This means more love, more attention, more daily rituals, lots of family time, family game nights, family movie nights, meals together, camping or other vacation trips, reunions, father-daughter night, mother-daughter night—less television alone in a room, less time spent without focus, less of life lived without parental and community love involved.

Judith Wallerstein's twenty-five-year study of children of divorce found the same thing in broken family structures—the more quickly the child could redevelop and newly develop healthy family bonds, the less the negative emotional impact. Two decades of what is called "resiliency" research echoes these findings: Children with healthier bonds and attachment do better, those with lack of bonds or insecure attachments do worse. Brain-based attachment research now shows us how the biochemistry of emotion operates in both secure and insecure attachments. The more insecure the girl's attachment, the higher her cortisol (stress hormone) levels, thus the more fragile the girl's normal hormone and brain cycles. In boys, higher cortisol more often leads to emotional problems manifesting in behavior issues—increased violence, for instance. In girls, higher stress hormone leads to more overt depression, self-cutting, and eating disorders.

Research from nearly every field, then, indicates what each of us may instinctively sense: The highest protection for a girl's emotional development—the best way to help her through the journey of malleability—is to surround her (not smother her) with a web of trusted relationships to which she can always turn. In most cases, no matter what the outside world throws at her, her close bonds will provide her the foundation for emotional development.

I call this simple, instinctive truth *The Anne Frank Principle*.

Anne Frank, who died at fifteen of typhus, hid away with her family behind a wall in a friend's home in Amsterdam during the Nazi occupation. Her diary is the story of the life of an adolescent girl living the normal strife of adolescence while under constant crisis, and uplifting herself, discovering herself, navigating her own malleability with healthy emotional development, even as she and her family hid for their very lives. How could a girl do this? The stress she was under—going to bed every night in terror of Nazi capture—was enormous; yet she grew up along a normal path of emotional life.

What she had—which quite often our own girls lack—was the

close-knit bonds of a family and extended family. My use of the term *The Anne Frank Principle* grew from noticing how emotionally mature—how able to handle her own fragility and malleability—a girl can be, *even under the highest stress*, when she is well bonded to family. Anne Frank's inspiring story illustrates the possibility of female emotional health for all girls. It also reflects, in a kind of reverse mirror, how strangely lonely the lives of our daughters can be. Anne Frank, who lived in a cage, experienced greater emotional health than Jasmine, whose life was, outwardly, so free.

When we look at girls' lives today from this perspective, we must at least cautiously notice that the greatest damage done to our girls' emotional development today is not done by media or by peer pressure—the buzz words of our time—but, unfortunately, by those of us who love our girls the most: the very families (and close communities) girls are raised in. We live a style of life that pulls parents away from children, and pulls children into isolation.

We do not live in a nature-based society. Let me give you an example that always startles me—from our school communities.

Some school districts so little understand female emotional development that they punish two girls for hugging each other in a hallway. Normal and natural bonding activity is not trusted, not encouraged. Said the principal, David Robbins, of his ruling at his Euless, Texas, junior high school, "Physical contact is inappropriate in school." In Pequot Lakes, Minnesota, teachers have been ordered to dole out reprimands and detention to students in elementary and middle school who hug each other. Ashley Bennett, a twelve-year-old who has been written up for hugging, told an Associated Press reporter, "But that's how people express their feelings. It makes people feel better." Perhaps like Anne Frank, Ashley has an intuitive grasp of human nature—she knows that bonds make for a good life.

Home, school, and neighborhood are our daughters' "Anne Frank" world. Each of us must assess how much bonding and attachment is going on in these worlds, especially between adults and children. And we must assess how our daughter is getting along in her female group, which I like to call "her pack."

## GIRLS NEED A PACK

The psychologist and storyteller Clarissa Pinkola Estes, author of *Women Who Run With the Wolves*, studied wolf biology. She saw up-close some similarities between wolves and human females that startled her into a very meaningful perspective on human female development. In her words:

"Healthy wolves and healthy women share certain psychic characteristics: keen sensing, playful spirit, and a heightened capacity for devotion. Wolves and women are relational by nature, inquiring, possessed of great endurance and strength. They are deeply intuitive, intensely concerned with their young, their mate, and their pack."

What parent of a daughter has not noticed this? Our daughters learn and grow within small packs of girls and women. How terrifying it is for them to feel "left out," "outcast," "not invited," "not popular."

Often families must do more than we realize to ensure this "girl pack" element of female emotional development. These girl packs—generally composed of same-age, older, and younger girls—contain an element of female emotional life that often, in our cultural dialogue, gets missed: *female hierarchies*. Female self-esteem often depends on how we help them learn to navigate these female hierarchies.

## THE FEMALE HIERARCHIES

The female psyche develops emotional structure in a complex web of female *hierarchies* within girl packs. Within these hierarchies, girls develop a great deal of their lasting sense of personal power. We adults can learn much about the nature of our daughter by observing (even overhearing) how she navigates pack hierarchies over the weeks, months, and years of development.

1. *Family Paradigm Hierarchies.* When girls play, they play games about family, agreeing or arguing about who is the mom, the dad, and so on. Generally, if they play "school" or "workplace," their fantasy hierarchies resemble family systems too. If an older girl in the girl pack is always mom and the younger girl never gets to be, tensions ensue.

2. *Moral Hierarchies.* Girls are very concerned with how "good" or "nice" another girl is. A girl who is incessantly not nice will probably have to go join or form another pack after a few weeks.

3. *Physical Appearance Hierarchies.* Female physical appearance is crucial to reproduction selection, and every girl, at some deep level, knows it. From a very young age, girls are hierarchically judging their own and other girls' appearances—clothing, eye color, jaw line, then breast size, buttocks, fatness/thinness. In highly competitive cultures like ours, female physical appearance becomes even more important because it is often the equivalent, in female power assertion, to physical aggression in male power assertion.

4. *In-crowd/Out-crowd Hierarchies.* In a group of girls—e.g., a school classroom—there are generally three to five packs of girls. Individual girls attach themselves to a pack (or form one, with a friend or two themselves). By including or excluding others the girls in the pack gain power.

5. *Male-Attachment Hierarchies.* Females, especially after puberty, gain a great deal of hierarchical status from their selection of males. This is why we instinctively want our daughter to "marry a successful man." This human tendency, by the way, is true in every world culture. Females and female culture will put up with a lot from males as long as the males keep their high status.

Females are very hard on other females who mess with the pool of available high-status males. Gail counseled a family whose seventh-grade girl was immensely athletic, as good at basketball as nearly any guy, and also very charming with the guys. She became respected by her seventh-grade peer *males*, especially athletic high-status males, and, as a result, became ostracized by seventh-grade *girls* who had become jealous. She presented to Gail with depression, so harsh was her pain and confusion at being rejected by not only "the girls," but also a lot of girls who had been her friends in sixth grade.

6. *Offspring Hierarchies.* Females base a great deal of their status on the status of their offspring. From the toddler years, lit-

tle girls are already pretending to be pregnant, and already caring for baby dolls like infants. This kind of hierarchical success is instinctive to humanity, and to females, which makes being a childless woman very difficult in any culture. Women who pass child-bearing age without reproducing almost universally report some form of sadness, confusion, and grief. This is true for many biological and sociological reasons, not the least of which is the unconscious realization that a woman without a child has greater difficulty feeling like she completely belongs in a community. She does not feel like she's part of the pack.

7. *Physical and Social Competition Hierarchies.* This is a relatively new hierarchical selection area for females, in which girls, like boys, judge one another by physical and athletic prowess, and later, during adulthood, by the ability to succeed in the competitive workplace. Many girls today are gaining status not available to their mothers or grandmothers by being good at sports. Many women say, "I am president of my own company!" gaining immense hierarchical status and sense of accomplishment.

8. *Tend and Befriend Hierarchies.* "Tend and befriend" is a phrase anthropologists use to reflect female manifestations of biological imperatives, in the same way they use the phrase "provide and protect" to talk about male manifestations of biological imperatives. Where males, dominated by testosterone, tend to move toward providing and protecting, females, dominated by estrogen and other female hormones, gravitate toward *tending and befriending.* They also gain hierarchical status by how successfully they "tend and befriend."

Picture a twelve-year-old girl and boy both walking toward a child who just fell off his bicycle. The girl is more likely to get down on her knees and help, tending and befriending; her male companion is more likely to ascertain that this kid on the bike isn't really hurt, and make a jesting comment—"Did you just learn how to ride?"—in order to elicit a laugh, and the injured child's quicker psychological recovery from the embarrassment of falling.

Both female and male strategies are essential to the growth of children and communities, and females gain status and power in their packs from their ability to give care, sympathy, and empathy. When a woman seems to lack the ability to tend and befriend, she is generally ostracized by women and men both. Highly masculinized women in the workplace—who rightfully dislike being called "bitches"—are often examples of this hierarchical selection process. They have gained status by their social competition, but they have lost status vis-à-vis the tend-and-befriend hierarchy.

Our culture's manifestation of what are biology-based female hierarchy processes allows our daughters a very rich landscape in which to experience the emotional dilemmas, pains, and growth that female hierarchy has always accomplished in girls. In their packs, and as they utilize all the different hierarchical systems at different times, girls constantly test each other, prod each other, judge each other, cause each other pain, help each other out of the pain.

In helping daughters emotionally navigate and grow in the girl-pack hierarchies, it is useful to focus on three things in particular:

1. Consciousness raising about the hierarchies themselves. Talk to daughters about all the ways they seek status and are tested (and even tortured) by other girls (and boys). Make this a conscious part of their life journey, for even as adults, female hierarchies will be a dominant part of their emotional lives; they need parents and caregivers to help them understand their emotional fragility and malleability within the packs starting at an early age—as early as three or four a girl can start noticing how she's behaving in her girl packs.

2. Provide a family and extended family system that occupies girls' lives so generously that they feel the pain of hierarchical competition but do not become depressed.

3. Provide "competition-management." This is a phrase I developed for a parenting framework in which parents specifically help girls balance competition activity with tend-and-befriend activity. If a parent sees that a girl is competing more

than tending and befriending (overemphasizing one kind of hierarchical activity and neglecting the balance of the other), the girl is probably off-kilter in terms of her basic nature.

## THE NEW NASTINESS AMONG GIRLS

Jeannie Corkill, a family therapist, recently talked about what she calls "the new nastiness and meanness among girls." She was referring to girls out of balance.

"I have a lot of female clients who, by about eighteen, feel guilty that they've been so nasty and mean during their adolescent years. When I was growing up, I don't remember being so mean, so cutting, so competitive with other girls. I'm constantly having to figure out how to help girls with this."

Everyone has perhaps noticed something like what Jeannie has seen. Many parents of daughters today are asking how we protect our daughters' emotional development in the face of increasing female in-crowd/out-crowd competition, and a trend toward a lack of decency and fairness among girls.

We certainly can't stop all the teasing, nor in fact should we. Teasing, judging, cajoling, even humiliating each other is part of the human process, and built into girls' (and boys') lives. In fact, a new study, just released in the *Psychological Bulletin*, led by University of California, Berkeley, researcher Dacher Keltner, found that most kids tease and test one another to show affection and learn social rules; by middle school, he found, *two-thirds of teasing builds friendships*.

Nonetheless, all of our ancestors—with no studies available— knew like we do that there are certain ways in which girls are very fragile as they move through hierarchies; they knew adolescence was a time of open fragility; they made sure to create family and community systems in which girls received constant interaction and support.

When your daughter comes home from school continually worried about friendships with Leslie, or Laura, or Leslie *and* Laura, and when this goes on day after day, it may be essential that you go to her teacher and learn more about why she is becoming so depressed.

When your daughter comes home repeatedly feeling snubbed,

excluded, or the recipient of "the silent treatment" from her own pack of girls, she generally needs you to:

- Take it seriously. "Tell me more about it." Assess what is happening.

- Admire specific qualities in her that offset the nastiness. "Tiffany made fun of your hair but I really like it."

- Ask her godmother, grandparents, teachers, and other adults she trusts to help her assess who she is, what she's doing well, what weaknesses in social skills she can adjust. She may well be causing some of the teasing by some of her actions.

- Teach her to ignore the snubbing—one of the reasons snubbing exists in child development is so that children can become adults who have learned the power of "moving on."

- Wonder aloud with her if there is another pack of girls, or even just one best friend, who would be better for her development at this time in her life.

- Help her verbalize her part in the nastiness so she takes responsibility.

- Ask her how she believes you and others can help her gain the strength and skill to stand up for herself.

- Tell her stories from your own past of being excluded.

- Use the opportunity to help her gain a harder "shell," so that she can have it as a positive outgrowth of the pain and use it later in life when a protective emotional shell will be necessary.

- Talk to her about *how girls do things*, and ask her to teach you what she has noticed—empowering her, thus, to become more conscious of her situation, and gain power through understanding.

Female hierarchies are so pervasive I hope you will find worth in both increasing your vigilance with your girls and also the understanding in your community the hierarchies themselves. Teachers, bus drivers, principals, parents, friends, employers, grandparents—all of us need to understand better the invisible web of female relationships. What a gift we give our daughters by giving the gift of this understanding to the communities that help us raise them.

We've explored so far some key themes of female emotional development: a girl's fragility and malleability, her need for three families, her journey through girl packs, and her very natural scheme of emotional development in all this. There is another area of profound importance to girls' emotional development: her physical body. Far more than we may realize, a girl's emotions are attached to her physical development.

## Protecting the Bodies of Our Daughters

When Jasmine walked into my office, one of the first things I noticed was her body—not only did I do a quick appearance check developmentally, noticing that she had finished her growth spurt and was physically a young woman, but I saw that she carried a number of implicit emotional attitudes toward herself in her body and appearance. As a therapist I must confess that I learn more from an assessment of initial physical appearance of female clients than I do from males. Boys who come in for therapy are more uniform in their costuming and posturing. Their issues are also generally hidden away from costuming. Females, more so than males, seem to costume their bodies to fit their hidden pains.

So when I saw Jasmine's slumped shoulders, saw that she was perhaps twenty to thirty pounds overweight for her developmental age and bone structure, saw that she had rings pierced into even her nipples, showing through her shirt, saw that she had well-bitten fingernails (and learned, later, that she had experimented with cutting herself), I saw a girl's "emotional body" unprotected and hurt, and could immediately begin to pinpoint ways in which Jasmine felt psychological disfigurement internally through the way she treated her body.

Like many girls today, weight was, for Jasmine, an issue. Let's explore it here.

## GIRLS AND WEIGHT

Jasmine was overweight and told me that she had been so since just before puberty. She said it worried her mother more than her, but it clearly worried her as well. Part of my job was to educate her and her family on some new discoveries regarding adolescent girls and body weight issues.

Because the male body—driven by testosterone—turns more of what it eats into muscle, males have a biological advantage, in general, in the area of weight management. An estrogen-driven system, the female body turns more of what it eats into fat. And because testosterone is an aggression hormone, males are more likely to manifest emotional problems by aggressive behavior; females, on the other hand, are more likely to "hold" issues in their cells. This circumstance is being exacerbated microbiologically by fertilizers, meat tenderizers, and animal feed, which increases animal size and economic profit to growers by use of estrogen receptors. Because the meat and vegetables a girl eats are laced with estrogen receptors, her own estrogen levels—and, thus, potentially her fat levels—increase.

For these very biological reasons, it is crucial to watch what girls eat—especially sugars, fats, and carbohydrates. If your daughter faces any kind of inordinate weight gain, Sandra Friedman's *When Girls Feel Fat* is a very fine resource. Robert Arnot's *The Biology of Success* provides a wealth of scientific material on how what we eat affects who we are. These books take a nature-based approach to girls' weight issues.

There is no doubt that, in general, *American families eat too much junk food and refined sugar for the health of many pubescent girls*. If your family genes lean toward thinness—both Mom and Dad—your daughter may get away with more than a few treats of junk food and candy. But especially if there are fat genes on either side of the family your vigilance starting from toddler years is crucial. By letting your children eat too much junk food and refined sugars from early on, you are setting your girls up to be obsessed with their weight from pre-puberty on. Given the fact that even foods like meat and vegetables eaten in a healthy diet carry weight-gain components, we cannot be too vigilant about junk food, which is so completely damaging.

Jasmine, like nearly every girl, watched huge amounts of television, read numerous teen magazines, and watched movies that gave her unrealistic expectations of the female body. Part of my therapy with her was to guide her and her family to better diet and less of the media imagery that fed her feelings of being "physically wrong." At the same time, Jasmine was a smart girl, and capable of understanding that her diet contributed to her problems. After two months of her receiving support to change what she ate, she began to shift her diet to healthier foods, and this helped her deal with her weight. She lost weight. In fact, she and her mother joined Weight Watchers together, an activity which both bonded them and dealt with weight issues.

## EXERCISE

Jasmine and I also discussed how important exercise and even athletics can be for an adolescent girl in general, and one dealing with weight problems in particular. Jasmine had dropped out of extracurricular sports, but she was willing to do Tae-Bo, a weight-loss form of martial arts exercise pioneered by former world karate champion Billy Blanks.

People often overlook the fact that while male biology does compel males to spend more time, on average, exercising physically and engaging in athletics for longer periods of time during a day, female biology craves exercise too—both for physical health and for mood stability. There is hardly anything better for improving mood during the female hormonal cycle than exercise. There is hardly anything better for fat cell management than exercise. And for many girls, athletics and organized sports not only fulfill these functions, but also boost self-confidence and bonding. If your daughter does not like athletics or organized sports, she still needs to be encouraged toward physical exercise.

If she has any hints of depression, exercise can give immense hope and therapy. In a recent study at Duke University, researchers found that three 30-minute workouts each week brought as much relief as antidepressant drugs! Exercise was also found to ward off reoccurrence of depression. Just under 40 percent of patients who had been relying on drugs became depressed again within six months of ending medication; only 8 percent of those who stuck to exercise regimens experienced reoccurrence. Medication can be essential, but so can exercise.

In my therapy practice, because it is nature-based, conversation about how a girl cares for her physical body always occurs early. We immediately link the body to emotional health. Girls, in earlier centuries and decades, got more natural daily exercise—they worked more physically beside mothers, aunts, grandmothers. Nowadays, girls' lives can be too sedentary for the effective management of female hormones, brain development, and, therefore, emotional health.

For today's six-year-olds who get lots of spontaneous running exercise, no other exercise program (like athletics) may be necessary; by eight, however, an organized program (karate, soccer, swimming) would probably be beneficial; by twelve, perhaps more than one. By fourteen or fifteen, a girl will generally make her own choices about whether to participate in athletics or not; but if, like Jasmine, she is developing physical issues, it is essential you try to *guide* her choice toward exercise.

## EARLY PUBERTY

Jasmine developed breasts at nine. This was earlier than her mother developed them, and qualifies as "earlier than normal." This became an emotional issue for her.

A study in 1997 of seventeen thousand girls discovered that 7 percent of white girls and 27 percent of African-American girls begin developing breasts or pubic hair by seven.

Puberty is coming earlier for many girls than a generation ago. There are many theories as to why—one involves our increase in female average weight at pre-puberty (which is directly linked to our junk food/estrogen receptor diet). Between 1979 and 1991, the percentage of children from six to eleven who were overweight went from 6.5 percent to 11.4 percent—nearly doubling. Fat cells produce leptin—a protein that helps trigger puberty. As girls become fatter, more leptin is produced, and earlier puberty becomes more likely. Certain genetic groups—African-Americans, and East Asians—are already genetically inclined toward earlier puberty. So genetics plays a part.

In some cultures, early puberty is far less an issue than in ours. In India, for instance, where I spent part of my boyhood, girls entered puberty earlier than in the West. Many of them entered arranged marriages at thirteen and began, soon after, to have children. They were mentored and parented constantly as they produced offspring; they were surrounded by intimacy, attachment, caregivers, and a sacred sense of their role as mother. Early puberty was an advantage, as the infant and child mortality rate in India was high—the sooner a family got started on reproducing, the more offspring would potentially live.

Ironically, the United States is now producing some of the largest concentrations of early female puberty in the world, but providing the *least* amount of family attachment and community support for these girls. Rather than surrounding these girls with family, our family systems tend to give more independence to nine-, ten-, or eleven-year-olds. There is nothing inherently wrong with either our way or the Indian way, but the problem for us arises in the biological pressure we are putting on girls—early puberty—a pressure that doesn't fit the society we have created by which to nurture the biological anomaly.

It is crucial that your family feel no compunction about getting medical consultation if you think your daughter is hitting puberty early. A girl entering puberty early may need extra help, love, and attention from the three-family system, especially understanding from Mom and respect from Dad. She will get a woman's body before she has a woman's brain. Boys will make fun of her at an earlier, more tender age than normal. Girls will judge her, be envious, be confused by her. Some older boys will try to touch her and have sex with her at an age so young, we can barely imagine it.

Jasmine would not discuss with me early on in her therapy something her mother did tell me—that when Jasmine was ten, a boy groped her. She had well-developed breasts and did not know how to stave him off. Later in our therapy, Jasmine wept over this incident.

# Harsh Experience: Emotional Crises
in Girls' Lives

Jasmine faced a set of experiences and emotional issues, most of which did not reach a crisis state. Yet in total, she was in crisis. During her childhood and adolescence, your daughter will certainly experience states of crisis, generally self-made, as she overreacts to life's pressures. She will also face emotional crises caused by combinations of factors in her family and the outside world. Most girls and most families navigate life crises successfully without significant interventions. But sometimes, no matter what we do, we need extra help. Jasmine needed that help to deal with harsh experience. Some girls need it even more than she did.

We've looked at some areas of physical vulnerability in our girls' lives. Let's talk now about crisis states. We'll look at specific areas of emotional and physical crises your daughter, or a girl she knows, may face. In each case, I will include resources for you. And in each case, we will notice that the crisis is *bio*-emotional—a state of mind we call "emotional," which in fact has a profound biological component.

By crisis states we mean:

- eating disorders
- self-cutting
- drug or alcohol use
- mental illness
- sexual, physical, and emotional abuse and violence
- smoking
- academic and athletic failure
- dealing with divorce

## KNOWING THE WARNING SIGNS

One of the secrets to raising a daughter through the crisis times is knowing the warning signs. If your daughter, or a girl you know, is involved in three or more of the following, you may well have cause to move quickly. These are ongoing and repeated events or states of mind that indicate worse-than-normal emotional ups and downs.

- Grades drop, homework isn't getting done, she loses academic motivation;
- Athletic performance and participation suddenly drop;
- She loses interest in normal, everyday life, claims to not care at all about anything;
- She mutilates herself (self-cutting, for instance)—often this is accompanied by cover-up clothing;
- She talks about suicide, or attempts suicide;
- She runs away more than once;
- She won't let you meet her friends, changes friends suddenly, loses all friends;
- She becomes violent, begins to rage as never before—sometimes this happens first with a pet rather than a parent;
- She loses herself in her computer, on the Internet, in television—replacing meaningful life with machine and image addiction;
- She is becoming very thin or very fat quite quickly—can't eat enough, or stops eating;
- Her sleep is affected more than is normal for a growing adolescent;
- She stops communicating with parents, and communicates emotionally with no other adult either;
- She starts smoking, drinking, doing drugs.

Another warning sign lives in your intuition. If, after educating yourself in what is neurologically, biochemically, and culturally within normal range for your adolescent daughter, you feel in your gut that something is very wrong, your intuition is usually right. You are the parent. You are attached to your daughter as no one else is.

## WHERE TO START

If your daughter exhibits the warning signs, you will almost certainly need to seek professional *and* extended family help. Not just one counselor, or one program, but your own friends, and other families, are crucial.

Carol Maxym and Leslie York have written a very fine book on troubled teens called *Teens in Turmoil*, which many parents of girls in crises find helpful as a start.

As soon as you understand that your daughter is in real crisis, confront her respectfully but relentlessly.

"Something is wrong; please tell me what it is."

"I notice you haven't been talking to your friends. Can I help?"

When a parent thinks her child is in crisis, "letting her have privacy" is secondary to finding out what is the matter. If your daughter is trying to lock herself away in a private universe, you are challenged to do the terribly difficult work—difficult because for a time she may hate you—of invading that dangerous universe.

Rarely is it useful to try to deal with her all alone. Crisis yearns for community, not privacy. Often a mother needs to bring a divorced father back into the situation, or vice versa. Often the help of grandparents, godmothers, family friends is needed. Sometimes a pediatrician or psychiatrist—and thus, medication—is necessary; if it is used responsibly, it can be life-saving. Family therapy can be a good starting place in dealing with crises girls face.

## SEEKING A FAMILY THERAPIST

When seeking a family therapist, it is generally useful to look for these qualities:

1. The therapist really understands adolescent girls—specializes in them.

2. She will help *the whole family*—she's a leader, not a sit-back-and-wait-for-the-family-to-figure-it-out-themselves therapist. When there is crisis, leadership is required.

3. She understands female biochemistry and can refer you to the right medications and knowledge bases.

4. She recognizes quickly that your daughter's warning signs are generally statements that she is under overwhelming psychological pressure—and can help discover the roots of the pressure.

5. She is an explorer into your daughter's (and your own) psyche, but she is also very solution oriented. She gives solutions to try as much as she helps everyone analyze what's wrong.

Sometimes a male therapist can be helpful, and often a male-female team can help; for the most part, however, therapists who focus on adolescent girls are women. Generally, male therapists, like myself, with a professional and personal commitment to women's and girls' issues, make sure to remain close to a female consultant so we can get intuitive advice from someone who has lived a girl's life.

Quite surprisingly, many female (and male) therapists—even those specializing in adolescent girls—*have never received training in female biology.* Just because the therapist is a woman does not mean she fully understands your daughter. When interviewing the therapist, you might respectfully inquire about her methods and knowledge base.

Let us look briefly now at some specific areas of crisis you may be facing with your daughters.

## EATING DISORDERS

Fortunately for Jasmine, she did not have an eating disorder; but many girls do. Both Gail and I have counseled girls with these disorders, and they are truly devastating. If your daughter suffers an eating disorder, you will want to get immediate professional help.

If she binges and then vomits, or if she refuses to eat, she has an eating disorder.

Eating disorders can be stimulated by media imagery, but media imagery of thin women does not cause them. They are neurological, and they are an estrogen/progesterone-based stress response. While some girls are under immense stress, even experience trauma, and don't get an eating disorder, others do—the mystery as to why lies in the particular brain's genetic and neurological vulnerabilities.

Just as we are producing more boys with attention and violence problems today, we are producing more girls with eating disorders (some studies argue that one in five females will struggle with an eating disorder in her lifetime). The human brain—whether male or female—is under far more stress now than ever before. It is reacting in gender-specific, neurological ways to the stress.

In most eating disorder cases, crucial attachment is missing in the girl's three-family system. The intimacy her growing mind and body seek is not being satisfied. She lacks a father in her life, her mother is relatively unavailable, she feels outside the female hierarchies, she has started dating early and can't handle the rejections by boys. These intimacy-related and attachment-related circumstances are not the only cause of the disorder, but they are crucial factors. Along with medication and professional treatment, one of the best ways to help a girl with her disorder is to marshal her family and friends around her in support, increasing her attachment and intimacy with trusted family and friends.

Invaluable resources are available to you if your family faces an eating disorder among your girls. Mary Pipher's *Hunger Pains* and Abigail H. Natenshon's *When Your Child Has an Eating Disorder* are both very helpful. The first includes essential theory; the second is a step-by-step guide to treatment.

## SELF-CUTTING

Around two million Americans—most of them girls and women—cut themselves purposefully. Self-cutting is a neurological stress-response in which these girls bring more relief to the hurting mind and heart than pain. Like eating disorders, self-cutting is a kind of addictive behavior, a compulsive/addictive way of dealing with psychological stress. Gail has noticed in her practice that in nearly every case, self-cutting hides deep psychological pain regarding family or friendship problems.

Popular girls cut themselves, girls who think they are ugly cut themselves, smart girls cut themselves. It can happen to any girl, if she is already neurologically inclined toward it when her stress hormone—cortisol—levels rise. Jasmine cut herself for a period of about three months when she was just turning fifteen. This behavior instigated her family's search for therapy.

*Cutting*, by Steven Levenkron, is a very important book if you suspect your daughter fits into this category. Professional help should be immediately sought.

## DRUG OR ALCOHOL ABUSE

If your daughter is using drugs or alcohol, family interventions are generally necessary. There is no single more important issue in her or your life than to make sobriety happen. Everything else is secondary to getting her off drugs and alcohol.

Interventions can be organized by one or more family members—generally a parent and an extended family member or good friend. A pack of loving, courageous family members and friends come together to confront the girl on her behavior. Girls without a complete safety net of attachments remain in crisis states longer. The intervention is a direct way to right the inherent bonding issue: It now provides the girl with a set of attachments through which she can navigate her healing. At least three to five of the individuals involved in the intervention ought to call her frequently over the next few weeks, spend time with her doing activities or just listening, and get to know her better.

This should be augmented by professional help, and sometimes inpatient treatment is needed.

## SMOKING

More and more teen girls are smoking, and they are smoking earlier. Sneaking a smoke, a drink, or a toke once every few months is probably just experimental behavior, and does not indicate a girl at emotional risk. But ongoing use of any addictive substance does. All these substances—*including tobacco*—affect brain development, and therefore intellectual and emotional processing—during the adolescent years. There is also increasing evidence that especially in girls, they can affect reproductive health.

If your daughter is smoking, she needs help. If you suspect she is smoking, no rules of privacy at home ought to keep you from searching her drawers or her purse. She may become angry that you don't trust her, "You're not letting me be independent, you're smothering me!" but when she is at risk, you must do your job. Within a few weeks, especially with professional and family help, she will generally understand why you invaded her privacy.

The National Center on Addiction and Substance Abuse at Columbia University released, in February of 2001, the results of a survey of American teens. The Center discovered:

"Teens of 'hands-on' parents are at *one quarter* the risk of smoking, drinking, and using drugs as teens with 'hands-off' parents.

"But only one in four teens in America (27 percent, about 6.5 million) lives with 'hands-on' parents—parents who have established a household culture of rules and expectations for their teens' behavior and monitor what their teens do: such as the TV shows they watch, the CDs they buy, what they access on the Internet, and where they are evenings and weekends."

If you have been a hands-off parent, it is more likely your daughter is involved in the kind of high-risk behavior that often begins with smoking.

The solution now begins in being "hands-on."

The National Center on Addiction and Substance Abuse at Columbia University publishes pamphlets packed with helpful strategies for helping deal with teen smoking and other addictions.

## MENTAL ILLNESS

Author Kate Williams writes of her daughter, Rachel, who suddenly didn't want to live. "At the time she was thirteen and in the eighth grade. We started going to a therapist immediately . . . for two years. Then, after Christmas vacation, in tenth grade, Rachel had a nervous breakdown. Rachel couldn't stop crying, she couldn't get off the couch, she didn't know what was wrong, and she said she couldn't think of any reason she wanted to live."

With this powerful description, Kate Williams begins her book, *A Parent's Guide for Suicidal and Depressed Teens*, which not only gives helpful advice to parents of girls facing mental illnesses, but also chronicles the five years of hard work and recovery (with renewed bouts of illness) that the Williams family went through with Rachel.

If you are parenting or mentoring a girl who suffers from depression, a personality disorder, suicidal tendencies, or an addiction that has become a chronic mental illness, you are probably doing your hard work—which will last many years—without enough support. It is a rare caregiver of the mentally ill who feels at home in the job.

Kate Williams's book is a very important resource, as are *Suicide: The Forever Decision*, by Paul Quinnett (Continuum, 1987) and Tonia Shamoo and Philip Patros's *Helping Your Child Cope with Depression and Suicidal Thoughts* (Jossey-Bass, 1996).

Because so many of the characteristics of female adolescent mental illness can be linked to hormonal difficulties, it is crucial for you to consult, also, hormonal solutions, like those provided in Deborah Sichel's *Women's Moods*.

As you search for solutions, one of the best gifts you give your daughter is your own sanity: Make sure to take care of yourself, get help from your extended family, and find a supportive therapist or other confidant.

## SEXUAL, PHYSICAL, AND EMOTIONAL ABUSE AND VIOLENCE

If your daughter has experienced physical abuse it will generally be from parents, thus you will most probably know it, even if you have difficulty admitting it. But if she has experienced sexual abuse, signals may be more subtle. She may show some of the warning signs listed earlier in this chapter, and she may also be clearly sexualized at a young age:

- she may flirt more than is normal;
- she may seek attention for her body, breasts, buttocks in inappropriate ways;

- she may verbalize sexual comments inappropriately;
- she may be promiscuous;
- she may gravitate toward pornography.

Professional help is essential, even if you only *suspect* violence, physical abuse, emotional abuse, or sexual abuse. Legal and police assistance may be called for.

Abuse and violence "rewire" brain chemistry in both girls and boys. If the violence is a single episode, it may not have lasting effect; if, however, a pattern of violence is repeated—even prolonged emotional abuse, constant verbal shaming, threats, harassment—the trauma is not only a trauma to a particular time period in the child's life, but to the child's future life; cortisol levels in the brain rise when it is experiencing abuse of any kind. If this rise in cortisol continues for prolonged periods, the brain rewires itself to be in a constant "emergency" neural state.

If your daughter is experiencing or has experienced abuse or violence, her brain may be rewiring itself, and she may have problems with anxiety, attachment, learning, and life skills.

Violence against girls is decreasing in some sectors today, but increasing in others. My hope for every daughter is that she will take a form of martial art until she has become highly proficient. Self-protection, through the confidence building and physical development of martial arts, is a potentially universal possibility.

Violence among our males is statistically practiced more often against other males, but nonetheless (especially in the case of date rape and sexual harassment) is practiced against our females; and in the U.S. there is more male-on-female violence (basic disrespect) than in many other cultures. We are a culture of violence.

Our males are not only watching violence-modeling in media and being raised, many times, to see violence as a first option, but they have also developed a frightening new kind of mental illness which I have named and diagnosed as Character Regression Syndrome (CRS). It has been seen most obviously in the school shootings: Columbine, Santana, Jonesboro, etc.; if we are to protect our daughters we must come to grips with it.

We are raising a generation of young males, some of whom are not receiving adequate attachment with a primary caregiver (usually Mom) in the first three years of life and with Dad in the first few years of adolescence. Because of inadequate attachment, brain development (which tries to make crucial developmental strides between birth and three, and ten and thirteen) is impaired—especially in the frontal and prefrontal lobes, which handle moral decision-making.

And while these young males grow up in a position of inadequate attachment, they generally also experience a life crisis—divorce trauma, sexual abuse, emotional abuse—which raises their cortisol levels over a long period of adolescence.

Because they are male, and therefore testosterone-based, they are more likely than females to become aggressive when crisis (cortisol increase) occurs.

Inadequate attachment and brain development, then trauma, then male hormones form a possible violent adolescent. Most males, by middle adolescence, have learned to manage their own aggressive impulses, even when triggered by bullying or some other new crisis of loss or humiliation. Males with CRS have not.

These males—like the males in San Diego; Littleton, Colorado; and Jonesboro, Arkansas—experienced a trigger in school environments, generally, from teasing and humiliation by peers. This trigger did not cause their violence; rather, it triggered regression of what humanity calls "moral character" to about a six- or seven-year-old's thinking process. In neural terms, neural firing in frontal and prefrontal lobes decreased (thus moral decision-making decreased) and firing in the lower limbic system and brain stem increased.

Like children, these young men experienced immature frontal lobe ability to assess consequences. Because they had access to guns, what would have been, in another young man's life, unrequited violent impulses, or simply the picking of a fistfight, became carnage.

Because we are creating a generation of males who potentially do not receive enough attachment from primary caregivers, we are creating increased possibilities of male violence, and male violence toward females. Those of us who advocate for girls will, as this violence continues to shock us over the next years, need to advocate for increased human attachment. It will not be enough to follow the superficial courses laid out by some experts and the media—for example, "If we could get boys to cry more, they wouldn't hurt people"; "If we could stop children from teasing, boys would be fine." While both these efforts are helpful to young males, neither teasing nor lack of tears *causes* violence. In Japan, boys are raised rarely to cry or talk about feelings, but violence in Japan is rare. Male repression of feeling does not cause violence. Bullying, which is reprehensible, is practiced on millions of young males who never hurt others or kill. It is not the cause of male violence.

All of us who love our girls need to unite with those parents who love boys to reconfigure our family and society as soon as possible toward greater attachment, or we will continue to see more young girls and women lost to brutal experience and more young boys charged as adults and lost to prison.

*Parenting 911,* by Charlene C. Giannetti and Margaret Sagarese, is a helpful guide to parents who are rescuing daughters from abuse and violence. *Your Anxious Child,* by John S. Dacey and Lisa B. Fiore, helps parents cope with the long-term anxiety of their rescued child. *Helping Children Cope with Stress,* by Avis Brenner, is especially helpful in showing parents and others how to lead the girl through the months, even years, of post-abuse stress and adjustment.

## ACADEMIC AND ATHLETIC FAILURE

Failing at school or stopping athletic activity are generally surface signals your daughter uses to call attention to deep issues of lack of meaning, mental illness, abuse trauma, divorce trauma, depression, or other crises. Quite often, when the deeper issues are healed, academic performance is renewed and, if your daughter is athletically inclined, she regains athletic motivation and enjoyment.

In some cases, however, a girl drops out of athletics or academics because she is experiencing failure-trauma in those settings. She may have a learning disorder, she may be unable to endure negative coaching. The school itself may not be set up for the way her brain processes information.

If you discover your daughter is failing academically or athletically, you might need to try a girls' school, home schooling, learning disability resources, and/or increase your advocacy in her school system. It is essential to remember that 99.9 percent of teachers graduate from their college, graduate school, and certification programs without being trained in the differences between how the male and female brains learn. We lose a lot of girls to classroom and athletic environments in which the instructor is not well enough trained in the kind of verbal encouragement girls need.

*Boys and Girls Learn Differently!,* which I wrote with colleagues Patricia Henley and Terry Trueman, is a guide for teachers and parents, and specifically helps with academic/athletic failure that may well be caused not by psychological issues in the girl, but schools and learning systems that don't understand the way your daughter's mind works. Advocacy groups like the American Association of University Women in Washington, D.C., can provide you and your schools with further information on girls in athletics.

## DEALING WITH DIVORCE

It is a maxim in the world of professional psychotherapy that the two most common correlations with children who live in emotional crisis—and are therefore brought to therapists—are 1) abuse and neglect, and 2) divorce and/or single parents.

If you are divorced, your daughter has a higher statistical likelihood of prolonged emotional crisis during adolescence. This is not a moral comment; it is a fact. While divorce is waning as a universal solution to marital problems, it is still one of the most prevalent family circumstances in our daughters' lives. How can we make it less difficult on them?

Edward Teyber's book, *Helping Children Cope with Divorce,* is a must-read for divorcing parents. There is also a very powerful program, put out by Practical Parenting Education in Plano, Texas, called *For Kids' Sake: Nurturing Children Through the Transitions of Divorce,* which takes on the courageous challenge of "training" divorcing parents, children, and extended family in how to most effectively stabilize family life, protect attachments, and therefore decrease crisis during the divorce process. Linda Johnston, Practical Parent Education Coordinator, the author of the *For Kids' Sake* handbook, told me, "Divorce is generally the most traumatic thing a child will go through, and parents generally want to reduce the trauma. We created our program so they could." Her program is based on decades of research which indicate:

- The crisis states experienced by children of divorce ease the more quickly the individual parents rediscover personal equilibrium and emotional health.

- The crisis states are ongoing as long as parents remain enemies with each other.

In other words, as we watch our children go into and through crises following divorce (crises they may not fully emotionally experience until a few years after the divorce), we are confronted with the fact that much of their healing depends, in most cases, on two people forgiving each other, as quickly as possible, for the noblest of reasons: the health of their children.

## Emotional Development Touchstones

Our daughters are evolving beings who need different things at different times. We don't have to give them all at all times, nor should we worry if our daughters seem to occupy themselves with behaviors that show a lack of emotional strength some of the time. Both we and they are experiencing the emotional web of our lives by trial and error. We and they together are finding ways to remain innocent while negotiating the reality of experience.

I hope the following collection of emotional development touchstones gives you a checklist of what to do and what to look for as you make the journey of innocence and experience with your daughter. These are meant to be general, but inspiring. If you are accomplishing just a few of these emotional touchstones at a given time, you and your daughter are probably doing fine.

- Be affectionate with your daughter. Develop rituals of affection—lying down together at night with younger girls, kissing your kids when you come home from work. Be spontaneously affectionate. Throw a bear hug in now and then. Kiss and hug middle and high school girls as much as they'll let you.

- Show affection to your spouse and others around you. Let your daughters see you enjoying the web of relationships and the experience of emotion and intimacy.

- When your daughter is afraid, ask her to share her anxieties verbally with you, and tell her about similar anxieties you have.

- Encourage healthy competition, in sports and other arenas, but within moderation. Don't let some external image of "what a successful girl ought to be" force your family to try to change (or shortchange) your daughter.

- No matter her interests or personality, help your daughter choose happiness. Show her that every moment, every day is filled with both the possibility of choosing to be unhappy, and the possibility of choosing happiness.

- Provide both criticism and praise when appropriate. Generally, criticism is most effective when it is about specific things—"Check your spelling on that word." Generally, it should follow, not precede, a statement of support.

- Watch for overpraising. Parents often think praising their daughters for anything and everything—i.e., praising them even when they haven't acted to earn praise—will "boost their self-esteem" or build stronger emotional development. Just the opposite is generally true. Your daughter knows when your praise is a lie, or a quick verbal substitute for your actual participation in the daily activity of her life. She wants to *earn* your praise. Earned praise—"Davita, you know something, for three weeks you didn't focus on playing goalie the way you wanted to, but this week you really watched that ball!"—is very powerful because it is very real.

- Teach your daughter to express her feelings in places and ways that are appropriate. When she inappropriately expresses feelings—throws a tantrum, whines, nastily labels someone else—it will not "crush her spirit" or hurt her developing emotional self to be shown what was wrong with her method.

- Teach her, also, that repressing her feelings is often the best thing to do. Let her learn, thus, the whole spectrum of how to handle emotions, and feel comfortable with all kinds of emotional responses. If she uses emotional manipulation—weeping on cue, for instance, just to get her way—do not reward it; rather, show her better ways.

- Let your daughter experience her emotions with as much privacy as she needs, but do not let her become an emotional recluse for longer than a few days. She needs and wants to talk to someone she trusts.

- Encourage her to take risks that fit her own development. Sometimes girls need us to keep them motivated and focused on doing what they might initially think they can't do.

- Teach your daughter to experience emotions within the framework of basic manners and social skills. For instance, a child's emotional needs—unless she's having an emergency—are not generally an appropriate cause for interrupting an important adult conversation.

- Provide stories, examples, and individuals who model healthy emotional life. Talk about these people. Talk about how people handle emotions in movies. Emotional health comes, to a great extent, from making verbal and conscious the hidden world of emotional life in the mirror images of people around us.

- Accept that your daughter's emotions are real to her. To minimize them, to say they are not real, to turn away from them because they are not convenient, can increase the emotive load her brain already feels. Helping her learn to repress her feelings, when appropriate, is not the same thing as saying, "Your emotions are not real" or "Your emotions are not worth bothering with."

- Listen carefully to your daughter's emotional conversation, and raise a daughter who knows how to listen carefully to emotions around her.

- When necessary, seek medical and biological solutions to emotional problems. Educate yourself, family, and community in the biology of female emotional life. Be patient with a girl's emotions, as you would be patient with a flowing river.

- Develop a sense of humor with your daughters. Whenever possible, teach through humor, not lecturing.

## JASMINE'S FUTURE

Weight issues, eating disorders, early puberty, self-cutting, and the other issues we've discussed in this chapter are issues of body, biochemistry, and emotions. Jasmine experienced many of these. After a few months of therapy it was clear to her and her family that the need to feel less alone, to feel more loved, was underlying most of her experiences. Protecting her body meant better nurturing her heart and soul. Her family adjusted itself back to her.

Her mother confessed, "Yes, we did just leave her alone too much." To her daughter she said, "I see how unloved you have felt." Jasmine's mother came to see that her return to full-time work when Jasmine was eight had been traumatic. Her father came to see that he had pulled away from Jasmine when puberty came early, confused by her. Jasmine understood ways in which she had overreacted to normal adolescent problems, especially with other girls. She also came to understand how she needed now, as a young woman, to better care for herself both physically and biologically. Finally, toward the end of our time together, Jasmine confessed to having done "terrible things"—shoplifting, lying, stealing from her parents. Through these confessions, she was able to deal not only with emotional issues but also with how she felt her character was developing (the subject of the next chapter).

Jasmine came back to say hello recently, now seventeen, a freshman in college, and, in her words, "relatively happy, I guess." She

wore only one earring in each ear. She was about ten pounds overweight, joking, "A girl needs a little extra for the cold days." She had
a boyfriend, but she didn't want sex yet. He had agreed to wait a
while too.

Jasmine carried a slightly dark, sardonic quality in her that I saw
now, two years later, to be not only a product of her tumultuous adolescence but also just "her." She had made it suit her. She walked
with her head up more than she had. Her nails did not look as bitten
as two years ago. She gave me a hug and I congratulated her on how
wonderfully she had grown up.

I hope I see her again but I may well not. I was a mentor for a
brief time in her emotional development; there were some ways in
which, if my daughters became like her, I would be very proud—
especially in her ability to take responsibility for her life, no matter
the odds.

I hope in this chapter you've glimpsed the hidden emotional world
of girls and seen that its wonder lies in its love of relationship, intimacy, caring, nurturing, feeling, embracing, curling up with, talking
with, listening with, waiting for, and doing with as much as it does in
developing self-esteem by conquering the external, social world. The
innocence girls enjoy and the experience they discover is laden with
emotional signals and clues, which echo in their minds and hearts
because of the people who surround them with love.

Now, as we move into the next chapter, let's link the emotional
world of girls with the moral. Let's look at the Heroine's Journey that
every girl is living—not in an epic movie of faraway adventures, but
adventures right before our eyes.

# 7

## THE HEROINE'S JOURNEY

### BUILDING CHARACTER IN
### OUR DAUGHTERS

*"We are not born all at once, but by bits. The body first, and
the spirit later . . . Our mothers are racked with the pains of
our physical birth; we ourselves suffer the longer pains of our
spiritual growth."*

—Mary Astin

*"We make stories about the world and to a large degree live out
their plots. What our lives are like depends to a great extent on
the script we consciously, or more likely, unconsciously have
adopted."*

—Carol Pearson

The Australian sun is bright blue and the air clear and dry. A
slight breeze advances across a desertlike plain where a village
of a few hundred people enjoys its daily work, play, prayer, and, on
this particular day, the joy and intensity of a character-building rite of
passage ceremony. A girl, twelve, has just begun her first menstruation. A group of women surrounds her, singing, talking to her, and
preparing to paint her body with symbolic colors and designs. The girl
has been looking forward to this day for years now; this is the day she
begins her woman's journey; this is the day that her good character,
and her excited, purposeful soul begin a second birth, a journey of
acceptance into the community of adults. From biological birth to this
moment, the girl has been a baby, a child, and a little girl, but now she

enters a kind of social "birth," and this birth too is surrounded by her community's delight, as well as deliberate planning.

The women now lead the girl to a small hut, built not by the men of the tribe, but by the women themselves, earlier in the year, under the direction of the girl's mother and grandmother. The girl is to stay in the hut throughout her first menstruation. She will be brought food, visited only by women, and spoken with, and listened to, as the lessons of life, of goodness, and of maturity are taught and recited back, in an intense four-day period of spiritual commitment to high purpose, high ideals, good behavior, and trust of nature, divinity, and community. The girl is told the stories of her people and explains to listeners the life of integrity she is, as a girl and woman, hoping to live. To aid her in her second birth, her mother, grandmother, and community of elder women lead her in traditional symbolic acts of character—fasting is one of these. Specifically, she does not eat meat while menstruating, for among these aboriginal people, the nature of the human female is directly linked to the nature of all life: These aboriginals believe that if a woman eats animal blood when she is menstruating, she can ruin that animal species' procreative process. The menstrual blood of the girl, and of all women, is considered so sacred by her tribe that women are forbidden to conceal it; the village knows when a girl or woman menstruates, and celebrates with her. In all this, the girl's life is being contextualized, by her elders and traditions, into a heroine's journey.

Now this particular young woman has completed her four-day seclusion and this four-day event of character development. She has gained experiential support for the female journey she'll live very consciously in adult life. Now the women take her out of the hut to a nearby river, where song continues, along with bathing, and celebration among the women. When her body has dried of water the girl is decorated with the paints prepared by the women. Her seclusion hut is destroyed, as both a symbolic and literal act of the ending of childhood and the birth into womanhood. When her body paint has dried, she begins the small walking journey back to the whole tribe, and is known now as a woman. When she sees the village gathered to receive her again, her heart fills with anxiety about the difficult life of a woman that lies ahead of her; but also with joy, for she knows her life is blessed by community, by spirit, by acceptance of natural design, and by the kind of inherent self-trust and self-love that grow from knowing oneself to be brave, meaningful, connected to spiritual Oneness, and good.

The anthropologist Robert Lawlor, who described an aboriginal rite of passage ceremony like this one in his classic study, *Voices of the First Day*, notes that adolescent female rites of passage are less somber, elaborate, and long-lasting than males'. In the aboriginal view, adolescent boys need far longer—sometimes years long—rites of passage, character development, and journey into manhood. Why? In the aboriginal view, nature has made them "not girls," and thus given them a different course in life. There is less they know about character intrinsically, and more they must learn from their tribe's traditions and culture. There is less they know about maturity intrinsically, and more they must learn. They are more aggressive, more impulsive, by nature, and thus need longer tempering. And their sacred role in life is less clear than a girl's, for they do not have a biologically sacred role—they must be taught how to seek the spirit of the male adulthood in the journey of the soul through a lifetime in ways girls inherently understand, and receive reinforcement for every month, in menstruation—and later, in childbirth and child-rearing.

In Lawlor's words, "With each child she bears and with each monthly menstruation, a woman accepts pain, depletion, and inner withdrawal. Her body and her state of mind undergo radical transformations and swings not only with the monthly cycle but also in the deep shifts of life roles. Women move from virginity to motherhood, and motherhood ends as abruptly as it began. The essence of death and rebirth are built into a woman's physiology. Her confrontations with pain, fear, and death are a necessary adjunct to her miraculous birth-giving role."

The aborigines of Australia, as well as not only tribal peoples everywhere in the world but each of your own ancestral peoples— whether you come originally from Europe, Africa, or Asia—did not have available to them the PET scans that show boys' prefrontal cortices maturing later than girls', thus giving girls earlier moral maturity; nor did they have the science of endocrinology to show them that female secretions of oxytocin, vasopressin, progesterone, estrogen, and prolactin directly affect the female's experience of empathy in ways males can only imagine. Yet without these sciences, they nonetheless knew the nature of girls and of boys. They constructed the female adolescent journey of growth in concert with the natural cycles, natural rhythms, and the natural song of blood.

We have "moved beyond" tribal times, constructing civilizations where once were desert huts, and perfecting sciences that allow us to at least appear to control nature. But still there is great wisdom in looking backward toward our ancestors' rituals and stories. There is much to learn by looking in aboriginal Europe, Native America, Africa, Asia, and Australia, where tribes focus more simply than we on basics of character and spiritual development, and adolescent rites of passage. Much of the human spirit—and the spirit of what we might call "female character"—awaits us if we will give it even the gentlest of exposures by looking to the past.

## "True" Stories

One of the most important parts of the girl's journey to womanhood are the "true" stories (not literally true but true because as a culture's primal story they capture life's meaning) she is told by her elders as she traverses her journey to womanhood. Aboriginal stories resemble the Grimms' and other fairy tales we told our children when they were quite young, depicted pleasantly in children's books. All of these are character and moral development stories, as well as spiritual hints for growing children. Most of the fairy tales—*Jack and the Beanstalk, The Ugly Duckling, Rapunzel,* and thousands of others— that we read to our children during infancy and toddlerhood were actually told by our ancestors to *adolescent* girls and boys as they made their journey into adulthood. A thorough read of nearly any fairy tale—from *Hansel and Gretel* to *Rumpelstiltskin*—will reveal the archetypal nature of each, and the character lessons each carried, in simple, clear terms, about how children should act once they are adults; how to persevere, to be fair, just, respectful, and respected.

One such story is *Cinderella*. The original and ancient *Cinderella* is a beautiful depiction of the development of female character (and useful for male character development as well), and one around which I would like to explore what it means to a girl to be moral and ethical, brave and truthful, fair and successful. *Cinderella* is a primal character story that would have been told to our daughters during their adolescent rites of passage centuries ago.

In a classic feminist work of the 1960s, *The Cinderella Complex*, this tale was analyzed from a feminist point of view as a patriarchal tale about the repression of women's individuality, the imposition of dependency on men, and values antithetical to modern women. That interpretation moved me when I was a young feminist. As a student of Jungian psychology, I was especially glad to see an archetypal approach to a classic female initiation tale. For many years, I shunned the Cinderella story, suspecting it of being corruptive, especially to my daughters.

But my daughters enjoy—even into early adolescence—this story of a girl who loses her parents and must live with a mean stepmother and stepsisters. Few fairy tales in our home have brought learning and pleasure like *Cinderella*. My daughters—independent-minded, assertive, self-reflective girls—gravitated toward the Brandy version of *Cinderella* on TV, the Disney animated classic, and the wonderfully modernized and gender-balanced *Ever After*, with Drew Barrymore, in which she rescues the prince before he later rescues her! When I saw my daughters' love of this tale, I began to reassess it, and noticed in it many reasons why it so resonates for girls.

Cinderella, the girl who is forced to clean everything around the house, including the cinders in the fireplace, is a girl of dreams who speaks with animals, remembers better days, and accepts her fate with dignity until she can reinvent her life. When she finds liberation she not only escapes her painful circumstances, but in fact becomes the queen of the land. She doesn't do it alone, but with the help of fairies, animals, and a prince; and always with the same attitude she's carried throughout—an attitude of immense strength and character.

This story depicts the female journey into high character, and it is a stunning rite-of-passage tale. Victorian storytellers, whom Disney followed, diminished the original European versions of *Cinderella* (in some five hundred pre-Victorian versions, according to folktale expert Jane Yolen, Cinderella actually involved herself in politics), so there is a lot hidden in the Cinderella story—a lot hidden in the versions we commonly know, and a lot hidden in the older versions. The full-blooded Cinderella story I will share with you here is one of the most popular renditions we have of the Heroine's Journey.

## The Heroine's Journey

Every girl, especially as she moves through adolescence, wants to be a heroine. She wants to be loving and to be loved in whatever grand and simple ways her heart desires. She wants to be wise, and looked up to. She wants to be powerful, in whatever form of power suits her personality.

She wants to be a woman both independent and interdependent, a woman respected, a beautiful woman, a woman of means, a woman of values, a woman of protectiveness—especially when her kin and children are affronted, a woman who makes good alliances. She wants to be a princess, but also a queen—in other words, she wants to be taken care of, but she wants the power to rule. She wants to be the apple of a man's eye, but she also wants to rule the man.

To be a hero, and to make the hero's journey—a term made famous by the Jungian thinker Joseph Campbell—is often seen as a somewhat simpler task, at least on the surface, than the heroine's. To be a hero is to be the center of an epic stage. Apollo, Romeo, a Western good guy, Neo in the sci-fi movie *The Matrix*—whole worlds need saving by heroes. Humanity's future is often and obviously at stake in the hero's journey. In the end, if we don't know who the hero is, we wait till he fights the bad monster, the bad guy, or the bad aliens. At that point we know: The hero always perseveres, thus proves himself to humanity. When he has won the day, he is more than a growing boy or adolescent on an adventure: He becomes a good man, and a leader.

Heroic ideals sit at the center of every boy's psyche and, to a great extent, every man's, because every man knows his body, his mind, and his hidden heart yearn for status, and also because women and human civilization as a whole need men to prove themselves heroic. A lazy, good-for-nothing, even mediocre man does not generally end up being selected by women, or rewarded graciously by his community. Performing toward heroism is wired into adolescent boys, and helps them become men. Both females and males generally like to see the hero not just *call* himself a hero, but *prove* it.

But is the hero a heroine too? Is Athena also Apollo? Is Juliet interchangeable with Romeo? Is Snow White interchangeable with the prince? Can we wait for the big fight, watch a young woman persevere, notice that by victory she has now proven her worth to humanity, and thus call her a woman, a good woman, a leader, a heroine?

In some cases, we certainly can. *Xena: Warrior Princess*—a popular Fox Network show, especially among adolescents—takes the male model of hero and, in changing the sex, makes it the heroine's journey as well. Her task is supported even by dictionary definitions of heroines: In *Webster's*, for instance, a heroine is initially defined as "a mythological or legendary woman having the qualities of a hero."

But Xena, and *Webster's*, are both, as we who care for daughters know, simply taking the easy way out. The heroine's journey is far more complex than "having the qualities of a hero." Kathleen Regan, the editor of a beautiful anthology of stories, *Fearless Girls, Wise Women and Beloved Sisters*, describes her years-long search for stories that showed the heroine's journey—the *female* journey to high character and female passage to mature, meaningful womanhood. She confesses that she expected to find Xena-type stories, but discovered that "as tales with female protagonists were found, a whole new class of heroines emerged. Some heroines did things that resonated with my innermost feelings but refused to be classified as heroic: a woman who sensed the importance of an insignificant-looking coin, a girl who loved to dance, or a woman who told a story. A simple conversation between two women when taken at face value could elicit a shrug of the shoulders. Yet underneath this ordinary conversation, the effort that women make to keep relationships alive in a family or a community swells like the incoming tide."

Heroes and heroines can overlap, of course, but they are as different as are boys and girls, and women and men.

So—what is a heroine? How do we see our daughters as heroines? How can they see themselves in this kind of meaningful light as they build character and mark the events of passage and maturity? Let's answer these question quite practically, utilizing various models of "heroine" that you and your family can talk about. Your daughters are, during their childhood and adolescence, developing each heroinesque identity at different times, like trying on different masks and costumes.

## LIKE A HERO

A heroine can be a female hero. Athena, in ancient mythology, was as "manly" as any man. Xena: Warrior Princess can best men at their own game. The advertisement for the highly violent video game *Perfect Dark* shows a futuristic setting and a warrior female besting all opponents. A voiceover intones: "The only person man enough to handle the job is a woman."

This kind of heroine is a girl or woman of our day who climbs Mt. Everest as well as any man, or outcompetes any boy or man. This kind of heroine is the best soccer player, the highly driven success story in the business world.

For the last few decades, this kind of heroine has been of great interest to social thinkers and to our popular imagery—it has been important to show that a female can be as warriorlike as a male. And yet, whether we refer to Athena, Xena, or *Perfect Dark*, this kind of warrior heroine is probably, if all world stories are put together, a smaller part of being a heroine than contemporary theories have tried to make her. Though she is very valuable in a girl's journey (my own girls, for instance, experience the warrior in themselves by taking karate and playing soccer), we would not want to limit the heroine's journey to her. Even when this female warrior is expanded to include girls who are very competitive in school, sports, business, there is also much more, and much more subtlety to your daughter's heroine's journey.

## THE WISDOM OF THE SMALL

Heroines, quite often, seek the wisdom of the small over the flourish of the large. They shine the light of their character into hidden, small places.

*The Princess and the Pea* is not *The Prince and the Pea*. Heroines move in a female sphere of neurological experience, making a heroine's awareness of the tactile irritation of a pea twenty mattresses below the surface a stunning metaphor for female sensitivity. What girl has not felt resonance with that "unheroic" but very "heroinesque" story of a princess on whose sensitivity to a pea the future of the kingdom hinges?

This heroinesque quality is not just about sensory experience. It is also about what things come within a woman's sphere of care. Women more than men—and thus heroines more than heroes—will let go of abstract, socially constructed principles if a single life is at stake. The hero's empathy is based more on large group principles than individual sufferings. Statistically speaking, a woman is less likely to call for the death penalty than a man. A heroine is more likely to protectively hide a small animal, a man more likely to kill it if duty calls. Intrinsic to the heroine's journey is the empathy and sensitivity on which civilization is based; just as intrinsic to the hero's journey is the controlled aggression on which civilization is based.

## DELAYED INDEPENDENCE

Heroines often seek and protect attachments even when those attachments might mean sacrifice of personal independence. It is more often the heroine than the hero who makes sure the complex web of human bonds is protected as the foundation of the society. While heroes will sacrifice their very *lives* for their communities, families, and leaders, heroines more often sacrifice their *freedom* to keep the social web strong.

In fairy tales this is often illustrated by the heroine's move away from her own family's village or domain and into her husband's (even oppressor's—e.g., *Beauty and the Beast*) home. This symbolic act of self-sacrifice has been seen, by some recent commentators, as an act of passivity women should disavow. On the other hand, who can say which sacrifice is superior or inferior? Is it better to give your *life* for the protection of the human world, or better to give up your *independence* for the protection of the human family? Are not both deep, abiding symbols of the moral requirements of human character?

Heroines are rarely asked to give up their lives (and this is especially true now that medical science protects females during childbirth) for the protection of their community. Heroes are more disposable and meet more quick deaths than do heroines. But a heroine's independence is indeed more often disposable than a hero's, especially in the initial stages of a relationship or alliance. Most often, after long patience, the heroine regains her freedom, or, just as often (as in *Beauty and the Beast*), reconstructs, subtly and gradually, her new surroundings to fit what she needs.

## CRAFTING THE SELF

Heroines often craft a self through relationships, patience, behind-the-scenes efforts, and hidden mysteries of female power. In archetypal stories, this crafting of the self is in itself proof of a heroine's maturity, as it was in the Indian story, *The Girl with the Moon on her Forehead*, with which we began Chapter 3. The self-knowledge this girl gained in the cave of the crone became her power, her self. Once she completed the gaining of the knowledge, she returned to her village and was known as a mature woman, and a leader.

Males, in the hero's journey, tend to craft a self through *performance.*

Heroines can craft selves that way, but generally craft a self differently. Where males struggle constantly with having to prove themselves worthy of respect in the larger world of power, females are intrinsically worthy from a nature-based standpoint—they can bear and raise children, the most inherently sacred act in the natural universe. Therefore, it is not the most crucial base-challenge in the female psyche to craft a heroic self in long journeys of physical ordeal; they already face the most challenging physical ordeal by their very nature.

However, females know themselves as malleable. Every girl knows she is, often, too easily swayed. "Holding on to herself" can be difficult. Malleable to the needs of others, especially children and loved ones, heroines seek to prove themselves not mainly through battles with enemies, but through battles with malleability, emotional fragility, internalized character development, and individual self-reliance. This battle generally goes on in intricate webs of intimate relationship, rather than, as often happens for heroes, independent acts of prowess.

Odysseus makes a long sea journey while Penelope confronts internal politics at home. Sleeping Beauty allies with her home-and-hearth mentors (the three fairies) to avoid succumbing to her vulnerability, fragility, and malleability—the prick of the needle that will put her self to sleep—while the prince makes an outward journey through kingdoms, on his horse, in battle, and using his sword against the undergrowth.

This crucial difference between the ways that boys and girls generally try to build character is not a limitation on either gender's journey. It is more important than that: It is a warning to all parents, mentors, and educators that there is a hidden feminine and masculine journey going on in children, which we ought not neglect.

A boy feels unhappy if he can't perform at something. He wants to be the chosen one in some field of play, work, battle, or intelligence. His unhappiness is his cry for help in finding areas of performance in which to gain social respect.

A girl feels unhappy if she can't find the interwoven social alliances she needs. Her unhappiness at not being chosen for the group, clique, or pack is her cry for help in finding social mirrors for her own character development.

Like the boy who isn't a hero, the girl who isn't a heroine feels left out, and afraid.

## SHE IS THE REASON FOR THE STORY

Heroines are often, by their very identity, the sacred goal of the human search. This archetypal fact has been missed, recently, by many commentators, who argue that when males rescue females in fairy tales, girls and women are demeaned. They are referring to the many fairy tales that often involve young women—*Jack and the Beanstalk*, or *Sleeping Beauty*—who are caged or trapped (by a giant, or an evil spell) and then rescued by a male hero. Both the rescue by the prince and the "happily ever after" marriage at the end of these tales are seen as inherently unfriendly to female development.

Better would be to see the heroine in it: In this view, *she is the reason for the story;* the prince serves as a supporting player. She carries the moral ideals of the domain; the prince, in rescuing her, rescues those ideals. And she has almost invariably, through her own ordeal during the story, become more loving, wise, and powerful. She, upon rescue, forms an alliance with a young male who through his ordeal has become more loving, wise, and powerful. During the story, both hero and heroine have gone through their rites of passage, their initiation into adulthood.

Furthermore, she is not only the moral object of the prince's search, but in compelling the prince to earn his way to her, she serves as a model for other young women who are best served as individuals, and best serve humanity, by waiting, watching, practicing romantic patience, and letting young men neither best them, nor ally with them too early, but instead prove themselves moral, courageous, loving, and thus worthy of a long-term alliance.

In this vision of the heroine, the "happily ever after" alliance, rather than a burden to her, is a reward, which she nurtures as she, now a queen, rules her domain, in partnership. And in the archetypal logic on which fairy tales, biblical stories, and world folktales are based, were the girl not a heroine, she would not be attractive to the hero for alliance. Were she not the moral center he sought to uphold, he would not look to her, but to some other, for the goal of his heroic journey. She is a heroine and so he seeks her. By the same token, he is a hero, and thus attractive to her. Our ancestors, such brilliant storytellers, did not waste time educating young people with stories of vacuous girls and boys. They brought to their children stories of heroines and heroes.

## THE CHILD OF NATURE

Heroines hear the multifaceted song of nature. It is no accident that Walt Disney animators have constructed so many heroine stories that involve girls and young women in spiritual contact with the animals and the foliage of nature. Snow White, who hears the birds, and Pocahontas, who talks to trees, are perhaps easiest to recall. Disney is following the archetypal patterns of the heroine's journey in the fairy tales of our ancestral cultures. While there are definitely some tales in which male heroes are similar to Pocahontas (for example, the Lakota story of *The Stone Boy*—a boy who hears rocks talk), these are more rare than heroine tales; just as, in "real life," St. Francis of Assisi, who hears the language of the birds, is a rarer male. Most often, when nature-oriented tales involve males, the males themselves are animals who understand animals (i.e., *The Lion King*), or males who do not understand the natural world as well as the females (i.e., John Smith can't hear Grandmother Willow like Pocahontas can). In this, again, Disney follows the old stories. It is usually the heroine who knows and is utterly allied with the rhythms of nature—her journey, like her own biological nature, is as much or more based on the grounding of the natural world, and human alliance with its rhythms (Pocahontas), than on the abstract principles or divinities of conquering civilizations (John Smith).

These are some of the primary characteristics of the heroine's journey. Your daughters are seeking to live a heroine's journey of their own.

- They seek the entrancement of nature, for they know themselves, especially when they're young, as daughters of nature.

- They seek to be the object of the human moral search, for even if unconsciously, they not only want to be good, truthful, and worthwhile, but they want others to notice their good qualities.

- They seek to learn the games of alliance, because they know that if they are to feel fully worthwhile in life, they will have to make alliances, learn how to depend on others, and protect attachments with fierceness.

- They seek to craft a self from everything available around them, and through the search within, for the spiritual center of their own lives. They know that generally they do not have to stray too far from home and community to find a self, but some among them will wander, and yet these women too will, one day, turn back home.

- They seek to be wiser in the myriad dances of everyday life than in the abstractions of principle. Many girls enjoy the abstract principles, but heroines often realize that what can be debated is somehow weaker, for them, than the intimate wisdom of a woman's intuition. Many girls enjoy physical aggression, but most, especially when they bear children of their own, experience an internal call for less aggression in the world.

How is your daughter living the heroine's journey? How can you help her live it better? How can you and your community help her moral and spiritual development in everyday ways?

I would like to help you answer those questions through the beauty and wisdom of a story. Especially in our age, when our daughters get so much of their self-crafting from superficial stories—on television, in magazines—and so little from archetypal stories based in human nature's search for spiritual truth, I invite you to join me now as we pursue, together, some of the keys to character development by evoking a classic story of the heroine's journey. Not by sitcoms or Internet chat, but by stories of archetypal character, like *Cinderella,* can we judge how our daughter is doing in her heroine's journey, her character development, and her search for belonging in the spirit of the universe.

## Cinderella

Once upon a time, there was a sweet and kind family with only one child, a very shy daughter. The father had acquired some wealth and the mother was well liked in the village, one of those women to whom others came for wise counsel. The daughter, who had few friends, was just becoming a woman when her mother fell sick. Both husband and daughter cared for the mother, sought help for her, loved her dearly, but to no avail. On the day she died, she called her husband to her, saying, "Promise me you will find a mother for our dear girl." He promised. And she said to her daughter, "Promise me you will face adversity with courage, and live with high moral character." Her daughter promised. "And promise me too when happiness comes, after hard times, you will seize it." The daughter promised.

The beloved mother died, and her husband and daughter were grief-stricken. It was a long time before they stopped their weeping, fully two winters, and they tended the mother's grave not only with beautiful flowers, but with tears to water them.

And yet there came a time when the father met a beautiful woman, and felt love grow in him, and recalled his wife's entreaty. He wooed this woman, though his business was becoming more scarce here, and he would need to spend a great deal of time traveling. He married her, happy that in his absences his daughter would gain the stepmother she needed, and also two sisters who were also just becoming women.

So it was that he and his daughter welcomed a woman and two teen girls into their house. At first, things seemed pleasant enough, but then when the father had to be gone, things changed. The bereaved daughter was little respected by her stepmother or her stepsisters. Nonetheless, she recalled that her mother had wanted her to have a mother, and thus respected her stepmother—perhaps more than she should have. Even when her stepmother ordered her to do one job, then another, then another, until the girl had to change out of her good clothes in order to protect them, wear a gray bedgown and wooden shoes, rise early in order to be able to carry the water, light the fires, do the cooking, and the washing, the loving daughter still strived to be a good child to this new mother, and was rewarded, at times, by shows of approval—for her stepmother, though a rigid woman, was not an ogre. As more and more work was piled upon her, the girl recalled her mother's words about hard times. These must be those times, she thought. She could endure them, for they had meaning. One night she was so tired, she actually fell asleep while cleaning the cinders out of the fireplace. From that day forward, her stepsisters called her "Cinderella."

What should we make of this sad opening to a fairy tale? A girl loses her mother whom she adores, and recalling her mother's admonitions, does everything she can to be the good daughter to a new mother. We might ask: How can Cinderella imagine that this kind of "being a good daughter" is within the job description of a stepchild? She must have extremely low self-esteem, we might say. She is certainly not assertive, confrontational, or competitive. More and more work is piled on her, she is abandoned by her father, she keeps just doing what she's told, no matter the consequences to her former, more self-respecting life. Only in our most generous reading of Jesus' "turn-the-other-cheek" would we want our daughter to live like this.

At the same time, the tale of Cinderella is a female character development model: a heroine's journey. From that point of view, there is far more here than may initially meet the eye.

This is a shy girl, very attached to her mother and father, who is now forced into psychological separation from her two primary caregivers. The wise woman whom she most trusts, her mother, provides her with a script for her character development, hints at the kind of heroine's journey she will have to endure—and elicits from her a promise to become, when her passage to womanhood is done, a woman of high character. Struggling in the wake of a dead mother and a father now absent, the shy girl tries to manage her own need for approval with the moral script she has been handed by the wise woman.

Her moral script has also, unconsciously perhaps, come from the moral script of her culture. In that script, a girl does what a woman in authority tells her to do. Good character is not measured by rebellion, but by patient fulfillment of the burdens elders give her. Cinderella is unhappy in the kind of psychotherapeutic way we are very used to discussing these days, unhappy because she is not a free spirit. She is, however, quite happy to be fulfilling what she believes is her journey of character. "She could endure the hard times, she knew, because they had meaning."

From this point of view, we might say that Cinderella has high self-esteem rather than low. She is focused, she is relentless. She has deep insight into her circumstance, and feels connected to a plan larger than her present moments of suffering. This kind of self-esteem is different from what we're used to discussing when we talk these days about "self-esteem." It is "character-based" self-esteem, rather than "feeling-based" self-esteem. The self that is esteemed is a "moral" self rather than a "feeling" self. In reality, a child's developing core-self is constructed of *both* feeling-based self-esteem (emotional development, see Chapter 6) and character-based self-esteem (in this chapter), thus both are crucial.

What do we mean by a "moral" self? I discovered in writing *The Good Son*, a book about moral development, that it was crucial to define words like "moral" and "character" in universal ways—ways shared by all of humanity, not just one culture—so that those words could be used with power and precision. In my study of thirty cultures, I was fortunate to identify ten moral competencies that all thirty teach as primary character traits: *decency, fairness, empathy, self-sacrifice, respect, loyalty, service, responsibility, honesty,* and *honor.* These thirty cultures also held a common seat of morality— i.e., in all of them the seat of morality is *compassion.* To have high character is to be compassionate. To do right is to do the most compassionate thing, given the circumstances, and the absolutes that apply. To do the wrong thing is to have just completed an unnecessarily uncompassionate act.

With compassion at the center of a developing character, and the ten moral competencies as the highest supporting players, we can come closer to defining what Cinderella's mother meant by "live with high moral character" and "be a good person." We have discovered the *character base* for her self-esteem. The feeling-base is one of sadness, but at the level of character she is in sync with appropriate development.

In this, Cinderella reflects a million moments in your daughter's life. Many times your daughter has been, is being, and will be challenged to "do the right thing" even when it feels bad, to "be a good person" even when it would *feel* better to do anything but. A child's moral development depends on maneuvering, in constant trial and error, between "feeling good" and "feeling well"—feeling she has done the right thing, and just plain getting a good feeling from an experience. Many times, the two will gel wonderfully; she will feel good because she has done good, and she will feel good because she has avoided acting incorrectly. Many times, though, she will be Cinderella, living a life of honor, duty, expectation, and very human need, and not feel "well" about it, but feel she is doing the right thing.

In every adolescent girl's passage to womanhood we can hope she experiences this inner conflict often, and constantly, so she can gather the strength, courage, and vision to see what is honest, what is fair, decent, empathic, compassionate, moral during her adult life, when so much will be at stake as she becomes an authority in her family, culture, and civilization. Obviously, we do not hope our daughters suffer the loss of their mother, Cinderella's apparent immense shyness, and the distance of her father.

As we help our own daughters through their character development, and aid them during their adolescent journey of passage, we are called to help them find duty, hard work, even hardship. Abusive hardship—the kind that destroys feeling-based self-esteem, and moral hardship—the kind that builds character-based self-esteem are, of course, not the same thing. It is interesting to note that in pre-Disney versions of *Cinderella*, the stepmother is not as abusive as we are used to seeing in Disney. Even in the Grimms' version, she represents the maternal continuation of the dead mother's moral scripting of the daughter's life. In these observations, it is the stepsisters who are abusive—hoping to destroy Cinderella's feeling-based self-esteem—and it is the stepsisters who provide a warning lens into the shadow of the feminine.

They appear next in our story.

## THE SHADOW FEMININE

As the story continues, let us recall that the stepsisters gave Cinderella that name because she fell asleep, one night, just beside the fireplace, cinders all over her apron, her dress, and her hair. The stepsisters forced Cinderella into the ashes over and over again. They did this by emptying her peas and lentils into the ashes, so that she was forced to sit, in a painful position at the hearth, picking the tiny objects out again.

One day Cinderella's father was set to come back to the house, after a monthlong selling trip through faraway villages. Sensing Cinderella's excitement, her stepmother instructed her to change back into her normal clothes, and to refrain from hyperbole about any difficulties in her life during his absence.

"You don't have it so bad," she reminded the young girl. "You have a home, work to do, people who look after you, and a father who provides."

Behind their mother's back, the stepsisters said, "It will go very bad for you if you do anything to make your father's visit unhappy. We'll get you after he's gone."

Cinderella knew that she could not get her stepmother's ear against her stepsisters, for they were their mother's blood children and she, herself, was motherless. She resolved to enjoy her time with her father, saying nothing negative.

While her father visited, she was, in fact, quite happy. Together, father and daughter walked to her mother's grave and laid new flowers there.

When it was time for her father to go again, he asked his daughter and stepdaughters what gift they might like him to bring home.

"Beautiful dresses, covered with baubles and bells," cried one stepdaughter.

"The roundest pearls and the brightest jewels," cried the other.

"And you, my dear, what about you?"

"Father," Cinderella replied, "break off for me the first branch which knocks against your hat on the way home."

When Father left, Cinderella returned to her old life. This time, her stepsisters were even nastier to her, tossing her food into the ashes, pushing her into the ashes, mocking her, "A branch, Daddy, bring me a branch," and turning their own mother as far as possible from her stepdaughter with lies of the foulest nature.

A few weeks later, the father's gifts arrived via a family friend. Father himself had to travel farther and would not return for another few months. The stepdaughters draped themselves with their clothes and jewels.

Cinderella discovered a note from her father attached to the hazel twig he had given her. "As you requested, my dear, this was the first twig that struck me as I rode through a green thicket on my way home. I'm sorry I had to turn back, but at least this will reach you."

Cinderella took the twig and planted it on her mother's grave and there she wept so much that her tears were the first moisture to water it, and she sat a long time, cloaked in the cinders that had become her constant companion.

This section of the story is rich with revelations of the shadow feminine, and the kinds of circumstances that allow the shadow feminine to flourish. By shadow feminine we mean, in simple terms, the dark side of being a girl. Just as, in all mythology, there is a dark side to being male—symbolized in *Star Wars* by Darth Vader—violent, ego-driven, seeking domination over the weak, hiding behind a mask or disguise and unable to show his true ugliness, prepared to kill whenever he can—there is also a dark side to the feminine—hyper-manipulation, lying, pretending nothing is wrong, excessive materialism, verbal nastiness, shaming of others' core self, and, sometimes, violence.

In mythology, stories of the heroine's journey always include episodes of the shadow feminine. One or more figures in the story mirror the dark side of being a girl. The heroine's character—in this case, Cinderella's—ends up shining brighter because she confronts the darkness in her stepsisters. While we might say she doesn't "confront" them at all—i.e., doesn't stop their shaming and violence toward her—she does confront it, by enduring and by waiting. Immersed in the shadow feminine, she experiences joy when she sees her father again, but then after he leaves, she discovers a nadir in her life, a single twig on her mother's grave her only solace, and even that evincing a torrent of anguish.

Once when my daughters were younger, and I was reading them the illustrated Cinderella story—the Disney version in book form—I asked them if they would ever act like the stepsisters.

"Oh no," they assured me. "Never."

But we all know there is a strong warning in this story about not only nastiness from stepsisters, but the dark side of the feminine in all our daughters' lives.

## FEMALE BULLYING AND VIOLENCE

In Blythe, California, recently, a three-year-old boy was smothered by his six-year-old sister and five-year-old cousin. According to Sergeant Mark Lohman, spokesman for the Riverside County Sheriff's Department, interviews with the girls show they intended to kill the boy.

"It was not an accidental death," he confirmed.

From Toronto, Canada, I recently received an e-mail telling me the story of a very sensitive six-year-old boy who had been bitten and taunted by two girls at school. No matter what the family did, the school did not believe girls could do those things uninstigated, and assumed the boy to be the one who started things. "We have finally taken him out of that school," the father wrote me.

Similarly, in a school district in my own state, a third-grade boy was picked on for having big ears by a group of girls. It went on for some time, and his parents taught him to ignore, to use his words, and to try to get adult help. One day, two girls pulled his ears until he cried out and he punched the ringleader girl. The school called parents in, said the boy needed to see a counselor, had aggression problems, and perhaps had a conduct disorder. The girls received very little attention from school—no mentoring to take personal responsibility. The parents were lucky to keep their son from being suspended.

These stories illustrate two key issues facing us as we strive to raise girls of high character: One involves physically violent behavior itself; the other involves taking responsibility for their part in violence with males.

Bullying behavior all over the U.S. is increasing, according to the FBI and Bureau of Justice Statistics (for both boys and girls), with marked increases in the bullying behavior of adolescent girls. At the Gurian Institute in Kansas City, our teachers have noticed this increase. Said one of our teachers, "The girls have changed from when I was in junior high. In every generation, puberty is a bad time for girls—the in-crowds, and out-crowds; everything becomes a crisis. But now we're seeing more girls in physical altercations, more hitting from girls. This is very different from when I was in junior high."

Her instinct is supported by statistics; females are becoming much more physical. Between 1985 and 1994, violent crimes increased 90 percent for women compared to 43 percent for men. In a classic study of over eight thousand families, conducted by the University of New Hampshire's Family Research Laboratory, it was found that 12.4 percent of women have assaulted their spouses, compared to 12.2 percent of men. This kind of result generally shocks people who think of men as the primary purveyors of violence in families. The statistics for "severe assaults" were 4.6 percent for women and 5 percent for men, again amazingly close.

Males, no matter the statistical parity of violent behavior, still cause more significant physical damage, but to neglect to notice the increasing violence in girls and women is to sweep the evil stepsisters under the rug, just as Cinderella's father (distant from family politics), Cinderella herself (intimidated by her stepsisters and holding to a maternally scripted idea of character endurance) and the stepmother all do. In our own homes, we are more responsible than we may realize for confronting the bullying, violence, shaming, and instigating that our daughters do. Violence is not only something that is "done to" our girls, but increasingly, they are acting out their loneliness and being led by media imagery, peers, and lack of supervision and guidance, to become more violent. Especially scary about this trend is the natural trends of violent behavior: i.e., the more violent girls become, the even more violent boys will become. Among all primate species, increased violence among females increases the violence-modeling for males. When males become more violent, the world is even more dangerous for females. This is a vicious circle we don't want to continue.

And so we are inspired by the stepmother's lack of action to be unlike her. When we see our girls instigating others, we are called to confront them.

When we see our girls becoming physically violent, we are called to redirect their behavior and, if necessary, punish them.

When we see our girls shaming and teasing others just to be mean, we are called to worry less about "protecting their self-esteem" (feeling-based) by "exploring with them why they might do that" and worry more about "protecting their character" by finding, in ways that fit our family, clear paths to the immediate end of the behavior.

The increase in verbal nastiness we discussed in Chapter 6, and the violence and bullying discussed here are, of course, not the only displays of the shadow feminine in our times. Another is displayed by the stepsisters' actions as well.

## THE STRUGGLE WITH MATERIALISM

"I want to be Barbie—that bitch has everything" reads a license plate frame in downtown Seattle.

When Cinderella's father asks his daughter and stepdaughters what gifts they want, his stepdaughters want beautiful clothes and jewels. Cinderella, representing the sacred feminine—the feminine of high character and spiritual search—asks for a natural object with which she can pay respect to her mother's memory. She is untouched by materialism, but her stepsisters are entranced by it. Later, they will get their comeuppance for their blind materialism—it will involve an immense humbling of their position in life.

Materialism can hit boys and girls both, but hits girls in a special way. Female biology and acculturation both enjoy the beauty of small objects and the increased status of material wealth. Doesn't the stepsisters' flagrant materialism provide a warning which all of us, especially in this age of material luxury, need to heed? While it is terrible for a child to have nothing, it is just as terrible for her to think she can have everything. Both lead to a kind of material madness that empties the soul of meaning.

My daughters, like yours, have their eyes on a million material things. Especially in a home where attachment to mother, father, and extended family is diminished, materialism takes a deeper hold. Often it seems like a girl's feeling-based self-esteem can correlate with material gain. Many girls just feel better when they are surrounded and ornamented by material. Sometimes the distant father—whether distant by divorce or work—takes the easy way of reconnecting by bringing material gifts alone, rather than also his affection and discipline. Sometimes the mother, if distant in some way from her children, or if herself a materialist at the core (as the stepmother, we will soon learn, certainly is), does the same.

The shadow of materialism extends deep into a girl's adult life. It can burden her relationships with mates and children, and it can rot her own soul. This it does, in symbolic terms, by playing a kind of masking role over true emotional and character growth. In other words, when this aspect of the shadow feminine has a large hold over a girl's development, her emotions, morals, and soul are actually being repressed. She never fully grows up because, distracted by materialism, she does not focus on the emotive, moral, and spiritual life journey. In the Australian aboriginal culture's story with which we began this chapter, the young woman is specifically put into a hut *without* her material possessions so that she can recall and discover who she is *without reliance on the material world*.

The Cinderella story pursues the theme of materialism in numerous symbolic ways:

The stepsisters—the shadow feminine—toss Cinderella's—the sacred feminine's—peas and lentils into the ashes. Cinderella is forced to fish the food she needs to eat from these ashes. In European fairy tales ashes are often symbolic of the emotion of grief. Cinderella's food is hidden in her grief. Her growth comes from delving deeply into the emotions of that grief, as well as holding fast to the character traits she has received from her mother who is the object of that grief.

On the other hand, the stepsisters are involved in no deep emotional activity; their "peas and lentils" are not the round vegetables of real food, but the pearls and baubles of self-ornamentation. They do not delve into the self-defining emotion of grief, nor do they focus on their spiritual inheritance. They want material wealth, pure and simple.

Peas and lentils versus pearls and jewels: The sacred and the shadow mirror each other symbolically, and the differences between ashes and rags (grief) and clothing and jewels (disguise and ornamentation) are intriguing. Cinderella is cloaked in an emotional and spiritual search; the stepsisters, at best, hide their selves (selves never seen, except in their nastiness) with clothes and jewels.

In all our homes and communities, the challenge of materialism is present. It is the challenge that requires curtailing purchases:

"No, Sally, you can't buy candy every time you go to the store."

"No, Mariah, you can't have that just because you want it."

It is, at its center, a challenge to protect the soul of a daughter. Whenever we say no to a material purchase, we are asked, in a spiritual sense, to say yes to some kind of inner dialogue, inner search for an emotional, spiritual, and moral center in our daughter.

"Why can't I have that?"

"Well, because . . ." and we must speak our own soul.

As a girl develops, she often gravitates toward measuring herself by the costumes around her. In protecting her character development, we are not just taking away costumes or limiting her material possessions; we are called to raise her with our own values, and spiritual focus. Often the building of character in a daughter is not just a matter of negating her impulses, but also a matter of *directing* her inner vision to matters of high character, service, and giving.

In many homes, for every material thing a child receives from parents, extended family, or peers, whether at Christmas, Hanukkah, a birthday, or any other time, she must give away a toy, piece of jewelry, stuffed animal, CD, clothes, or other personal item (that is in good working order—she can't give away something she would throw away) to a charity. We practice this in our home. Our daughters actually have come to enjoy choosing toys and clothes to give to others who need them.

## HANDLING SIBLING RIVALRY

Vigilance with our daughters that they do not join the terrible nastiness of peers and vigilance regarding materialism are two of three aspects of the shadow feminine that this section of the story reveals. The third, in which the first two often collide, is the area of *sibling rivalry.* Like so many girls, Cinderella's stepsisters are each other's rivals. In our own homes, a lot of what we don't like about our daughters—a lot of their shadow—shows up in nasty sibling behavior.

What do we do to stop nasty sibling rivalry? And even further: How do we make *sibling respect* an important part of character development?

The basic philosophy behind a nature-based answer is this: The family environment is meant to be the safest place a child will experience in her lifetime. Brain, biochemical, social, and spiritual development require that a child's home be the "safe place" in her life.

Anything that negates that safety is suspect. Alcoholism negates that safety. Drug addiction, abuse, sexual molestation all negate that safety. And, at times, sibling rivalry goes much too far, negating that safety.

In the end, then, the job of the parents is to help girls be responsible, as siblings, for assuring one another's sibling safety in the home. This is *sibling respect.*

Gail and I use, and coach, this philosophy. We expect our daughters to be friends, and we nip in the bud, very quickly, nastiness between them. There are enough opportunities for each of them to compete in the greater world, enough opportunities for each to develop the skills of the rival, the opponent, the aggressor—they do not need to emphasize that skill development with each other. Our home is, ultimately, a safe place because it is a place of parental authority and childhood friendship.

One reason for the very nasty sibling rivalry in our culture (it is not as flagrant a problem in most cultures of the world) is our culture's lack of guidance toward sibling respect. Our culture's inherent competitiveness is another. And even more deeply felt—but less noticeable—is the breakdown of family, especially the three-family system. Our children do not get enough love and guidance. They show their pain by making their siblings hurt. And they feel, most acutely, the pain of having to compete with siblings for the affection and guidance that seems to them, so often, to come from a shallow well.

When children feel loved (provided with affection, discipline, and family activity as the center of life) they have less need to compete with one another for parental affection. Archetypal stories often speak to this. The shadow feminine comes out when there is a loss of affection in the home. In the Cinderella story, this is symbolized by the father's nearly complete absence from home life. When a parent is distant (and when children get little affection from other family members), affection is a commodity too little in stock, and rivalry for it ensues. Thus, concerned parents and extended family need to not only curtail nasty rivalry but preempt its necessity by being devoted to our families.

Some practical strategies can be very useful in dealing with sibling rivalry. I hope you can employ these directly as you face the shadow of rivalries in your home:

1. Call a family meeting when arguments (and physical violence) have become shrill. Discuss issues, front to back, and discipline when necessary.

2. Reward the girl (or boy) who stops the fight. Sometimes this makes it possible to waste less energy on determining who started it.

3. Many arguments can be removed from your presence, i.e., "Go argue out back," or "Go argue in your room." Often, arguments diminish when there's no audience.

4. Intervene, as much as possible, in the early stages of the fights between siblings. This can often prevent escalation. And then there is nothing wrong with insisting, "Say you're sorry," watching your children say it to one another, then moving on.

5. Consistently promulgate (repeating often) what the rules for rivalry and respect are in your home. For instance, let your children know they must always apologize if they've hurt someone.

6. Constantly explain your definition of a safe home, and your children's responsibilities to ensure it. This makes sibling rivalry a

character issue. Your daughters' character—sense of responsibility and family honor—is on the line.

7. It is just as often useful to take sides as not to. Follow your intuition. If one side is very clearly wrong, be the wise one and show allegiance with the right. If, however, you can't figure out what's going on, don't get enmeshed; don't take sides.

8. Remember that time is your ally. Many disagreements will solve themselves. Pick your interventions wisely.

9. Raise your children to expect to play with each other, and to develop some common interests—an easy way to model and encourage this is to play family games together one night a week. A child does not always "have to have a friend over." Parents can encourage their children to develop ways of enjoying each other's company. Admittedly, this works better with sisters than with a sister and a brother.

10. Teach your daughters to express when their feelings have been hurt, and to say *why*. A girl from about four onward should be able to attempt, and most often accomplish, an explanation of why she feels what she feels. Quite often, when the sibling understands how she or he has caused pain—understands it clearly—the sibling feels regret. The quick grief that regret brings helps rebuild sibling alliances.

## Female Mentors, the Language of the Birds, and the Dance

Having delved into some aspects of the shadow feminine, let's return now to the story. Some new challenges await us.

It came to pass in the kingdom in which Cinderella lived that the king and queen of the land, who were getting older, and who had a son, a good young prince, knew it was time for him to show that he had become mature by marrying and taking on the responsibilities of manhood. The prince, however, had not found a particular young woman of interest. His parents determined to help him find her by holding a dance in which all the young women of the kingdom could participate.

When she first heard of this event, Cinderella was excited, but soon she knew her stepsisters would not let her go. "This is a ball for real princess material," they said, "not cinder girls." And now her stepmother, who had been a distant but decent parent, seemed to turn on her as well. Now protective only of her biological daughters' chances for love and power, the stepmother gave Cinderella impossible tasks. With the help of beautiful birds, with whom Cinderella had always been able to converse, she fulfilled her stepmother's requests. But finally her stepmother just locked her in a room, and with her own daughters, set off for the ball.

Cinderella, at first helpless, heard a voice, and then noticed a fairy, flying with the birds. This fairy godmother, who looked so much like her own mother, used her magic to construct for Cinderella a carriage out of a pumpkin and horses out of mice. Her rags became a dress, her face and body transformed to the beautiful young woman she had, over the course of the last few years, actually grown to be.

When she appeared at the ball, everyone noticed her, including the prince and his parents. The prince could not get enough of dancing with this princess who would not tell him anything about herself! All the other young women and their parents watched enviously, but did not know who she was either. Not even her own stepsisters and stepmother recognized her. Cinderella danced and danced, hearing both whispers of approval and recrimination but feeling, in her heart, her mother's words: "When happiness does come, seize it." This was the moment, she thought. And for a while, it was.

But midnight struck, and she suddenly realized she would be found out—her fairy godmother had told her the magic would only last till the last hour of the day.

Rushing out of the dance, she lost a glass slipper, and by the time her family came home, she had returned to being the rag-wearing Cinderella.

In many fairy tales, as in most marriages of our ancestral pasts, marriage arrangements—often developed at birth between families in power—negated any possibility of romantic attraction as a basis for alliance, intimacy, and harmony. Social balance was ensured by the religiously sanctified act of marriage itself, not by the spiritually evolving union of two selves attracted to each other.

The Cinderella story is one of those archetypal tales with roots deep in old traditions but wings capable of great flights of freedom. The great ball as a place to meet an attractive mate is a wonderful innovation for its time; it shows human culture moving toward the kind of intimacy we now strive for—free intimacy, based on two selves touching romantically, bonding emotionally, and keeping that spiritual bond alive throughout life. This very spiritual approach to human love (my book *Love's Journey: The Seasons and Stages of Relationship* is an exploration of twelve stages of this kind of love) is a recent phenomenon, a few thousand years old, and especially an innovation of the last few hundred years. Our girls now have the ability, in their exploration of love and mating, to reach spiritual heights even their own grandparents, often living less in luxury and more in brute survival, could not reach. This is a good time to be an adolescent girl—it is a time of immense personal freedom.

On the other hand, it is a very complex, pressure-filled time to try to learn how to love. For this reason, the Cinderella story holds keys to survival for our girls—it is not just an old-fashioned tale, but in fact a wonderful reflection of what every adolescent girl needs as she begins to make the journey of self-revelation that adolescent and adult love is.

## THE ROLE OF THE MENTOR

Researcher Pegine Echeverria has written a book called *For All Our Daughters: How Mentoring Helps Young Women and Girls Master the Art of Growing Up*. In it she reports her discovery, intuitive to all of us, that girls are desperate for mentors to lead them through the tumultuous years of adolescence. Mentors exist throughout girls' lives—teachers, tutors, older siblings, family friends, grandparents or other relatives, coaches. But some mentors are special to the girl.

These are the mentors who become like the fairy godmother to Cinderella. They are the keepers of a certain distinct portion of the girl's self. In unconscious motions, they help their protégée learn who she is and plan how to reveal who she is to the larger world.

As girls become nine, ten, and older, their cognitive and emotional systems—both from brain growth and from hormonal structure—*need more than Mom and Dad.* When they were infants or little girls, Mom and Dad, and a second mother—a day care provider or grandma—might have been enough for most self-development and character needs, but later the adolescent mind, blood, body, and soul become larger than just a two-parent creation. It is a self that needs many mirrors, many guides.

Some of these will be provocative, even painful guides—like the stepmother who jealously guards her own daughters' freedoms. She is a "shadow mentor." All our daughters will meet shadow mentors in their lives—hopefully, these will be restricted to coaches who are rude or teachers who are unfair. Vigilantly we protect our daughters from truly dangerous shadow mentors—rapists, abusers. Our vigilance is necessary because sometimes shadow mentors are like the stepmother—sometimes they seem so nice, concealing their rough edges masterfully.

As much as possible, we try to provide our daughters with "sacred mentors." These are like the fairy godmother: The teachers, friends, coaches, godmothers, and other elders—some being men, and many being women—who are charged, though they may not consciously realize it, with helping our daughters reveal a hidden aspect of self and soul. Some families today find it useful to "build in" a fairy godmother, from as early as their child's birth.

My own daughters, for instance, have a godmother, Pam Brown, who is Gail's oldest childhood friend. Pam has been like a second mother to our daughters since their birth and now, as Gabrielle and Davita navigate adolescence, Pam helps them develop who they are by her presence, her answers to their questions, her reflections on our family, her admiration of their skills, her critique of their actions. Pam is like a mother, slightly removed.

The fairy godmother in *Cinderella* is like this also. She carries the ideal of the mother (in Cinderella's case, the deceased mother) without herself being the mother. In a spiritual sense, the girl, during her second birth—her adolescence—has room to grow in the mentor's symbolic womb because it is not restricted like the mother's literal womb was. Cinderella's mother is gone, cannot help her with a dress, slippers, and so on; but her agent, the mentor, can. Sometimes there are things Gail can't help our daughters with, but Pam can. The mentor becomes a kind of transitional parent. Cinderella needs a female mentor to get her prepared for the grand ball, which is a major rite of passage for her. The fairy godmother fulfills this task.

There is always magic associated with the mentor, and the reason is simple: Some of the magic of the mother, which the infant and young girl felt so fully, has now dissipated—the adolescent girl is almost obsessed, at times, with how little magic Mom carries anymore. The mentor, on the other hand, is not Mother and is therefore exotic. She has powers to persuade that Mom now lacks. She has keys to certain rooms of the social house, or even the self—a self Mom tries to open but often merely irritates. "Oh, Mom . . ." the fifteen-year-old girl laments. But when the mentor teaches the exact same thing, the girl listens with rapt attention.

Each of us is called to ensure our daughters a world not only of parents but of good mentors.

And each of us may well be called to notice, too, the power of mentors who are not literally human.

## THE LANGUAGE OF THE BIRDS

Cinderella has other helpers besides the fairy godmother—she has the birds, who help her fulfill the impossible tasks, and who befriend her through great tribulations. Like your daughter and mine, she is a child of nature; she senses herself to be one with the many spirits that surround her. When she was younger she made birds and other animals into characters (that word is no accident) in her own imagined worlds of play in which she measured and developed her own character. As an adolescent, still she loves to commune alone with the natural world. At times, she gets more out of imagining the spirit-filled world of a book than from living her everyday life. Many of her mentors are utterly spiritual in nature, even if she lives in the middle of a city and rarely "gets into nature." Still, in the world of books, stories, and religion she imagines her communion with invisible guides.

Cinderella pays special attention to birds as do so many stories you might recall—most Disney movies, for instance. The language of the birds is an ancient language in all religious and spiritual traditions. In the ancient Middle East, storks (whom we canonize as the bringers of babies) were said to speak to and guide travelers and new mothers. In Chinese traditions, flying "firebirds" (dragons) are spiritual guides. Among the Norse, the language of the birds is the symbolic and sacred language that heroes receive access to only after they have vanquished dragons. In the *Qur'an*, "people who have learned the language of the birds *(ullimna mantiq at-tayr)* will have all favors showered upon them."

The language of the birds (of spirits, of imagined beings and souls) is a language of sensitivity to hidden things and to nature. It is a language of flowers and of beauty. It is a wonderful alliance in a girl's growth and in her development of character. Cinderella shows symbolically—by her ability to talk to birds (and all the animals)—what your daughter seeks literally: a feeling of belonging, not just in one's immediate family, but in the larger natural and spiritual world. Your daughter came from nature and does not, at the level of soul, want to feel alienated from her creative center. Nor does anyone, male or female, child or adult.

While the most obvious mentors you nurture in your daughter's life are people, the Cinderella story of character development encourages us to expand definitions of mentors in our girls' lives. The more a girl is attuned to the possibilities of conversation with pets, angels, spirits, birds, and invisible guides the more she develops imagination. In the human journey, success is generally most possible when imagination is a primary element of developing character. Imagination leads to greater compassion—for it increases a developing self's ability to feel and empathize with another's experience; and it leads to social success, for on imagination all mechanical design and social creativity depends. So even if a family does not use the words "religious" or "spiritual" or even "God," still the Cinderella tale opens the girl's life to the possibility of hidden conversations, so that the life of the mind itself expands.

## THE REVELATION OF THE SELF

The Cinderella story has been very much about a girl, burdened by pain, who builds moral character—builds a self—through the help of personal experience and those who both care and do not care for her. When the prince calls the grand ball, and we see Cinderella moving out of her small family world into the larger society, we now see the story transform into one about how she can and will *reveal* the self— the personal character—she is developing. A central question of the ball scene itself is this question of self-revelation. *At what pace, in what ways, and for what intentions shall a girl, a young woman, reveal herself to another?* Cinderella rushes away from the prince at midnight—she does not reveal all of herself too quickly.

In these next few pages, we will approach the question of self-revelation from a number of practical angles. It is a crucial question in every adolescent girl's life. There is no single answer or formula for how all girls should reveal themselves, especially to boys, and then to the larger society. A basic part of each girl's strategy—like Cinderella's—depends on her previous life-experience. And yet there are some basics to female character that we see throughout the ancient and world literature. What are these?

Especially when a girl has suffered, she may choose the course of hiding herself, for a time, until she builds trust in a friend, a family member, or a potential lover. This shows strong character. Rather than rushing into the arms of another who will solve her problems, she remains a generous listener, dignified, but somewhat distant. Sometimes this holding-back will "turn off" her potential mates or friends. In the case of the prince, it is very attractive. He does not know how much Cinderella has suffered, thus does not think out the psychological facts. He knows only that she is beautiful and mysterious.

Every one of our daughters is beautiful and mysterious to someone like that prince at some time in adolescence, and more than once to more than one. Our daughters do not need to have suffered as Cinderella did in order to show the common sense to remain a bit mysterious. It is one of the most age-old and effective techniques young women have for protecting their own character self-development and expression of that character in the world. The gradual revelation of self is a basic component of the heroine's journey a girl lives. To reveal everything of oneself immediately is to lose the inherent power of mystery. It is to give the malleable self over to another for manipulation. It is to say, "I exist now for you, I am an open book to you, take me as you wish" far too early in a relationship.

Later, in the months and years in which a relationship grows, more complete revelation of self will hopefully occur between friends, partners, even lovers. And gradually, as potential life-partners are assessing each other, both romantically and socially, each reveals aspects of their own worth in gradations of intimate experience. But to reveal oneself on the first night? That would throw the female story—indeed the human story—far out of whack.

So it is in this archetypal tale of our daughters' journey to moral character that sexuality, sensuality, and romance are withheld at first by Cinderella. The prince is left, at the end of the evening, with only a beautiful glass slipper. This slipper is filled with symbolic meaning. It is a reminder of Cinderella's fragility—so that he must build a sense of her that constantly involves compassion. It is a "piece" of her self, not the whole—so that he may keep trying to learn her identity. It is a unique reflection of her self (i.e., only one foot will fit this shoe) by which he can be certain, later, that he has not been fooled into loving someone less worthy than her.

In archetypal tales about romance and courtship, this element of *worthiness* (self-worth, and worth-to-other) is almost always present. Strangely, it is almost always *not* present in our contemporary sitcoms and other stereotype-laden shows and films made for adolescents. Whereas among our ancestors both the female and male parties had to prove worthiness to each other *before* mating occurred, among our contemporaries, mating occurs quickly, and the gradual proof of worthiness is attached onto an already sexually and romantically consummated relationship. This latter way is, in the short term, more exciting for the adolescent partners, but it contributes to the breakdown of the intimacy imperative in the long term. Intimacy becomes not a journey that never ends but a series of actions—often sexual—which, once accomplished, deceive the participants into thinking they know the other self. Adolescent intimate relationships often do not last more than a few weeks or months, and adult marriages do not last more than a few years, after the deception takes hold.

So we strive to teach our daughters how to make the revelation of self *a gradual journey*, in which their characters lead them to reveal only some *aspects* of the self, while retaining some mystery at all times. As our story continues now, we'll become even more specific about how to help our daughters practice this not as a game, but as a ritual of love.

## The Prince Searches for Cinderella

The concluding section of the Cinderella story—perhaps one of the most famous concluding episodes in our culture—involves its heroine in a tearful run home, and her stepfamily's arrival there, full of fun stories about the ball. Cinderella remains demure, continuing in her role of the left-behind keeper of the hearth.

The prince, however, has fallen in love. He reveals to his parents that in his conversations with the mysterious princess, he met a young woman "of the purest heart." His only clue to her is her slipper, and so he sets everyone in the land to finding what girl's foot fits that slipper.

In early versions of the Cinderella story, she meets with the prince and is courted three times before she finally disappears. In these early versions, Cinderella goes to her mother's grave and prays there for help. She confides to her mother how pure of heart she finds the prince, and how worthy of love. The birds and her fairy godmother provide her with new clothing, the prince sees her, gets to know her, spends the day with her, even taking her to his family's castle; yet she always flees him at night. On the third courting, the prince puts pitch on the staircase, and her glass slipper gets stuck in it as she runs away. In these pre-Disney versions, the glass slipper comes into his possession after an extended courtship, not after just one dance.

In both the early and Disney versions, once the prince has the slipper, he searches the land for his love. His staff and he himself travel from home to home. When they come to Cinderella's home, the stepmother locks her away. The stepdaughters try on the slipper but their feet become bloody from forcing the imperfect fit. Cinderella (with the help of her spirit-mentors) escapes her prison. Though she is dirty with ash and dressed in wooden shoes, she gives the slipper a try.

In earlier versions of the story, Cinderella's father returns at this point. In one version, the father has come home and is shocked to see how his daughter's been treated. In another, he is so cowed by his wife, he joins in keeping his biological daughter enslaved and away from the prince.

Even despite, however, the obstacles of stepmother, locked door, and some versions of father, Cinderella perseveres, sits for the prince (who has the wisdom to see through appearances), and once the shoe fits, confesses who she is. She recalls her mother's final words, and knows that now her time of happiness has come. She and the prince are married and she becomes queen of the land.

There are perhaps a hundred different versions of what happens to her stepmother, stepsisters (and father). We will choose the most uplifting and magnanimous, in which Cinderella orders them to become keepers of the hearth—castle servants—during her reign as queen.

And so ends the story of Cinderella, as the new Queen and King live happily ever after.

## YOUR DAUGHTER IN LOVE

So much beautiful symbolism and wisdom occurs in the final section of the Cinderella tale. Cinderella finds her magic at her mother's grave, with the help of the spirits and her mentor. She does not reveal herself too quickly to the prince, but compels him to court her.

Though he is desperately in love with her, he must be patient. He must take the time to learn how he feels in her presence, and he must learn to *listen* to her. As he listens to her he learns who she is—her character—that essence of self that reassures a person of how high is the quality of a possible mate. She takes the time, also, to get to know him, and learns that he too is of high quality. She feels her mother bless her union.

In this simple, archetypal framework for a girl's portion of what we call young love, we see the continued revelation of character. Our daughters want to "get to know" a prince before they commit to him. They want to be listened to. They want the prince to reveal himself. When we, as parents, don't let our daughters date till they're sixteen, we are saying to them, "we support you in making the *gradual* journey of self-revelation." If we let them date (by "date" we mean boy and girl alone) at fourteen, we are generally missing the fact that female (and male) character needs to be *developed* before it can be *revealed* (at fourteen, a girl's character is not yet developed enough for the self-revelation process that dating is), and that its revelation should generally be a process watched over, for as long as possible, by caring adults (as the king and queen construct processes by which to introduce their son to dating).

It is worth remembering that *in no culture on earth* is adolescent dating considered "not the business" of the adults. Certainly none of our ancestors considered it off-limits. In our own time, though there is some pressure to "let the kids be," that kind of blanket isolation from parental authority is not really what adolescent girls want. They want us to provide them with structures within which to reveal character to a young man—curfews, dating limits, phone-time limits, and even, in cases of danger, the forbidding of a certain date. Gail has told our own daughters the story of her mother, who, suspecting a boy wanted to have sex with Gail when she was fifteen, forbade her from going out of the house that night. In retrospect, Gail sees that her mother was right, and is grateful.

Cinderella dates, within limits. This is the symbolism of her leaving the prince after each meeting, much to his consternation. She not only dates in a structured way, but she reveals herself in limits. She wants revelation back from the prince! Why should she reveal her character without him revealing his? A girl who gives everything of herself without receiving revelation back is set up to be manipulated and controlled. When Cinderella's mentor reminds her (as in Disney) that "the carriage will turn back into a pumpkin by midnight," her mother-figure is saying, "You are not his to control." The wisdom of the story's lost-glass-slipper plot element echoes this sentiment, saying, "Leave a little something behind so that he must keep coming to you. Let him keep revealing his character and his love to you."

## SEXUAL MORALITY, AND THE CRISIS OF CHARACTER

In today's culture, there has been a wonderful freeing of the male-female conversation, so that our daughters have "male friends" or male "platonic" friends with whom romance is not an issue. These boys are friends but not boyfriends. These boys are good sounding boards for the revelation of self and character our girls seek. Often they themselves are less masculinized, more feminized, than the kind of boy or young man our daughters would actually seek for romance. These kinds of group-peer relations and nonsexual male-female relations are very useful, especially before dating, to get girls and boys accustomed to one another in intimate conversation; and during and after dating, to help young women and men gain trusted peers to talk to about love traumas and delights.

At the same time, most daughters will seek a prince, and that prince will not be a platonic one. When this moment comes, it is essential the girl has in place a family system and friendship infrastructure that supports her in the major "character trauma" of relationship with the prince. While love-relationships are certainly *emotional* traumas, crowded with every feeling from pain to joy, they must be seen as *character crises* as well. A girl will test her morality and values in young love like never before. She will discover moments of moral crisis.

Cinderella has her mother's memory—the wisdom to guide her; she has mentors; she has guides; she has access to her own magic; she has dignity; she is self-reliant. She has been through everything and is very strong, that strength constantly supported by her aides.

Before your daughter dates, your family is challenged to make sure she has parents, mentors, and her own supports in place. While you can't ultimately control the dating, you can always stand with her, talk to her, listen to her, carry on moral debates about premarital sex with her, answer all her questions, even questions like "When is oral sex okay?" and "If I did have sex, would you want me to be honest and tell you?"

Dating ought to be a healthy character "crisis" *for the whole family*—a social rite of passage that everyone helps out with—in the same way the girl in Australia is led back to her people to discover boys and men within the boundaries of her social world. Our culture, highly individualistic, has seen dating not as a character rite of passage for the adolescent *and family*, but as a "child's right," to be protected whenever the child asserts it. We think we are making lives easier for our daughters and sons, but there is another way to see this: Given that whether we notice it or not, dating is a character crisis, the crisis is made doubly traumatic in homes where there is not open discussion about all issues of romance and relationship, and where structures and people don't support and mentor the process. Our daughters are facing character crisis alone.

## UNDERSTANDING GUYS

In my school-based research, I've had the opportunity to poll hundreds of girls. Nearly all put at the top of their "need to know" list: how it is that boys and men think, what they want, what they need, how to communicate with them. I've put all this into the term "Understanding Guys," and wrote a book for girls thirteen and older that speaks directly to them about boys and men called *Understanding Guys: A Guide for Teenage Girls*. As you help your daughter gradually reveal herself, and as you are honest in your conversations with her about her own sexuality, self, and search for love, I hope this resource will also be of use.

Its primary purpose is to help young women understand how young men are trying to reveal themselves and their character. It is about the journey the prince is making toward your daughter. While talking about how the male brain and body think and act, it goes further, into the male spirit. I've received many letters from teen girls who have read it in that vein, and many have said things like: "After reading about how guys think, I've decided to act differently with them." It is a strange phenomenon in our culture that though we seem to know everything and have access to all information and data, our girls are still Cinderella, trying in spurts to understand the prince, and the boys are like the prince, so confused by their new love.

So it is that just as our infrastructure must help our girls protect themselves, reveal their character and needs gradually, and help them deal with any character and emotional traumas that confront them in their love relationships, it must also provide them with ideas, wisdom, knowledge, and spiritual depth about what *males, masculinity,* and *men* are. Feminine and masculine are, especially to adolescents, the most interesting mirrors of each other.

## MODESTY, SEXUAL MYTHS, AND A GIRL'S REPUTATION

Boys and girls are very different in their adolescent journeys of character revelation. This is something we all intuit. Cinderella and the prince are very different people. How deep do the differences go? Cinderella's mentors know she must be a girl of modesty. For them, that is obvious. For us these days, modesty is not considered a virtue for adolescent girls. Is this wise?

Girls can experience a kind of shame boys will never quite understand, a character trauma of epic proportion, in which the heroine loses herself. This shame has its roots in misuse of her own nature and biology. Girls get that at a very deep level, and so do societies.

Wendy Shalit has written a very useful book on this subject: *A Return to Modesty.* Modesty, she claims, is a lost virtue. From a nature-based standpoint, the loss of it is especially dangerous to the core-self development of our daughters.

A girl's malleable self risks making character and self-crushing decisions in order to attach, especially if a girl feels emotional trauma in other parts of life (and even, often, when she's just under normal adolescent hormone and psychosocial stress). To put this more plainly, adolescent girls often feel driven to do whatever it takes to get the affection of someone who is attaching to them.

Every one of us can remember back to our adolescence and recall one or more girls who—in the language of our era—"had a bad reputation." These were girls and young women whose selves were malleable and who, often through sexual activity, encouraged boys and young men to manipulate them into losing self. In our own daughters' lives, even with renewed cultural interest in abstinence and virginity, there is terrible pressure to attach to boys who demand sexual activity; and even more subtly, there is an increase in internal female sexual pressure because of overwhelming sexual imagery which permeates media in late childhood and early adolescence.

The Cinderella story is one of great depth and wisdom specifically because it depicts a girl under terrible emotional stress who nonetheless has the character (and the support) to retain her self. She stays focused on what she believes is right: values taught to her by her mother.

When our girls miss this, when they give up modesty, and when they are not taught how to sustain self-restraint (even when boys are saying, "If you loved me you'd give me a blow job"), they risk the kind of loss of self that means the loss of the heroine's journey (at least for an important part of life). The heroine's journey is tested as Cinderella does the gradual mating dance with the prince. Every adolescent girl can feel the heroine's journey at stake as she dances. The self-control of sexual conduct is part of being a heroine.

How can we help our girls see it this way? The author Susan Chappell, in *American Girl*, created a list of "sexual myths" our daughters need us to talk to them about. It is a list that helps build modesty and sexual self-restraint.

1. If a girl has sex with a guy, he'll begin to love her.

2. Having oral sex is no big deal, and you have to do it if you want to have a boyfriend.

3. Girls fall into two categories—those who have sex with everybody (sluts) and good girls.
4. Good girls don't fantasize about sex, but bad girls do all the time.

This list is, of course, only the tip of the iceberg. As we acknowledge the importance of honest sexual conversation in the female adolescent journey of character, we discover that our daughters need help understanding everything from contraception to abstinence, and the interplay of their hormones with their sexual desire.

A number of good books can be helpful. In our family we've found three books, *Venus in Blue Jeans: Why Mothers and Daughters Need to Talk About Sex,* by Nathalie Bartle, *Beyond the Birds and the Bees,* by Beverly Engel, and *Sex and Sensibility,* by Deborah Roffman, particularly wise. A parent who invests in the wisdom of these resources becomes very able to protect the character development of her daughter through the "character crises" that even the most normal dating entails.

Presumably Cinderella's support system was revealing to her both sexual myths and sexual mores as she gradually revealed herself to the prince and found him gradually revealed. We can be certain that of primary concern to Cinderella's support system was her *reputation*. By this they would mean her "sexual character." Her support system knew intuitively the biology that makes female sexuality so crucial a part of female character building, and her sexual decisions so important.

In specific terms, that biology dictates that in a lifetime, a human female will produce approximately three hundred eggs. She has three hundred potential children in her body's life cycle. This may seem like a lot, but not when compared to the male, whose body will produce trillions of sperm, each a potential life. Every culture has seen this: the relationship between female biology and female character. Some have overreacted to the connection—like the Afghan Taliban government, which under the guise of Islam did not allow women to even sit in a car with a man who was not of their family. Others underreact to the connection—our culture qualifies here—those who do not teach girls completely enough that they are sexually *sacred* beings, instead teaching them to do whatever they want in romantic and sexual terms.

Throughout history, "a girl's reputation" has been a way society could help young females manage expectations of their own sexual character. Cultures "imposed" sexual character on girls by imposing the edict on them that they not sleep around.

Our culture, yearning to free girls of any personal restrictions, has experimented with the idea that "no matter what a girl does, she should be respected." In other words, her reputation should not depend on her actions, actions which are restricted by patriarchal cultural mores. If she wants to have sex with a lot of boys, so what?

This view, unfortunately, does not fit female biology. Like so many ideas about women and girls we've experimented with recently, it is not nature-based. And like so many feminist innovations, it better fits male biology. While a sexually promiscuous girl may well be surprised by a "bad reputation," resent it as a cultural imposition, and garner sympathy for lowered self-esteem in the face of socially imposed mores—she and her support system might also gain by seeing it as not merely an imposition, but a protection. It is a way societies can try to monitor sexual activity.

A family came to Gail with a difficult situation: Their fifteen-year-old daughter had a boyfriend who lived in Portland, Oregon (a one-hour plane ride away). His father was a pilot, so he could fly anywhere anytime. He was seventeen. The mother and father did not want their daughter having sex with him—he was very worldly, and though he was a nice young man, early sex did not fit their values. But their choice was either let him sleep over at the house when he flew into town on weekends or say no, but accept that the young couple would be having sex at a motel or friend's house. The family knew what it wanted to do—forbid the sex, and even the relationship—but the girl was ready to run away. As a sounding board, Gail helped the family determine if the girl was using birth control, and tried to engage the family in issues surrounding its discipline systems and expectations. Since the girl wouldn't come in, therapy ended.

In retrospect, Gail recalled feeling stunned by how quickly—by the time the girl was thirteen—that family's attachment to its daughter's character development had careened away from the family's center. Following that case, she became more vigilant in talking to our daughters about our own family's policies, ideas, and values. She and I both have utilized the "moral debate" format with our children, at the dinner table, or during long car trips. We discuss moral and sexual values, as they are developmentally appropriate, and ask the kids to debate us on topics such as:

- When is it right to have sex?
- Does "No" always mean no?
- Why does someone have sex?

We make sure to share our own stories as much as possible. Our daughters become embarrassed, very appropriately, especially if I'm around and there's too much "sharing," so we follow their lead on what they need us to share.

We hope to give our girls what the family of the fifteen-year-old could not: wise, nature-based sexual values a girl can hold on to as she enters the phase in her character development that will involve a very insistent young prince.

## The End of the Story

After a long journey of courtship, following a long personal journey of emotional and character development, Cinderella makes the promise of marriage to a worthy man, and becomes queen. The story of her adolescent character development—the adolescent episode of her heroine's journey—is coming to an end. As it does, Cinderella gains authority, new respect and power, and new purpose: She joins in a ruling partnership. She has earned her new purpose and power through a life of travails, endurance, and compassion. Even as she wields her power—first, over her stepsisters and stepmother—she remains a person of magnanimity and high character, just as her dying mother admonished her to do.

This is what parents generally wish for daughters: the kind of power that comes from compassion, the kind of self-confidence that comes from not only praise but also tough experience, the kind of dignity that comes from holding to a worthwhile vision of how to live, the kind of strength that comes as much from resisting temptation as from accepting new freedom.

I hope you've enjoyed this rendition of the Cinderella story, and my attempts to bring out some of its archetypal lessons. As Cinderella finds the happiness her mother's vision promised, and as she looks back on a life of stress and pain, she can certainly say that she is now at a worthy place in her life. She can certainly feel that she is a morally developed human being.

That is one of the greatest gifts she'll receive in life.

My daughters are heroines, and so are yours. In their passage from girl to woman, they learn the qualities of the heroine they possess. They know what they themselves are capable of—learning both their sacred qualities and their shadow sides. In each girl is a greedy stepsister, just as in each girl is a dignified, patient Cinderella. In each of our daughters is a yearning for the prince, just as much as a sense of completion in moments alone, in nature, or in another solitude. Our daughters seek to learn the story they are living, and seek to know many stories of self at once. They make many clear rites of passage during their second decade of life, and they experience many hidden ones as they make the life journey.

Looking at the journey to womanhood, Clarissa Pinkola Estes, the psychotherapist and storyteller who wrote *Women Who Run With the Wolves,* says, "We all begin with the question 'What am I, really? What is my work here?' " This is two questions as one. What a girl is and what she will do to reveal who she is: This is her character. From early puberty to late adolescence she is deciding who she is and what her work will be, and we are her guides.

Heroines, unlike heroes, don't as often have to journey far from home to learn their own inherent and developing character. Where the Australian aboriginal male must travel far into the desert and into dreamtime to "find himself," the adolescent female goes into a hut constructed nearby. An American mother often feels her adolescent boy pulls farther away from her than her adolescent girl. But just because she may not journey as far into the geographical unknown, she is as complete a heroine as he is a hero. She has her own obstacles, and must find strength in her own way. She has her own fears, and must find her own courage. She is as capable as anyone of living with a shriveled, jealous heart, and so must find her own journey through and beyond ego.

Everyone who helps shape a girl helps shape her character. There is not one "right" family structure or religion or rigid set of social codes that makes a mature woman out of a young girl. It can be done by the kind of alternative family Cinderella lives in. It needs mainly that the adults around the girl understand their task, and focus on it, protecting her moral development as much as her emotional, and showing her paths to worthiness of which they themselves would be very proud.

## Looking Forward: The Issue of Women's Roles

As this chapter ends, we end four chapters of very specific practical application of nature-based theories. I hope you have discovered a template for ensuring the healthy development of all the imperatives in your daughter's life, including especially her desire to love and be loved. We have focused in these last chapters on that intimacy imperative especially, even as we looked at everything from doing chores, to spanking, to diet.

There remains, however, another crucial element of female development with which I'd like to end this book: the issue of what role, in society, your daughter, as a woman, will find unfolding for her. As you read the next chapter, I hope you'll join me in envisioning and ensuring for her a "woman's role" that, because it is based in her nature, is as unlimited, free, and self-fulfilling as any imaginable.

# 8

## WOMANISM:

### GIVING GIRLS A SACRED ROLE IN LIFE

*"There is one thing stronger than all the armies in the world and that is an idea whose time has come."*

—Anonymous

I first used the word "womanist" by pure accident when Gabrielle, eleven, came to me in my study with a troubled look in her eye. About an hour earlier we had all been talking at the dinner table about women's issues, feminism, and the pressures girls are under these days.

She had not asked if Gail and I were feminists; not until now, as she entered my study. "I just asked Mom," she reported, grinning a little. "Mom gave me an answer, but said not to tell you. She said to just ask you, and see what you said."

I stalled, repeating the question aloud, "Am I a feminist?" and watching a host of images play out in my mind—my mother, a feminist, taking me to rallies, myself and Gail at a feminist protest of violence against women, donations I had made to feminist causes, media and academic forums I had participated in. I recalled myself, at a conference in a hotel ballroom in Izmir, Turkey, in the late 1980s, explaining to participants, in sensitive but also forceful ways, how American feminism had a great deal to offer Turkish society, and the Muslim world.

But I saw images also of so many moments within feminist subculture that forced my withdrawal, and my distrust, especially as I felt a parent's protectiveness of his daughters. I recalled Gail and I sitting with friends just a week before, talking about how ironic it was that we who had daughters were looking for other ways of thinking about girls than feminism offered.

In the wake of all the images, with the simple voice of intuition, I said, "You know what? I think I would call myself a 'womanist.' That's the term that fits me better."

"Womanist?" Gabrielle said. "What's that?"

I avoided an immediate answer; instead, I said, "So now tell me what Mom said."

"Mom said she used to be a feminist, but now wasn't sure what she was."

"Give me twenty-four hours," I told Gabrielle, "and then let's you and I talk. I'll tell you what I think womanist means. Okay?"

She agreed, and left my study. I sat back, having stumbled onto a term (a term I later learned had been used by Alice Walker, the author of The Color Purple, fifteen years before). This term brought a vision, one that needed time for conversation with Gail, reminiscences and hopes late that night and into the morning as, with Gail's help, I wrote a statement by which to explain to my daughters not only the blessings and the burdens of feminism, but now perhaps the excitement and the compassion of a new framework for how girls and women, as well as the men who support them, can think of themselves as activists and passionate participants in a global dialogue about the state of women and girls. Later that evening, after a lot of talk and writing, Gail and I both knew that the most important judges of our ideas would be our daughters, and so we tried to make sense of our vision for their sake.

When, the next evening, we shared our womanist perspective with them, Davita, too young, listened patiently, and Gabrielle, just on the edge of loving the intellectual challenges of adolescence, asked pointed questions. As we had interacted with them the previous evening concerning feminist theory, we interacted with them now concerning womanist vision. This interaction lasted beyond one conversation, and in the end even Davita helped us form our ideas.

In this chapter, I will detail a vision, not a fact, in hopes that this vision helps the millions of people who are, like my family, passionate for women's rights and the rights of children, but dissatisfied with our present, conventional, politically correct language. I hope you will utilize my attempt at envisioning a *nature-based* logic for women's lives as a foundation on which to build your own logic. Mine is not a final statement.

No matter where a family raising girls ends up, I deeply believe that it must, actively, passionately, and verbally, engage its daughters in talking about their sacred roles in life, the politics that surround their roles, and the challenges girls and women face. To be a girl is to become a woman who hopes to feel that she is performing a sacred, purposeful role in life; and to be a woman of our day is to be confronted with where she stands on issues at the center of our vibrant, democratic politics.

## What Is Womanism?

And so Gail and I explained to our daughters, womanism is three things at once:

- A return to the basic-rights philosophy of women's suffrage—i.e., wherever in the world that women do not possess basic rights to physical safety, voting booths, reproduction, and education, women's suffrage seeks to protect them;

- An embrace of the economic politics of feminism (women who want to reach economic parity with men should have opportunity to do so, and wherever in the world or in our culture women live in desperate circumstances, they shall be protected); and

- A new vision of the unlimited possibilities for the women's role in the new millennium (one in which women now have the evolutionary luxury to *stage* their life-journey to fit their internal *nature).*

We spoke with our daughters about the history of the women's movement, from Susan B. Anthony to Gloria Steinem to Naomi

Wolf, and I promised my daughters a kind of grid to help them understand differences between feminism and womanism.

I hope the following comparative model is useful to you and I apologize to everyone, especially to feminists whom I deeply respect, for its simplicity. Here, then, are examples of differences in beliefs.

| WOMANIST POSITION | FEMINIST POSITION |
|---|---|
| 1. Positive change for women once came from a victim philosophy, but now that philosophy actually keeps women one-down from men. | 1. Positive change for women comes from proving that women are victims of men, and thus politically polarizing men and women toward ultimate gains for women. |
| 2. Women and men are fellow victims of a fear- and violence-based social system, and have different but equally painful wounds. Girls and boys suffer equally, though often differently. | 2. Women's suffering, despair, and pain as individuals and a group is greater than men's. Girls suffer more than boys. Boys and men are more privileged than girls and women. |
| 3. The educational system is biased against girls and boys both, with boys now the worse off. | 3. The educational system is set up to hurt girls and help boys. |
| 4. Key words: self-knowledge and service. | 4. Key words: power and empowerment. |
| 5. The ideal situation for a woman is one in which she is valued equally for work within and without the home. | 5. The nonworking woman is not financially independent, thus is potentially a victim of men, thus is not ideal. |
| 6. The study of male and female biology is crucial to the understanding and nurturance of girls (and all others). Nature is our best guide as we seek wisdom to live by. | 6. Ninety percent of why males and females are the way they are is socialization, so the study of biology is relatively unimportant. Feminist ideology is our best guide as we seek wisdom to live by. |

| | |
|---|---|
| 7. Masculinity is mysterious and we need to understand, clarify, accept, and shape it meaningfully, rather than fearfully. | 7. Masculinity is defective and dangerous. Females must react against it. |
| 8. We need to get help for women and men who are hit, and for the hitters. Violence is perpetrated by both men and women. | 8. Men hit women and must be punished. Women are mainly victims in domestic violence and child abuse, not participants. |
| 9. Marriage is sacred and essential to human progress, especially when a couple is raising children. Achieving stable, healthy attachments is the hardest work of our civilization. | 9. Marriage is an inherently flawed institution, and secondary to the needs of a woman. Female independence is of paramount value, and achieving it is the hardest work of our civilization. |
| 10. Women and men are not, nor ever will be by nature, the same or function in the same way. Human life is passionate and progressive as much because of difference as similarity. | 10. Our goal as a human race should be gender androgyny. |

A powerful, narrative illustration of the difference between a feminist approach to social issues and a womanist approach was recently provided by a report of the Institute for Women's Policy Research, which, in November of 2000, graded the fifty states and District of Columbia on the best states for American women. It graded states on women's economic autonomy, women's participation in professional and managerial jobs, abortion rights, access to contraceptives, and political participation.

*A woman's ability to attach, in a stable and ongoing way, to her children was not studied,* nor was her ability to develop healthy extended family support, and successfully work part-time (or make another useful adjustment) during child-raising. Apparently these were not considered useful measurements of a woman's life.

As we move toward a broader womanist philosophy, we will ulti-mately raise higher in public consciousness the notion that most women and men are parents or grandparents (and that it is most humane for those who do not have children to nonetheless help nur-ture other people's children). Thus corporate CEOs will look more closely at corporate day care and one-year maternity leaves as pri-mary issues in their workplace. Most of what is useful, noble, and essential about human life is the care of children; thus that care must be reflected at *all* levels of personal and philosophical dialogue, as well as sociological study; it must certainly be primary in a study of women's policy, and corporate life. The womanist philosophy is, in large part, based in the idea that protecting a mother's (as well as father's and extended family's) graceful attachment to children is the most important job of both home and business. Throughout human history, one of the best ways to judge the health of a civilization has been the careful determination of how it supports the mothers of its children.

In making this statement, we must not flinch from seeing human equity differently than we have these last few decades. Ideas like "gender equity," which have permeated legislation, are often helpful, but they are just as often dangerous to children. When equity as a concept rises above child attachment as a concept, the law deems political correctness higher than the careful love of children. I recently learned of a case that illustrates this profoundly.

A mother, who is also a business executive, wrote me from New York. The judge, during her custody battle over her infant daughter, told her to stop breast-feeding, in hopes the child could get used to the bottle, so that the father could take her on a trip for two weeks (the child was four months old). The mother's staged, biologically driven attachment to the infant child came second to a social idea about gender equity. In this case a mother's biological bond with her child—one the child and the mother need—was undercut by a judge who put ideology (and his interpretation of the law) above the needs of the infant. As the womanist philosophy is more discussed in the culture, we hope the biological and developmental characteristics of human attachment will become paramount in lawmaking. Thus, this father (and judge) will understand the potential destructiveness of both separating a four-month-old girl from her mother's milk, and separating a four-month-old child—whose primary attachment figure is her mother—from that mother for two weeks. It is the forced separation of an infant from her primary attachment figure that should be illegal.

By the same token, this father should be legally supported in taking the daughter out of state for two weeks *later* in life, when she is of school age. Understanding the developmental nature of children and parents helps everyone better care for them. Had the father and judge understood a child's nature, their compassion would hopefully have aided them in constructing a plan by which the father stayed close and facilitated breast-feeding, and the mother enjoyed the father's closeness with the child, so that he bonded with his daughter in preparation for the times when, after infancy, he would have her for long periods without Mom. This New York case is one of those where feminist calls for gender equity backfire on women. This backfiring, ironic as it is, will become more and more the norm the farther our culture swims away from human nature and into ideology. More and more women will be pulled farther from their children, in myriad ways, and soon the majority of women will not find the long-term stability of mates, nor the closeness and attachment with children, nor the financial security that the intimacy imperative, so important to female life, draws them toward as they mature.

## CAN WE EXIST WITHOUT FEMINISM?

In expressing a womanist philosophy, we are implying that there is danger to women, and therefore to their families, if the feminist approach continues to dominate social dialogue. Because its call for "equity" is founded in reactivity to men and masculinity, it certainly can help daughters be independent of dangerous men, but it can also harm daughters, most of whom seek, by their very human nature, love, companionship, and trust of men and masculinity. Because it is founded in a search for economic power, it can certainly help women develop as independent beings, but it can also harm daughters, most of whom seek, at a very natural time in their lives, to find their self-worth in their attachments with children and family. In expressing a womanist philosophy, we are calling on women, men, and the culture, to look beyond the limits of feminism.

At the same time, it would be counterproductive for human civilization to exist without the feminist agenda. When it comes to facing specific ways in which men are dangerous to women and girls, and male groups exploit women and girls, the womanist philosophy is not as directly powerful as the feminist. While the womanist philosophy focuses on the attachment and development needs of the majority of girls, the feminist philosophy focuses on the protection of the minority of girls—girls who are beaten, exploited, systematically victimized, and destroyed. The womanist philosophy is too tame, in comparison, to immediately combat the situation in India's eastern state of Bihar, where women are still, to this day, killed as "witches," or in many parts of the Middle East, most obviously Afghanistan, where girls are not allowed education. When I lived in India and saw women physically attacked by men (in fairness, this is a rare occurrence in India), it was the militancy of feminism that rose up in me. When I lived in Turkey and traveled into the far east of that country, talking with girls and women who would never go to school (in fairness, most girls in Turkey do go to school), it was the militancy of feminism that I felt could best help.

Feminism as a philosophy takes the risk of crossing cultural boundaries in search of women's safety, girls' education, and thus, human progress. It is also a philosophy with the militancy and political base to help disenfranchised, marginalized, and impoverished women and girls in our own, comparatively wealthy American culture. In our discussions with Gabrielle and Davita, Gail and I expressed to them our hope that, as our civilization transitions to a womanist philosophy, it will do so in respect and support of the areas where feminism is better suited to prevail.

May our family's discussion of the characteristics of womanism and feminism inspire you to actively discuss the politics of femininity with your own children. As you do this, you may well find yourself immersed in a kind of ultimate conversation with your daughters concerning their sense of the sacredness of their life experience—the sacred roles they will take on in their lives. A discussion of this kind can bring great meaning to the lives of girls, especially adolescent girls who are searching for themselves.

## A Sacred Female Role in the New Millennium

Gail and I have taught our own daughters what we can about the sacredness of their lives by lining conversations with the kinds of philosophical dialectics that began this chapter. We do it not only so our girls will be savvy individuals in a very dialectic culture, but also because by helping them think out who they are and verbalize where they fit into both the female and the human drama, we help their brains grow and their self-confidence, as members of this society, build. Given the incredible amount of information a girl faces from media, schools, peers—and in her own self-reflection—critical thinking skills—specifically about who a girl is and should become—are essential to the development of daughters.

The fact that my daughters have taken to debating with me on social issues, personal goals, and "the female role" makes me feel that, though they and I, Gail and I, and they and Gail don't always agree on the fine points, we are nonetheless navigating together the same ship through today's vast, complex ocean of information and possibility.

In the final chapter of *The Wonder of Boys,* I provided ten principles of a sacred male role, and my daughters have found this intriguing. "Dad," they said, "what are the principles of a *female* role?" Which ones would be the same, they wonder? Which ones would be different? They sense already what every girl and boy senses—that they must become *women,* just as boys become *men,* and that in that becoming the human mind seeks organizing principles.

Thus, in part as a gift to my daughters, and beyond that, as a gift I hope will help every parent, I have searched through the literature of thirty cultures, including our own, to discover universal principles for female development. I hope you will find benefit now as I present the results of that research: a model of a sacred role for girls and women based on principles shared in all cultures. It is presented first in one word, and then in ten organizing principles.

## MOTHERING

Not surprisingly, all cultures hold up the function of the *mother* as the most sacred aspect of female life. Cultures differ in how expansive or limited is their definition of that word, and the sacred role it implies. Among the Japanese, for instance, it is very common for the mother in the family to be handed, by the husband, his paycheck, and utilize it as she believes the family needs. Sometimes, in an "innovation" Americans—individualists to the core—would consider crazy, she gives her husband an allowance out of his own paycheck!

Among the natives of certain parts of New Guinea, women do not gain full status until they have mothered a child—a common practice among tribal groups who exist at survival-subsistence and must put the production of children as the tribe's highest priority. A woman (or man) who does not have children is seen as dangerous to the society, a freeloader not doing her essential part.

In Japan, New Guinea—indeed, everywhere in the world, including the U.S.—mothering is a constantly evolving, vigorously innovative, and sometimes cripplingly limited role. In our culture, we would generally not give allowances to the fathers of our children, nor condemn childless women. However, we are no less innovative in constructing the role of mothers for our women, and even as I study world cultures, it strikes me powerfully that we are, should we choose to assert our ability, capable of helping to innovate a sacred role for girls and women that is among the most unlimited, and also among the most well ordered, in the world.

This new female role can find its most expansive and most powerful expression in loyalty to the word *mothering*, which is one of the most etymologically various words in any language. The English word "mother" grows from Middle English, Middle French, Greek, and Latin, and even mirrors ancient Sanskrit. In all languages—whether *moder, mater, meter, maternus,* or *matr*—mothering is the highest ideal in female life, the most universally respected. And one etymological fact that is perhaps of greatest interest to us in the wake of thirty years of experimenting with the possibility that women didn't need to define a sacred role for themselves is this: In its linguistic roots, *mothering* is associated with being *a woman of authority* as well as being a female parent of children. For our age, this expansive definition of mother seems most fitting.

It implies the sacredness of female authority. It ensures focus on the needs of female parents. It makes obvious what most people have noticed, clearly and even by hidden intuition: that girls seek to be *both* caregivers to those in need, *and* authorities in their circles of influence, whether those circles be large or small, hierarchical or intimate, within family or without, corporate or alternative. Girls are focused, from very early, on being *mothers of the human experience*; this is true in every culture for biological reasons we defined in Chapters 2 and 3, and of course because every culture—whether in well-defined ways like the Japanese or in more happenstance and confusing ways like our own—directs its girls to become "mothers of the world."

Women who never have children are still mothers—they mother communities, other people's children, the earth itself. Women rarely shirk the responsibility to nurture and care for people. Young women who "couldn't care less about bonding with kids" generally discover chinks in their armor as they grow through adulthood. Women, like Catholic or Buddhist nuns, committing never to have children, mother other people's families and communities. In a stunning example of this, my college debate coach, Sister Margaret Mary Conway, who retired in 1998, a woman in her eighties, left Gonzaga University, where she had taught for decades, and returned to her order's headquarters in Wisconsin, where she would join her sisters in one-hour prayer cycles twice a day. She told me, "By praying for others I am, in God's eyes, a mother." Even in her lexicon, after eighty years of life without the biological practice of mothering children, she sensed the primary, visceral role within herself.

The word *mothering* provides, I hope, an inspiring foundation for a sacred female role. From that foundation, let me offer ten principles which can serve as a way of defining what a "good mother," in its most expansive sense, can be. In order for a girl to reach high personal expectations, it is important we teach principles to her from very young, by our example, by choosing communities for her which teach them to her, by the didactic practice of teaching itself, by listening to them develop, by nature, in her own voice as she grows.

The following principles constitute, of course, only one model of a sacred female role. I hope they inspire you to create your own "womanifesto" for your daughters of what you believe makes a girl's, and a woman's, life most sacred to humanity, and thus most successful and happy.

## TEN PRINCIPLES OF A SACRED FEMALE ROLE

The basic principles of female and male roles are similar, in a universal way, but the gender-specific challenges to each will often differ. We may have the same basic goals for girls and boys—that they will live lives of successful work and service, nurturance of family, and personal, soulful development—but we ought not expect either gender, during their journeys to and through adulthood, to achieve the expectations in completely the same way. Womanhood and manhood are, thus, not different in status, but considerably different in how each girl and boy becomes what we dream for all children: that they grow into loving, wise, and powerful adults.

> PRINCIPLE 1. *Seek lifestyles, communities, and helpmates that afford you a balance of personal spiritual development, family devotion, and life-sustaining work.*

A woman is going to juggle many different selves in one self—that is a given. A girl learns this very early, as she seeks success at school, in sports, in clubs, while feeling responsible to help raise younger children, or to baby-sit others. This juggling, if one remains conscious of its rewards and does not fall prey to overemphasizing, for too long, one single element, allows a woman to experience the best of life through her own spiritual path, through devotion to her children and devotion to those in her extended family, and through work in society that stimulates her. It is crucial that our girls seek and choose mates, institutions, and lifestyles that will allow them to juggle and to journey in ways that fit the natural stages of their lives as women. Working most of the week away from home and never seeing one's children is not balance, and is rarely enjoyed by a mother. Staying at home, purposelessly, while children are at school is the other extreme—it can lead a woman to loneliness, a sense of inner shame, and lack of meaning. A woman's soul asks of her life that balance be ensured, as much as possible, for in finding balance—whether a woman has biological children or not—a woman becomes a mother.

PRINCIPLE 2. *Provide for, protect, and nurture those you are called to love.*

A mother nurtures, protects, and personally manages the provisions required for her own children (and her community's children) to grow in safety. She is fierce in her devotion, provides unconditional love, lessons in respect, hands-on care, and opportunities for exploration that children—and/or coworkers, friends, other family members—need. Every woman is a mother in this regard, for every woman is called to the sacred role of loving others who need her.

PRINCIPLE 3. *Actively participate in not just one but three families.*

A mother is always mother to many. Her responsibilities do not begin and end with her own blood kin. She stands at the center of three families: her nuclear family (or, if she is single, her self alone); her extended family, including non–blood kin—friends, schoolchildren she helps, her friends' children, younger people who need mentoring in the workplace; and her communal family—her faith community, neighborhood, workplace. A mother is not only parent to her children but mentor to many others. Her life is a journey of attachments and intimacies through which she produces what she, and her world, need in order to flourish.

PRINCIPLE 4. *Live in concert with the natural world.*

A woman cannot help but be a child of nature, and a mother *knows herself as this child;* she understands the part she plays in the interdependent web of organisms and systems and souls. Part of a mother's integrity comes from her ability to live in concert with the rhythms of her own nature, and thus the nature around her. Nature is the place from which she came and to which she will return after the brief journey of her particular mind and personality in this life. When she is unclear on how she is doing as a woman, the beauty and challenge of nature can be her therapy.

PRINCIPLE 5. *Seek equal partnerships with men and male culture.*

A woman approaches romance like a mother discovers deepest love, by practicing her love as a mature spiritual discipline—with rules and codes of conduct, and a deep sense that the life of the soul is at stake in human relationships. She keeps boundaries clear but does not punish her mate with remoteness. She seeks a spiritual path, and asks her mate to join her, but does not condemn his times of separateness. When she experiences the primal urge to dominate and the equally powerful urge to be excessively compliant, she discerns the source of her desires, seeks help in managing her confusions, communicates as openly as possible with her mate, and makes decisions about love in the same way a mature congregant makes decisions about faith in divinity: with questions, with doubts, but if at all possible, with commitment to the sacredness of loving bonds themselves.

PRINCIPLE 6. *Seek a female kinship system.*

Among first, second, and third families, a woman needs other women to support her. Her reaching out to them and their reaching out to her is a sacred community. Together, the community of women admires femininity by bringing new women into the adult community—girls who are growing up, women who have recently arrived. An emotionally and spiritually vital community of women shapes women into mothers. Mothers feel their elemental connection with mirrors of themselves. It is difficult for a woman to be a mother if she betrays other women. Women must always be there for other women.

PRINCIPLE 7. *Be an agent of service, social dialogue, and, when necessary, social change.*

A mother participates in her society's evolution. In her everyday life, and no matter the supposed smallness or the grittiness of her service, she is a visionary. What she does shapes the future of humanity. By her intimate acts, she is partly responsible for the human conscience. When a woman comes to a time of service well beyond her three families, she is fearless in this pursuit, but accomplishes it in balance with her everyday life.

PRINCIPLE 8. *Know the story you are living.*

A woman who is conscious of the life story she is living often becomes a mother to the stories of many others. Her consciousness of her own life journey makes her wise. Through her understanding of herself she can fully take personal responsibility for her life and actions. Her long memory of her own ancestors, her understanding of the season of life she is presently in, her wrestling with tradition, her visions of new possibilities are all parts of her invaluable life story. It is a story others need to hear, especially as she becomes an elder, and especially nowadays as so many young people live in confusion about what stories make a life worthwhile. It is, ultimately, and no matter her language—even if she is an atheist—a story about her female journey through life's mysteries, which, for most people, are ultimately spiritual in nature. Most often, she is supported by rituals that sustain her through the busyness of life, and give strong binding to the book her life is writing.

PRINCIPLE 9. *Enjoy the fruits of your labors.*

A mother is a woman who can play ecstatically. A woman who cannot enjoy the fruits of her labors will not feel whole. Life is a joyful journey, though pain-filled and, sometimes for years on end, lived as if in a series of terrible storms. No life is without the promise of the dance that follows harvest. Whether on a daily basis, or after the children are grown, or after retirement, or in a million ways of character and devotion throughout a woman's life, a woman experiences herself in the sacred role of the mother when she notices how little it matters if others watch her dance disapprovingly. She simply knows that by hard work of mind, heart, and hands she has earned the right to dance.

PRINCIPLE 10. *Be open to change, even major changes in values.*

Adaptability is the finest path to happiness. A mother is a woman who can hold on tight, and then can let go. She knows when the flower has fully opened; she waits to pick it until then. She knows when the flower has withered, and throws it to the wind, where it can do other good. A mother holds fast to her values, to her beliefs, to her commitments; she is the essence of conviction. But she is also capable of constant wonder and unbridled anticipation. If a new way is best for her children (whether children of her blood or her neighborhood) she explores it, and if she finds it worthy, refines her life and intentions to include its uses.

The sacred role of the mother is available to every girl through the attention of those who raise and care for her. If you neglect teaching your own version of a sacred role, you may be neglecting the spiritual life of your daughters. It is possible you are feeding them, clothing them, buying them things, giving them a good, solid education—but not helping them discover a deep framework for their existence as girls and as women. It is natural in our time to neglect to teach girls a sacred role; we are busy people, and we live in a time of immense social transition regarding gender. Many people hope that we need never use the word "role" as regards girls and women, so clear is our memory of times in the recent past when the female role was one of subservience to men.

Yet, to neglect the final piece of our daughter-raising, and to live in fear because we fear the past, is to incompletely prepare a girl for life. It is to neglect to give her the gift without which happiness is impossible: a template for personal meaning. Our daughters want to grow to be women who live a life of spiritual worth. They want to look back on their adulthoods with the sense that they have been strong women, loving mates, and good mothers. We can begin them on their journey toward that kind of meaningful certainty by constructing in our own families, workplaces, and communities new paradigms for what a healthy female role can be.

This certainty is not only our daughters' right; it is our right as well.

# EPILOGUE

*"We can only speak of the things we carried with us, and the things we took away."*

—Barbara Kingsolver

I t seems like just moments ago, toward the beginning of a dream, that we ourselves were children. Our hearts and minds were occupied with the minutiae of how to grow up ourselves, not on being the wise ones who would raise the next generation. Men and women of our era, we ran through our culture's decades of transition with hunger and energy to burn, trying on new ideas like new coats. Our closets are full, to this day, with possible selves.

Somewhere in all this we had children, and these children came to look at our closets, questioning us about what each coat meant. Our children always assumed that our accumulation of ideas and colors and traditions and new values were evidence of our wisdom; they never for a moment imagined we might have felt inadequate to the task of raising our daughters. They did not come into our families knowing of a culture in transition, or of gender politics; they came in knowing only that they yearned to love and be loved. They did not wonder over the difficulty of their future journey because we held them in our safe arms.

Each of us has made a journey toward our children with as much vigor as our children have journeyed toward us, and each of us knows that to raise a daughter in today's world is a huge challenge. Each of us has felt, at times, inadequately prepared for the task. I must admit that when Cheryl McKenzie, the mother of four, wrote me her letter about her daughters with which I began this book, and when she asked me, so directly, to help her parent these girls, I felt inadequate to the task—I am an imperfect father, and whether as a family therapist, researcher, or social philosopher I've always found, when matters are of the utmost importance, that humility is a better stance than omniscience.

But *The Wonder of Girls* grew in me, and with the help of Gail, my daughters, and many others, I hope I have helped you to shape loving, wise, and powerful women. The challenges girls face today are confusing ones and, as they have in every generation, our girls are turning to the wise ones. You and I have become those wise people—perhaps we didn't see it coming, but here it is. The next generation is in *our* hands. In writing this book, I hope I have helped you cut through the millions of distracting ideas around you and focus on the basic, simple, and heartfelt needs your daughters are showing by their gestures, their moods, their words, and their behavior. If your daughters are like mine, they like to be mysterious; but even more so, they like to be understood.

May your road to understanding be easier now. As you listen to your daughters asking the age-old question, "Who am I?" may you be better able now to answer what part you can before you let them go into the world where they will fill their own closet with their own intentions, attachments, dreams, and responsibilities.

Let me end this book with these words inscribed on the wall of Mother Teresa's Home for Children in Calcutta, India. They have been an inspiration to my daughters, hanging on our refrigerator door; I hope they will be an inspiration to you and yours.

*People are often unreasonable, illogical, and self-centered.*
*Forgive them anyway.*

*If you are kind, people may accuse you of having selfish, ulterior motives.*
*Be kind anyway.*

*If you are successful, you will win some false friends and some true enemies.*
*Succeed anyway.*

*If you are honest and frank, people may cheat you.*
  *Be honest and frank anyway.*

*What you spend years building, someone may destroy overnight.*
  *Build anyway.*

*If you find serenity and happiness, people may be jealous.*
  *Be happy anyway.*

*The good you do today, people will often forget tomorrow.*
  *Do good anyway.*

*Give the world the best you have and it may never be enough.*
  *Give the world the best you've got anyway.*

*You see, in the final analysis, it is between you and God.*
  *It was never between you and them anyway.*


Bless you in whatever work you do to raise your daughters and care for the girls around you. They need you now more than ever.

# APPENDIX

## Books and Movies That Help Girls Grow

Girls love to read and to watch movies. But how do we tunnel through the millions of books and movies to find the really good stuff, the gold? What books and movies really help our girls' brains, bodies, hearts, and spirits grow in healthy ways?

I hope you'll find these twenty-five books and twenty-five movies useful to you as you plan family reading time and movie nights. If you can, engage with your girls in discussions about these films and books, using them as teaching and learning tools. I am presenting them in developmental order, with a book or movie appearing in the age group it is first appropriate for (it may well be watched or read by girls of older ages). You may end up disagreeing with my placements—your middle-school daughter may have already seen something I put in the high school section! I hope you'll use my list as a starting point, not an end. It contains only twenty-five books and movies, knowing full well that there are far more out there that girls need.

I've chosen very carefully with advice from Gail, Gabrielle, and Davita, offering this list with two underlying intentions in mind—to protect and enhance your daughter's growth as a human being; and to help your family bond together more actively through the use of sacred stories that are *needed* as a family grows and interacts. Thus I have chosen mainly contemporary movies, avoiding the possibility that your daughter will find the choices "dated."

I hope I have found twenty-five books and movies that are needed by families, that help to build success and intimacy in girls' lives, and that provide basic protection. The American Medical Association, American

Academy of Pediatrics, American Psychological Association, and American Academy of Child and Adolescent Psychiatry have all determined that what our children learn from media directly affects their development, behavior, and relationships. The stories our girls read and see are not trifling matters.

I am not including on this list the sacred texts of the world, such as the Bible, the Koran, and other religious texts. It is my assumption that these would already be on a family's list of books that help children grow.

## Twenty-Five Movies

*Special Note:* The American Academy of Pediatrics suggests no visual media for children two years old and under. Brain research shows that the infant brain can be damaged by fast-moving screen images, especially images that include violence.

### FOR GIRLS YOUNGER THAN SIX

POCAHONTAS (1997)  Girls love to watch this movie of an immensely capable young Native American woman who knows the language of birds, falls in love, and saves her tribe from violent destruction.

THE LION KING (1995)  Perhaps the quintessential animated movie, *The Lion King* tells the story of a boy who must become a good man. It inspires character in both boys and girls, and the fact that his girlfriend, Nala, is so quick-witted and competent, just makes the story even better for girls.

MULAN (1998)  When her father cannot serve in the military his daughter disguises herself as a man, and makes the most heroic of heroine's journeys, showing every girl how to reach even beyond what she might have thought herself capable of.

THE PRINCE OF EGYPT (1998)  My daughters thoroughly enjoyed the spiritual themes of this biblical story, animated almost perfectly by Dreamworks. Lessons about friendship, personal courage, and the power of faith inspire girls to explore their own beliefs, and to seek the safety of spirituality.

THE WIZARD OF OZ (1939)  Some parents will feel this film should wait until elementary school. It is scary, in a primal way, for young children. Dorothy has an adventure that is an allegory not only for the growth of a girl but for the maturing of any child. And she goes to some amazing places along the way.

## FOR ELEMENTARY-AGE GIRLS

### FIRST THROUGH THIRD GRADE

ALASKA (1997) A young girl and her belligerent brother must work together in the Alaskan wilderness to rescue their father, a pilot, who has crashed in the mountains. Not only is the girl a strong female lead, scientifically knowledgeable, and filled with conviction, but the nature scenes in this movie are breathtaking.

CHICKEN RUN (2000) Disguised as a fun "escape-from-prison" film, this claymation classic shows what a young woman can do to lead her community, and herself, to freedom.

EVER AFTER (1998) This Cinderella story, starring Drew Barrymore, might be too mature for some younger kids. It beautifully shows Cinderella surviving and succeeding, finding herself and then finding love.

FAIRY TALE: A TRUE STORY (1996) In a village in England, two girls take a photograph of actual fairies. Their love of these spirits and sprites comes to the attention of Sir Arthur Conan Doyle and Harry Houdini, who set out to prove, or disprove, the veracity of belief in fairies. A very sweet spiritual tale.

FLY AWAY HOME (1996) When her mother is killed, a girl must go live with her estranged father. At first, they have difficulties, then as the girl becomes surrogate mother to a flock of Canadian geese, father and daughter work together to fly them to a haven in North Carolina. Every girl and family can find wisdom in the tensions and then triumphs of this film.

THE MIRACLE ON 34TH STREET (1947, 1994) Both versions are quite inspiring at Christmastime (along with the classic It's a Wonderful Life). This story of a young girl who experiences the miracle of Christmas—a miracle of family and faith—guides girls and their families to make a year-ly reunion with the true meaning of Christmas.

### FOURTH THROUGH SIXTH GRADE

PRINCESS MONONOKE (1999) Nearly every primal theme moves through this Japanese epic of a forest girl who must team with a young man to save the forest, and perhaps humanity.

THE LITTLE PRINCESS (1998) A father is lost in the war, a daughter goes to live with other girls in an orphanage. Conditions are hard, and there is a sweet magic to life nonetheless. Happiness is earned, and many good lessons learned.

## FOR MIDDLE-SCHOOL GIRLS

THE COLOR PURPLE (1985) This film about the black South, mainly involving the lives of women, is gut-wrenching at times. It is a film to see and then to talk about with girls. Cruelty, poverty, male/female relationships, female hierarchies—so many themes are engaged by this film.

CROUCHING TIGER, HIDDEN DRAGON (2000) Ang Lee directs this Chinese epic, which won several Oscars, and mainly features female warriors in a past Chinese society. This is an unforgettable, magical portrait of girls and women living behind social disguises, and trying to find both true love and personal perfection under almost crushing circumstances.

THE LION IN WINTER (1968) Katharine Hepburn stars with Peter O'Toole in one of the finest films in cinema about the jealousies, egos, emotional fixations, and moral ambiguities of family life.

PLACES IN THE HEART (1984) Sally Field plays Edna Spalding, a woman, suddenly widowed, who tries to hold on to her farm with the help of her growing children. A very powerful film.

TITANIC (1997) This is an American classic about a young woman and young man on a sinking ship who fight for each other against fate. The young woman survives and with her survival comes immense maturity.

WORKING GIRL (1988) This film, well acted and well directed, can lead to some very interesting discussion about the kinds of facades a woman has to put on to make it in a male-dominant working world.

## FOR HIGH SCHOOL GIRLS

AGNES OF GOD (1985) A young nun gives birth then kills her baby. Was she sane? Was she hearing God's voice? Jane Fonda plays a psychiatrist who must discover the truth. This movie leads to powerful discussion about life and death, religion in women's lives, sanity and insanity, and personal responsibility.

THE AGE OF INNOCENCE (1993) This is a love triangle in which everyone learns lessons not only about love, but about what to expect from society as one seeks to understand how to love, and how to fulfill one's yearnings.

CONTACT (1997)  Jodie Foster plays a scientist whose father's encouragement helped her find her chosen profession. She is a very strong character, one of the best female leads in contemporary cinema. The film raises crucial questions about how science and religion collide.

THE CONTENDER (2000)  Joan Allen plays a senator who has been tapped for the vice presidency, only to find herself the target of scandal mongers and backroom politics. She is accused of inappropriate sexual conduct and chooses the highest moral road she can find: neither to deny nor confirm, but to say, "You wouldn't attack a man this way, so I as a woman won't give you the satisfaction." The price of good character is not too high for this heroine who inspires all our daughters to bravery and moral conviction.

MEN DON'T LEAVE (1990)  Jessica Lange plays a mother whose husband has died, leaving her to raise her two teenagers. This movie powerfully depicts the tensions a single mother faces.

PERSONAL BEST (1982)  As girls become women, the theme of lesbian life is of greater interest. This film handles this theme with grace, and shows a young woman as a successful athlete in the midst of many intense personal decisions.

THE PIANO (1993)  In this disturbing film, seen from a young girl's point of view, and set in New Zealand, director Jane Campion depicts a mute pianist who is supposed to be a mail-order bride but develops a complex friendship with another man. The movie delves into the theme of how right and wrong sometimes become relative, and are defined by a society.

NORMA RAE (1979)  Sally Field won an Oscar for her role as a blue-collar union woman who takes on unfair bosses and an unfair system.

SHAKESPEARE IN LOVE (2000)  In one of the finest love stories put on film, Gwyneth Paltrow disguises herself as a male actor in order to play the role of Romeo in William Shakespeare's new play. She ends up finding freedom from a troubling, impending marriage, and learns what love truly is.

# Twenty-Five Books

## FOR GIRLS YOUNGER THAN SIX

AESOP'S FABLES.  Each of these old fables carries a moral, easy to recognize and full of meaning and wisdom for growing girls.

THE BUTTER BATTLE BOOK by Dr. Seuss. It is always difficult to pick a favorite Dr. Seuss book. All are generous to the growing minds and imaginations of children. This one carries some very deep messages about why people fight, and why they shouldn't.

THE LEGEND OF THE BLUE BONNET by Tomie dePaola. This is a touching story of a girl who gives her most valuable possession to save her people. It brings tears to the adult reader's eye, and teaches the young girl what's really important in life.

LOVE YOU, FOREVER by Robert Munsch. This tender, heartfelt tale of a daughter who is beloved by her father begins with her grandmother's devotion for the father as a boy, a teenager, then a young man. Though the book spends most of its time on the mother and son, it is universally heartwarming. Few books make a young girl feel as safe and loved as this one.

THE TWELVE DANCING PRINCESSES retold by Freya Littledale. This is just one of hundreds of fairy tales in children's bookstores, illustrated well, fun to read aloud, and full of hidden messages of growing up a girl. In this tale, girls are going underground in order to dance.

## FOR ELEMENTARY-AGE GIRLS

### FIRST THROUGH THIRD GRADE

ALISSA (THE STARDUST CLASSICS) by Jillian Ross. These fantasy books about girls are best read aloud to this age group. The girls in them are heroines who live life both to its most heroic and to its littlest detail.

THE MAGIC TREE HOUSE SERIES by Mary Pope Osborne. There are more than two dozen of these wonderful books about a sister and brother who have adventures, both in the past and the future, learning about science, spirit, and themselves along the way.

MOTHER-DAUGHTER TALES retold by Josephine Evetts-Secker. These can be read to preschoolers, and are especially nice for first- through third-graders to read aloud. These poignant stories of mothers and daughters are beautifully illustrated.

THE DEAR AMERICA SERIES. We can begin reading these aloud to girls at this age, then they can take over as they get to be reading proficient. These books capture girls during American history growing up in all sorts of conditions, places, and economic straits.

## FOURTH THROUGH SIXTH GRADE

ARE YOU THERE GOD? IT'S ME, MARGARET by Judy Blume. This Judy Blume classic, about a pubescent girl going through many challenges who opens up a dialogue with God, has been life-changing for some girls who have read it. A truly inspiring book.

ALANNA: THE FIRST ADVENTURE by Tamora Pierce. This is the first of a four-part series about an eleven-year-old girl in medieval times who disguises herself as a boy in order to try to become a knight. Girls learn a lot about self-discipline and determination from this book; they also sense, through Alanna, that they themselves might have hidden gifts.

CHARLOTTE'S WEB by E. B. White. A spider named Charlotte is a kind of spiritual overseer in the imaginative animal world of this classic novel. Charlotte is the essence of dignity and self-sacrifice. The web she weaves teaches any girl about life, especially if we talk to girls about the story, and listen to their take on it.

GUTSY GIRLS by Tina Schwager and Michele Schuerger. The subtitle of this book, "Young Women Who Dare," says it all. This is a very supportive collection of stories about girls and young women who climb mountains, fossil hunt, even skydive, sure to inspire confidence especially in a physically oriented daughter.

HOPE FOR THE FLOWERS by Trina Paulus. This is a powerful spiritual allegory about the climb to success, the price we pay, and the hope for love and intimacy that interweaves into all of the human endeavor. It brought tears to my own and my daughters' eyes.

ISLAND OF THE BLUE DOLPHINS by Scott O'Dell. Karana, a young girl, is forced to live alone on a deserted island. She discovers what she's capable of—both in areas of strength and skill, but also in her basic character. In an era when girls are distracted so much by media, video, and the mall, this book is a breath of fresh air that focuses a girl on the stripped-down essentials of life.

I THOUGHT MY SOUL WOULD RISE AND FLY by Joyce Hansen. Subtitled *The Diary of Patsy, a Freed Girl,* this fine book in the wonderful *Dear America* series is written journal-style from the point of view of a black slave girl in slave times. Not only does the book stir the heart and mind of a growing girl, but it leads to important discussions in families and schools about slavery and prejudice.

OUR OWN MAY AMELIA by Jennifer Holm. May Amelia is the only girl among a bunch of brothers, but she ends up finding herself in special ways. An easy book for any girl to relate to, and especially valuable for a girl who feels overwhelmed by boys.

## FOR MIDDLE-SCHOOL GIRLS

TO KILL A MOCKINGBIRD by Harper Lee. A young girl becomes embroiled in racial struggles in the South as her father must defend a black man, and is ostracized. A book of universal importance, Lee's novel leads to discussions about some of life's most crucial themes.

CHILD OF THE OWL by Laurence Yep. Some older elementary-age girls will be ready for this book about a twelve-year-old Chinese-American girl who visits her maternal grandmother and learns about her own identity. This book can lead families to rich discussions about assimilation, and about each individual's ancestry and heritage.

THE DIARY OF ANNE FRANK. One of the most important stories of our century, it can be read by many upper-elementary-school girls, but I suggest it for middle-school classrooms and homes of middle-school girls (and boys) because by this developmental time, some of the universal themes in this story of a girl hiding from the Nazis can fully unfold in an adolescent's consciousness.

SOPHIE'S WORLD by Jostein Gaarder. Sophie looks in her mailbox one day only to find a letter that asks her two questions: Who are you? And: Where does the world come from? This book inspires girls and those around them to make a philosophical search both into the basic tenets of our civilization and into each of our own identities.

## FOR HIGH SCHOOL GIRLS

CHINESE HANDCUFFS by Chris Crutcher. Jennifer Lawless is a victim of sexual abuse. She experiences life in all its unfairness. In her friendship with Dillon she finds some hope. This book is a powerful gateway into discussion with girls about some of life's harshest lessons.

INTERPRETER OF MALADIES by Jhumpa Lahiri. This book of short stories, set in Boston and India, won a Pulitzer Prize in 2000. Each story is not only beautifully crafted, but each raises questions in the mind of a growing young woman about relationships, personal achievement, getting old, trying to stay young, and moral character.

MIDDLEMARCH by George Eliot (Mary Anne Evans). This classic from the last century challenges young women to more deeply understand relationships with each other and men, and just how complex adulthood is for a woman.

PRIDE AND PREJUDICE by Jane Austen. This is a love story about the human ego striving to transcend itself and learn to fully love. Some girls will find the language (as in *Middlemarch*) too archaic, but others will see themselves and others in this finely told story

SNOW FALLING ON CEDARS by David Guterson. Amid the snowfall of western Washington, in an ocean community, a trial transpires in which a Japanese man is accused of a murder. The trial takes the reader back in time, during WW II, into a love story between a Japanese young woman and an American young man. Girls are often transfixed by this story, so well written, of love both possible and impossible, and of social conditions that lead to prejudice.

*Special Note:* THE BOOK OF DISTINGUISHED AMERICAN WOMEN by Vincent Wilson, Jr., is a great resource for parents and teachers looking for female role models from history.

# Additional Resources

These are selected books about situations of interest to parents and caregivers of girls.

## ADOLESCENT GIRLS/TEENS

*A Field Guide to the American Teenager* by Michael Riera and Joseph Di Prisco (Perseus, 2000)

*Our Last Best Shot* by Laura Sessions Stepp (Riverhead, 2000)

*The Romance of Risk* by Lynn E. Ponton (Basic Books, 1998)

*Don't Stop Loving Me* by Ann Caron (HarperPerennial, 1991)

## BUILDING CHARACTER/MORAL DEVELOPMENT

*Building Character in Schools* by Kevin Ryan and Karen Bohlin (Jossey-Bass, 2000)

*Building Moral Intelligence* by Michele Borba (Jossey-Bass, 2001)

*The Moral Child* by William Damon (Free Press, 1988)

*Teaching Your Children Values* by Linda and Richard Eyre (Fireside, 1993)

## GIRLS AND COMPETITION

*Will You Still Love Me If I Don't Win?* by Christopher Anderson (Taylor, 2000)

*The Cheers and the Tears* by Shane Murphy (Jossey-Bass, 1999)

## GIRLS AND COMPUTERS/MEDIA

*Deadly Persuasion* by Jean Kilbourne (Free Press, 1999)

*The Failure to Connect* by Jane Healy (Touchstone, 1998)

*Computers in the Classroom* by Andrea R. Gooden (Jossey-Bass, 1996)

## GIRLS AND EDUCATION

*The Educated Child* by William Bennett (Free Press, 1999)

*How Girls Thrive* by JoAnn Deak (National Association of Independent Schools, 1998)

## GIRLS AND SUCCESS

*How to Father a Successful Daughter* by Nicky Marone (Fawcett, 1988)

*See Jane Win* by Sylvia Rimm (Three Rivers, 1999)

*What Teens Need to Succeed* by Peter Benson, Judy Galbraith, and Pamela Espeland (Free Spirit Publishing, 1997)

### ETHNICITY/CULTURAL DIVERSITY

*Radical Equations* by Robert P. Moses and Charles Cobb, Jr. (Beacon, 2001)

### FATHERING/SINGLE FATHERING

*The Common Sense No-Frills, Plain-English Guide to Being a Successful Dad* by Ronald and Gay Klinger (CSF Publishing, 1995)
*The Father's Almanac* by S. Adams Sullivan (Doubleday, 1992)
*Fathers, Sons and Daughters* by Charles Scull (Tarcher/Putnam, 1992)
*Father Time* by Christopher Scribner and Chris Frey (Insight Output, 2001)
*Live-Away Dads* by William Klatte (Penguin, 1999)
*The New Father* by Armin Brott (Abbeville, 1997)
*The Solo Dad Survival Guide* by Reginald Davis and Nick Borns (Contemporary Books, 1999)

### GRANDPARENTS

*Grandparents as Parents* by Sylvie de Toledo and Deborah Edler Brown (Guilford, 1995)

### THE MOTHER-DAUGHTER RELATIONSHIP

*Don't Stop Loving Me* by Ann F. Caron (Holt, 1991)
*I'm Not Mad, I Just Hate You!* by Roni Cohen-Sandler and Michelle Silver (Viking Penguin, 2001)
*Mothers to Daughters* by Ann F. Caron (Owl, 1998)
*Mothers and Daughters* by Evelyn Bassoff (Plume, 1989)
*Mothering Ourselves* by Evelyn Bassoff (Plume, 1992)

### STAY-AT-HOME MOMS

*At-Home Motherhood* by Ciny Tolliver (Resource Publications, 1994)
*The Stay at Home Mom* by Donna Otto (Harvest House, 1997)

# NOTES AND REFERENCES

Some of the cultures and subcultures I have personally experienced are Italian (*Naples*), Irish (*County Fermanagh*), Israeli (*urban and kibbutz*), Indian (*South Central*), French (*Paris and Quenet*), English (*London and Southern England*), Turkish (*urban and rural*), Kurdish (*urban and rural*), Egyptian (*urban*), Nubian (*rural*).

American subcultures I have studied include:
Hawaiian and Samoan, urban and rural United States (*all regions*), Native American (*Southern Ute*).

Some of the cultures and subcultures in which I have done scholarly work are:
Australian Aboriginal, Shavante (*Brazil*), Ndembu (*Africa*), Japanese (*urban*), Chinese (*urban*), Papua, New Guinea, Native American (*Lakota*).

For additional information about The Gurian Institute, check www. gurianinstitute.com.

## PART I:
## Why Girls Are the Way They Are

### INTRODUCTION
Many of the epigraphs for the chapters of this book, like Marilyn Sewell's words, come from a beautiful book on women's spirituality, *Cries of the Spirit,* edited by Marilyn Sewell (Beacon Press, 1991).

## 1: BEGINNING OUR SEARCH: A NEW LOGIC OF GIRLS' LIVES
### LOOKING BEYOND FEMINISM: OLD MYTHS AND NEW THEORIES

The poll I referred to was released by Youth Intelligence. See the article, "Trading Career for Casseroles," by Lori Borgman, of the *Indianapolis Star* (July 23, 2000). Sixty-eight percent of three thousand women ages eighteen to thirty-four said they would prefer domestic to corporate life.

Similar polls from years past can be found in *Who Stole Feminism?* by Christina Hoff Sommers (Simon & Schuster, 1996) and *Backlash* by Susan Faludi (Crown, 1991).

Conversations with Mary Pipher, Carol Gilligan, and Christina Crawford took place in Spokane, Washington, and Lincoln, Nebraska; West Stockbridge, Massachusetts; and Spokane, Washington, respectively.

*Reviving Ophelia* by Mary Pipher (Ballantine, 1994), p. 116.

The FBI crime statistic was provided by Christina Sommers, author of *The War Against Boys* (Simon & Schuster, 2000).

### A THEORY FOR SOME, NOT FOR ALL

National Institute of Mental Health statistics, as well as Department of Justice and Department of Education statistics, are generally available by checking the departments' Web sites. Keyword: Department of Education, for instance, generally gets you access.

## 2: HOW HER MIND WORKS: SECRETS OF THE FEMALE BRAIN

This chapter and the next gain their research base from over two decades of primary researchers—like Ruben and Raquel Gur, Laurie Allen, Roger Gorski, Camilla Benbow, Paul MacLean, and many others—who have provided laboratory findings to researchers like myself for application in the culture as a whole.

Good sources for original laboratory research in neural science are:

*Brain Sex* by Anne Moir and David Jessel (Dell, 1990);

*Sex on the Brain* by Deborah Blum (Penguin, 1997);

*A Celebration of Neurons* by Robert Sylwester (Assoc. of Supervision and Curriculum Development, 1995);

*Neuroscience* by Mark Bear, Barry Connors, and Michael Paradiso (Williams and Wilkins, 1996);

*Essentials of Neural Science and Behavior* by Eric Kandel, James Schwartz, and Thomas Jessel (Appleton and Lange, 1995);

"Your Child's Brain" by Sharon Begley, *Newsweek*, Feb 19, 1996;

"Fertile Minds," *Time*, February 3, 1997.

Also see *Boys and Girls Learn Differently* by Michael Gurian with Patricia Henley and Terry Trueman (Jossey-Bass, 2001).

I follow a particular method, presented in *The Wonder of Boys*, when applying neural and biochemical research to the lives of boys and girls.

1. I like to check to make sure more than one laboratory researcher has come to the same conclusion about the neurotransmitter, brain section, or hormonal system's effect on behavior.

2. If possible, I check the neural or biochemical research outside the U.S. In order to move away from too-heavy reliance on the idea that "girls are the basically the way they are because the U.S. socializes them that way," I see how girls in other parts of the world do or don't resemble ours (generally, they do). By taking a multicultural approach, it is possible to make some nature/nurture distinctions. While all researchers are in agreement that both nature and nurture play a part in shaping children, a multicultural approach hones in better on what part of girlhood is, simply, natural to all girls.

3. I check all research against what we know from the fields of developmental and child psychology.

From this base, I also apply simply intuition and common sense. If a researcher is saying something that just doesn't ring true, especially once I've checked it against my own observations in personal and professional work, I avoid using it.

## 3: THE HIDDEN WORLD: THE BIOCHEMISTRY OF GIRLS' LIVES

As with brain science, biochemistry is a field whose studies generate from the laboratory and then, once made available to outside researchers, become a part of the culture's larger dialogue. I am particularly beholden for this chapter's biochemical research to the aforementioned *Brain Sex*, as well as *Women's Moods* (William Morrow, 1999), mentioned in the text. I am also grateful for the research provided in: *The Anatomy of Love* by Helen Fisher (Fawcett Columbine, 1992); *Human Sperm Competition* by Robin Baker and Mark Bellis (Chapman and Hall, 1995); *The Moral Animal* by Robert Wright (Vintage, 1994); *Beyond Estrogen* by Laura Powlak (Biomed General Corporation, 1998).

### THE TREE OF LIFE: FROM MIND TO HORMONES

The conversation with microbiologist JoAnna Ellington, of Washington State University, took place in Spokane, Washington.

Kristi Boylan has written a wonderful book about the spirituality of female hormonal life: *The Seven Sacred Rites of Menarche* (Santa Monica Press, 2001).

### THE FOUR STAGES OF A MONTHLY CYCLE

No two girls or women are exactly alike in their cycle, so any attempt here to create a "pattern" is not to be considered a final statement. All information about hormones must be adjusted to the individual female hormonal system.

### FEMALE HORMONES AND THE INTIMACY IMPERATIVE

I heard Bob Obsatz speak at the University of St. Thomas, in Minneapolis, Minnesota, in the fall of 2000.

The biological material in this book is directed toward heterosexual female development. *Brain Sex* includes very interesting information on homosexual female development.

## PART II: What Girls Need

## 4: THE ARTFUL MOTHER: WHAT GIRLS NEED FROM MOM

### THE ARTFUL MOTHER IN STAGE 1: BIRTH TO FIVE YEARS OLD

*Becoming Attached* by Robert Karen (Warner, 1994); *Oneness and Separateness* by Louise J. Kaplan (Touchstone, 1978); *The Earliest Relationship* by T. Berry Brazelton and Bertrand C. Kramer (Addison-Wesley, 1990); *The Motherhood Constellation* by Daniel N. Stern (Basic Books, 1995); *A Secure Base* by John Bowlby (Basic Books, 1988).

### PROVIDING DISCIPLINE IN STAGE 1

*What to Expect When You're Expecting* by Arlene Eisenberg, Heidi Eisenberg Murkoff, and Sandee Eisenberg Hathaway (Workman, 1984) (These *What To Expect* books are being constantly updated); *The Good Son* by Michael Gurian (Tarcher/Putnam, 1999).

### THE ARTFUL MOTHER IN STAGE 2: SIX TO TEN YEARS OLD

*Your One-Year-Old* by Louise Bates Ames and Frances L. Ilg (Dell, 1976). These books go all the way into the teens, year by year.

*Backtalk* by Audrey Ricker and Carolyn Crowder (Fireside, 1998) is an invaluable resource on discipline.

### THE ARTFUL MOTHER IN STAGE 3: ELEVEN TO FIFTEEN YEARS OLD

*Don't Stop Loving Me* by Ann Caron (HarperPerennial, 1991); *A Parent's Guide for Suicidal and Depressed Teens* by Kate Williams (Hazelden, 1995); *Between Mother and Daughter* by Judy and Amanda Ford (Conari Press, 1999).

#### RITES OF PASSAGE

*The Heart of the Family* by Meg Cox (Random House, 1998).

ICA Journeys is a premier rite-of-passage coordinator. Their Web site is www.icajourneys.org.

### THE ARTFUL MOTHER IN STAGE 4: SIXTEEN TO TWENTY YEARS OLD

*You and Your Adolescent* by Laurence Steinberg and Anne Levine (Harper, 1994).

For help with the rules of co-ed sleep overs I am beholden to Amy Dickinson (*Time*, January 8, 2001), and the assistance she received from J. D. Moss, 17, of Falls Church, Virginia.

#### HOW TO BE AN ARTFUL STEPMOTHER

*The Courage to Be a Stepmom* by Sue Patton Thoele (Wildcat Canyon, 1999).

## 5: THE GIFTS OF THE FATHER: WHAT GIRLS NEED FROM DAD

*Father, Sons and Daughters* by Charles Scull (Torcher, 1992).

#### FATHER ATTACHMENT

*Fatherneed* by Kyle D. Pruett (Free Press, 2000).

#### OUR FATHERLESS DAUGHTERS

*Fatherless America* by David Blankenhorn (HarperPerennial, 1995).

#### GIFTS OF THE FATHER

*Father Courage* by Suzanne Levine (Harcourt Brace, 2000); *First Mothers* by Bonnie Angelo (William Morrow, 2000); *Fathering* by Will Glennon (Conari Press, 1995); *Beyond the Birds and the Bees* by Beverly Engel (Pocket Books, 1997).

#### FATHERS, DAUGHTERS, AND DIVORCE

*The Divorced Dad's Handbook* by Robert Bornstein and Richard Worth (Blue Bird, 1995); *Divorced Dads* by Sanford Braver and Dianne O'Connell (Tarcher/Putnam, 1998); *Vicki Lansky's Divorce Book for Parents* by Vicki

Lansky (Book Peddlers, 1996); *Second Chances* by Judith Wallenstein (Ticknor and Fields, 1989).

## 6: INNOCENCE AND EXPERIENCE: PROTECTING THE EMOTIONAL DEVELOPMENT OF OUR GIRLS

### GIRLS AND SELF-ESTEEM: A DIFFERENT VIEW
*All That She Can Be* by Carol Eagle and Carol Colman (Fireside, 1994).

### THE ANNE FRANK PRINCIPLE
*The Diary of a Young Girl* by Anne Frank (Doubleday, 1991); "School Officials Up in Arms over Hugging," *Associated Press*, February 23, 2001.

### GIRLS NEED A PACK
*Women Who Run with the Wolves* by Clarissa Pinkola Estes (Ballantine, 1992).

### THE NEW NASTINESS AMONG GIRLS
Jeannie Corkill is a family therapist in Spokane, Washington.

### PROTECTING THE BODIES OF OUR DAUGHTERS
*When Girls Feel Fat* by Sandra Friedman (HarperCollins, 1997); *The Biology of Success* by Robert Arnot (Little Brown, 2000).

### EXERCISE
The Duke University study was reported in *Newsweek*, October 9, 2000, p. 84.

### HARSH EXPERIENCE: EMOTIONAL CRISES IN GIRLS' LIVES
*Teens in Turmoil* by Carol Maxym and Leslie York (Viking, 2000).

### EATING DISORDERS
*Hunger Pains* by Mary Pipher (Ballantine, 1995); *When Your Child Has an Eating Disorder* by Abigail H. Natenshon (San Francisco, 1998).

### SELF-CUTTING
*Cutting* by Steven Levenkron (Norton, 1998).

### SEXUAL, PHYSICAL, AND EMOTIONAL ABUSE AND VIOLENCE
Character Regression Syndrome is a diagnosis I have named; it does not appear in the *DSM V*.

*Parenting 911* by Charlene C. Gianetti and Margaret Sagarese (Broadway, 1999); *Your Anxious Child* by John S. Dacey and Lisa B. Fiore (Jossey-Bass, 2000); *Helping Children Cope with Stress* by Avis Brenner (Jossey-Bass, 1997).

### SMOKING
All statistics come from the CASA 2000 teen survey.

### DEALING WITH DIVORCE
*Helping Children Cope with Divorce* by Edward Teyber (Jossey Bass, 1997); Practical Parent Education can be reached in Plano, Texas.

## 7: THE HEROINE'S JOURNEY: BUILDING CHARACTER IN OUR DAUGHTERS

*Voices of the First Day* by Robert Lawlor (Inner Traditions, 1991).

### THE HEROINE'S JOURNEY
*Fearless Girls, Wise Women & Beloved Sisters* by Kathleen Regan (Norton, 1998).

### THE SHADOW FEMININE
Statistics from the FBI and Bureau of Justice are available from their Web sites or by writing to them. Keyword: Bureau of Justice should give you access.

### FEMALE MENTORS, THE LANGUAGE OF THE BIRDS, AND THE DANCE
*Love's Journey* by Michael Gurian (Shambhala, 1994); "The Language of the Birds" by Rene Guenon (*Parabola*: Fall 1995; Issue Title: Language and Meaning).

### THE ROLE OF THE MENTOR
*For All Our Daughters* by Pegine Echeverria (Chandler House, 1998).

### UNDERSTANDING GUYS
*Understanding Guys: A Guide for Teenage Girls* by Michael Gurian (Price, Stern, Sloan, 1999).

### MODESTY, SEXUAL MYTHS, AND A GIRL'S REPUTATION
*A Return to Modesty* by Wendy Shalit (Touchstone, 1999); *Venus in Blue Jeans* by Nathalie Bartle and Susan Lieberman (Houghton Mifflin, 1998); *Sex and Sensibility* by Deborah Roffman (Perseus, 2000); *A Fine Young Man* by Michael Gurian (Tarcher/Putnam, 1998).

## 8: WOMANISM: GIVING GIRLS A SACRED ROLE IN LIFE

Conversation with Sister Margaret Mary Conway took place in Spokane, Washington.

## APPENDIX

*The Oppenheim Toy Portfolio*, by Joanne Oppenheim and her family, is a very detailed guide to contemporary media and toys.

# INDEX

abstract thinking, 41
  a young woman's abstract searches,
    48–49
abuse, 46, 159, 194, 218–21, 220, 222,
  279
  discipline, abusive, 173
  sexual, *see* sexual abuse
academic performance, 159, 189, 212,
  221–22
acetylcholine, 79, 90
adolescence: eleven to fifteen years old
  (stage 3):
  brain development, 32, 38–48
  caring for daughter's brain growth,
    42–43
  decision-making by, 46
  early puberty, 209–10
  father's affection during, 170–71
  hormonal changes in, 75
  mothering, *see* mothers and
    mothering
  physical development and body
    image in, 176–78
  sexual activity in, 46
  skills learned from, "sticking" or
    "reappearing" of, 39–40
  social and emotional changes, 40–42
  stress responses in, 46–47
adventure, father's gift of, 167–68
affection, 224
  of fathers, 169–72, 176–77
  between spouses, 224

Afghanistan, mistreatment of women
  in, 270, 282
African-Americans, early puberty in,
  210
aggression, 71, 207, 220
  testosterone levels and, 81, 90
alcohol abuse, 48, 194, 212, 216
*All That She Can Be: Helping Your*
  *Daughter Maintain Her Self-*
  *Esteem* (Eagle and Colman), 191
American Academy of Child and
  Adolescent Psychiatry, 298
American Academy of Pediatrics, 117,
  120, 297–98
American Association of University
  Women, 18, 222
*American Girl Magazine,* 133, 269–70
American Medical Association, 297–98
American Psychological Association,
  298
Ames, Louise, 120
Anderson, Jennifer, 113
Angelo, Bonnie, 164
anger, 71, 84, 127–29, 130
Anne Frank Principle, 197–99
anorexia, 17–18, 19, 21, 194
Anthony, Susan B., 277
anxiety, 71, 80, 196, 224
appetite, 80
approval of father, 169–70, 224
arguing during adolescence, 41
Arnot, Robert, 207